TRADITIONAL HOME I

BY

Stephen Fuller

Traditional Home Plans

By

Stephen Fuller

Eighty-Five Distinguished Designs
from
Design Traditions Home Library

HOME PLANNERS
TUCSON, ARIZONA

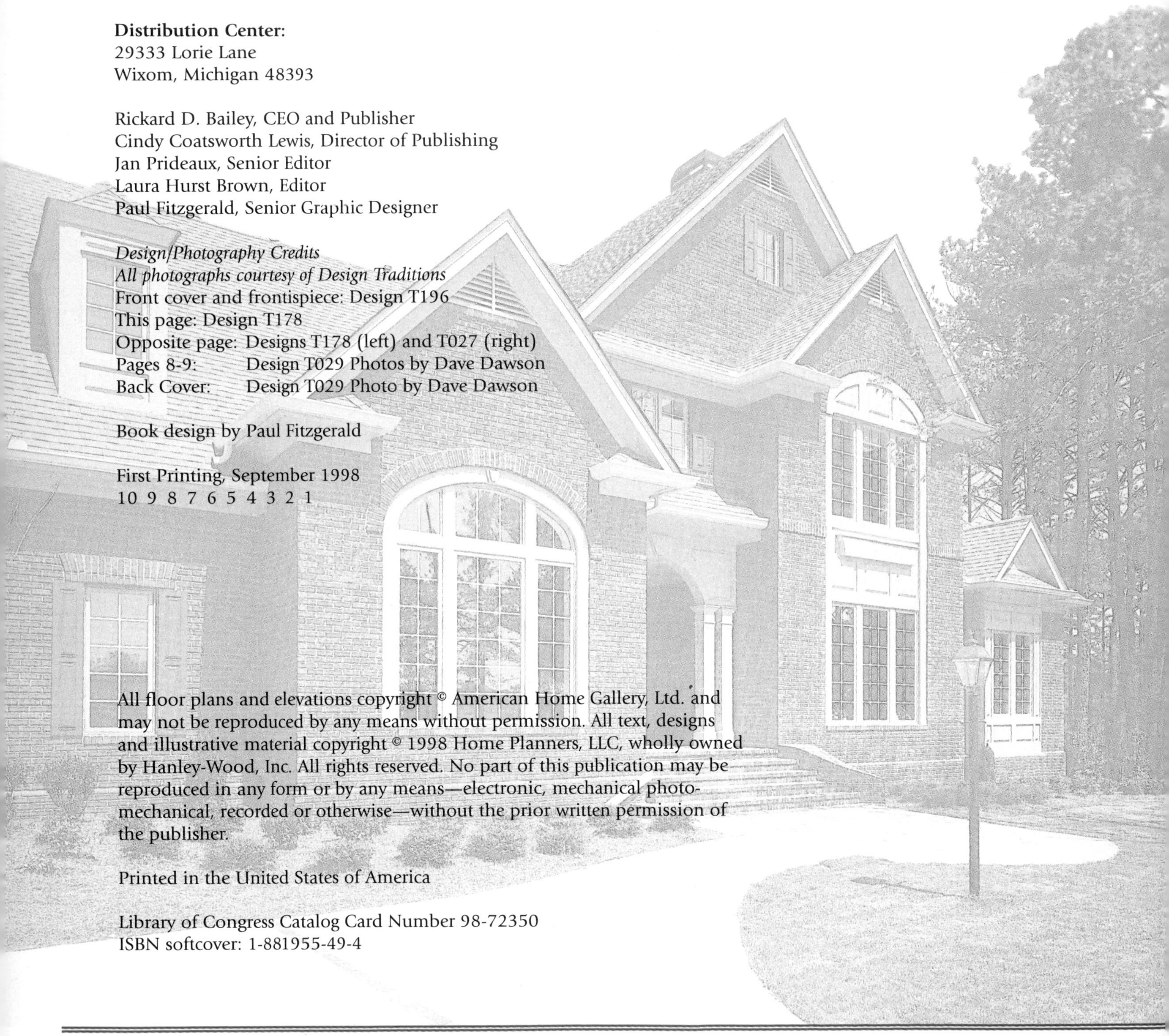

Published by Home Planners, LLC
Wholly owned by Hanley-Wood, Inc.
Editorial and Corporate Offices:
3275 West Ina Road, Suite 110
Tucson, Arizona 85741

Distribution Center:
29333 Lorie Lane
Wixom, Michigan 48393

Rickard D. Bailey, CEO and Publisher
Cindy Coatsworth Lewis, Director of Publishing
Jan Prideaux, Senior Editor
Laura Hurst Brown, Editor
Paul Fitzgerald, Senior Graphic Designer

Design/Photography Credits
All photographs courtesy of Design Traditions
Front cover and frontispiece: Design T196
This page: Design T178
Opposite page: Designs T178 (left) and T027 (right)
Pages 8-9: Design T029 Photos by Dave Dawson
Back Cover: Design T029 Photo by Dave Dawson

Book design by Paul Fitzgerald

First Printing, September 1998
10 9 8 7 6 5 4 3 2 1

Printed in the United States of America

Library of Congress Catalog Card Number 98-72350
ISBN softcover: 1-881955-49-4

CONTENTS

WELCOME

Photo courtesy of Design Traditions

Home. Few words hold such meaning. Few thoughts are as cherished, and few places hold such literal power to shape our lives. The place we call home reminds us of what is real and lasting: the love that we bear and receive from family and friends.

For these reasons and more, Design Traditions is committed to creating homes that enhance the lives of all the people they embrace. Great places show both exuberance and subtlety, as well as a quiet complexity that leaves room for the marks of time that families etch into a home's surfaces and spaces.

Our approach to residential design has always been what one might call fundamental, melding the classic architecture of the past with a sense of contemporary life. Elements rich with historical detail enhance rooms dedicated to modern comfort, while open, flowing spaces rethink the traditional visions of style.

The integration of aesthetics and function, beauty and form, is not an easy mix to master. But it has been, in a sense, the heart and soul of what we do. For over 20 years, we've created homes that quietly express the character of the people who live in them. The result is a portfolio of homes that are classic in inspiration, comfortably stylish outside with open, eminently *livable* interiors. I've added a personal note on some of these pages, to call up a bit of history or explore an architectural detail—just for the pure fun of it.

Traditional Home Plans is an important milestone for me and for all of us at Design Traditions. Here, we celebrate a lifetime of commitment to everything the word *home* stands for: shelter and support, love and inspiration. We hope this unique collection of plans will fuel your dreams as well as your imagination, and we think you'll feel at home here—now and down the road.

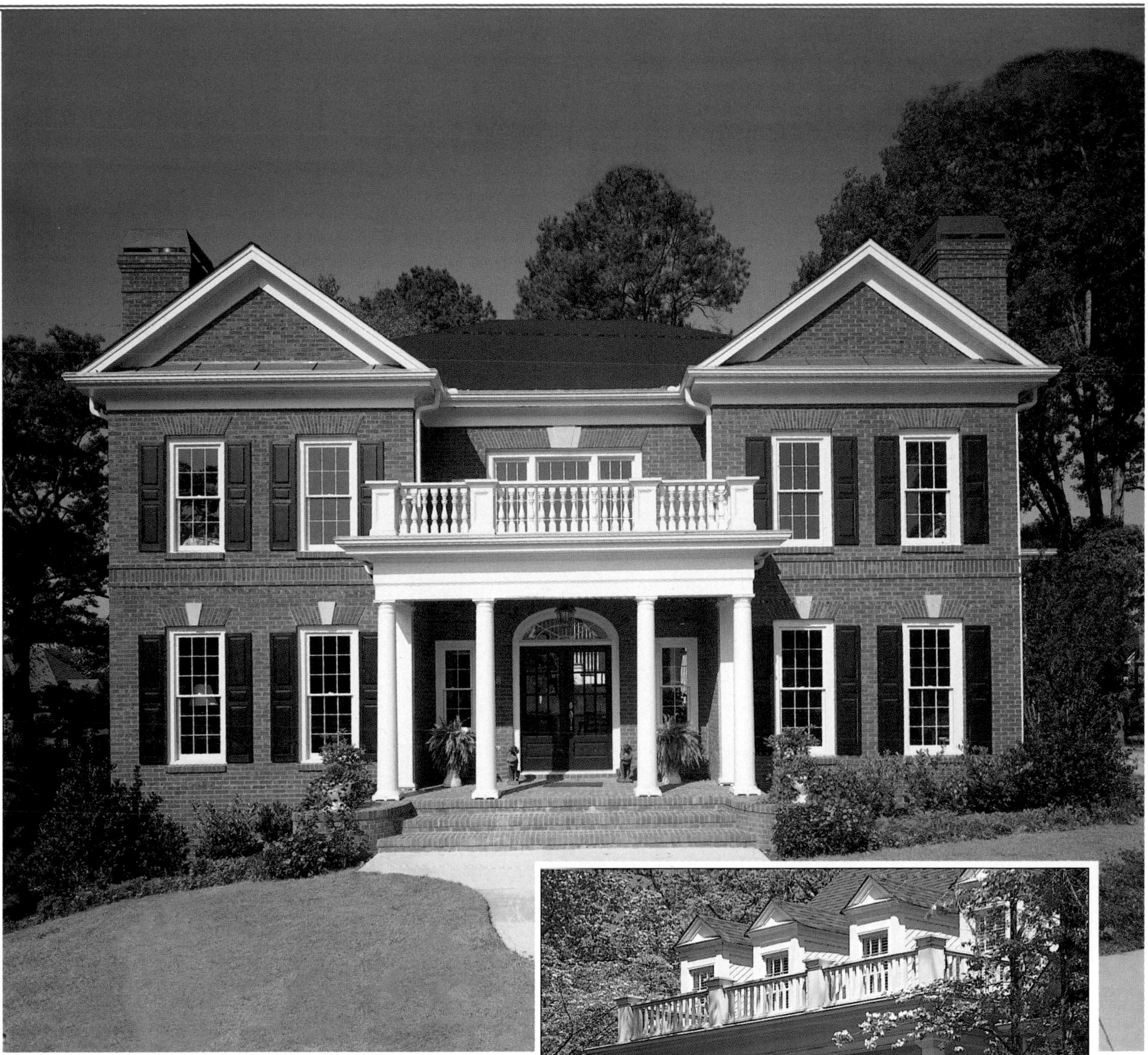

To view floor plans of these homes, please see pages 66-67 (Magnolia Place, top) and page 108 (Piedmont Family Home, right).

Photo by Dave Dawson, courtesy of Design Traditions

To view floor plans of this home, please see page 109 (Maple Glenn). Interiors as shown in these photographs may differ from the actual blueprints. For detailed information, please check the floor plans carefully.

THE LANGUAGE OF HOME

This presentation of timeless, traditional classics—from 1,600 to 6,000 square feet—melds elements that draw on the past with a sense of both luxury and comfort. Double-columned porches and triple windows are set off by fanciful copper seam roofs and fanlight transoms. At once formal and friendly, this collection of designs is an eloquent testimony to the durability of classic architecture.

Stephen Fuller's designs have always reflected a stunning blend of past and present, preserving elements of historic architecture while providing the flowing interior spaces and private areas that have become vital to the way people live today. Historic details speak softly of our American heritage but also point toward what we hold priceless in this moment.

Traditional Home Plans represents several of America's most loved styles, from Georgian Revival homes to New World Chateaux. Bold horizontal lines, Palladian windows and graceful arched entrys complement eclectic blends of stately brick and lap siding in our "New American Classics" section.

In "Georgian & Revival Styles," raised-panel shutters and jack-arch window treatments introduce engaging interiors that offer distinctive formal rooms but aren't short on casual space, with plenty of comfortable amenities.

Elements of the "Colonial-Spirit Homes" include pedimented porticos supported by classical columns, with a transom over the front entry door. Finally, our "New World Chateaux & Cottages" reflect a myriad of European influences, from English Tudor to French Country. Steeply pitched roofs, gently flared eaves, arched dormers, massive chimneys, bays and oriels are common ingredients of these styles.

Within a uniquely American vernacular, this collection sets its own plural definition of classic style—with a bevy of elements drawn from our rich history. Each home pays homage to traditional influences in style, detailing and materials yet is utterly progressive. This is vital architecture that will transcend the new turn of the century, creating beautiful, gracious homes that will help make time stand still.

Photo by Dave Dawson, courtesy of Design Traditions

New American Classics

With a large gabled roof over the double entry, this home has a touch of a mountain retreat or country house look. The simple main gable is an enchanting symbol of home.

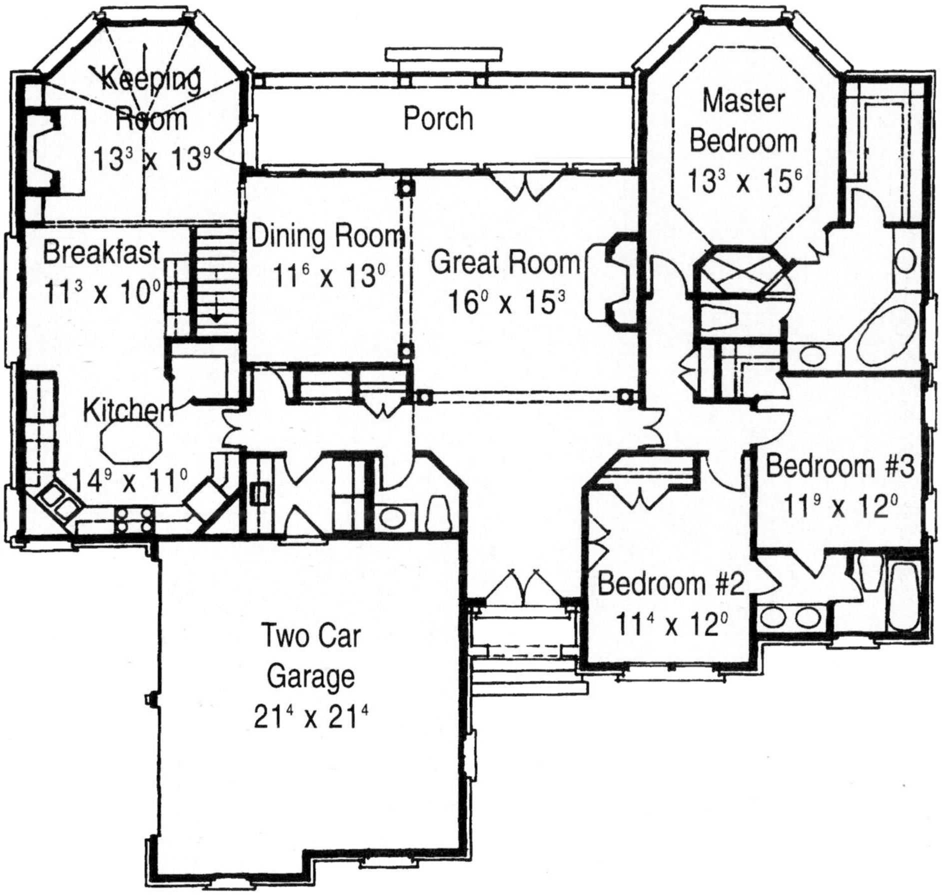

Width 63'-0"
Depth 59'-6"

Design T208

Square Footage: 2,150
Bedrooms: 3
Bathrooms: 2½

WOODSIDE WALK

A recessed entry creates a warm welcome, while the jack-arch window detailing adds intrigue to this charming exterior. The foyer, dining room and great room are brought together in an open interior arrangement that's casually defined by decorative columns. The abundance of windows throughout the back of the home provides a grand view of the rear property. The master suite enjoys a garden tub, a large walk-in closet and two vanities, for a perfect homeowner's retreat.

TIBURON MANOR

Design T215

Square Footage: 1,733

Bedrooms: 3

Bathrooms: 2½

A brick facade combined with a columned front porch establishes this home's early continental origins. Continuing the theme, the double-hung windows are crested by cut-brick jack-arches. The foyer opens to a large great room which emphasizes the open and airy floor plan, and offers French doors that lead to a back deck. Convenient to both the great room and dining room, the kitchen opens to an attractive breakfast area with a bay window. The luxurious master suite offers a garden tub, a separate shower and a double-bowl vanity.

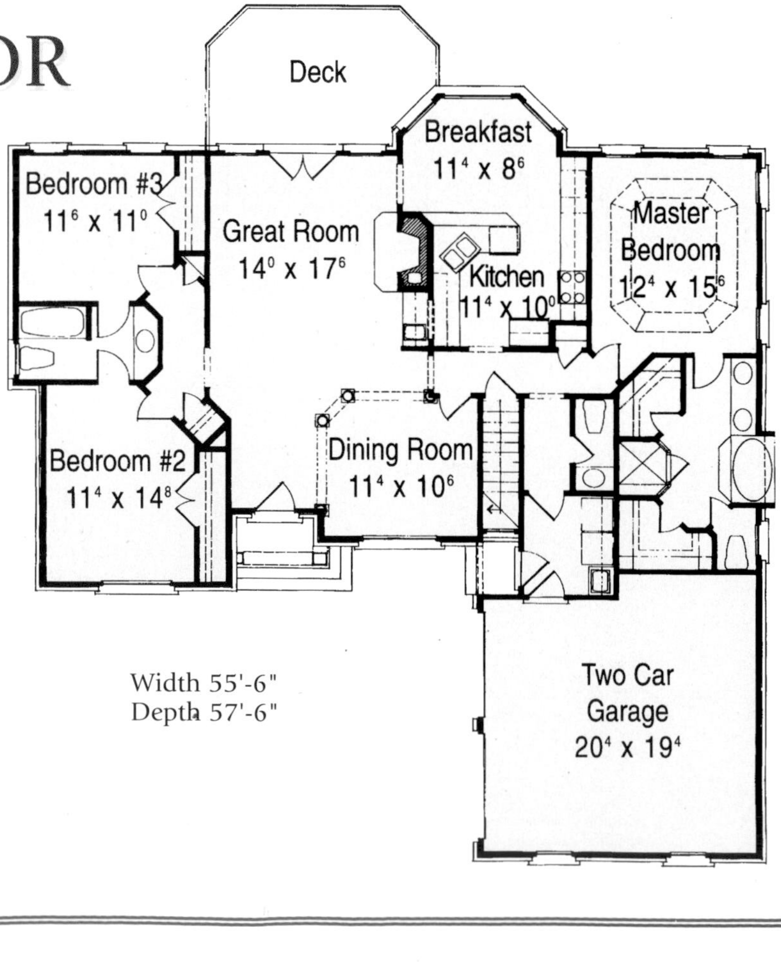

MAYFAIR COTTAGE

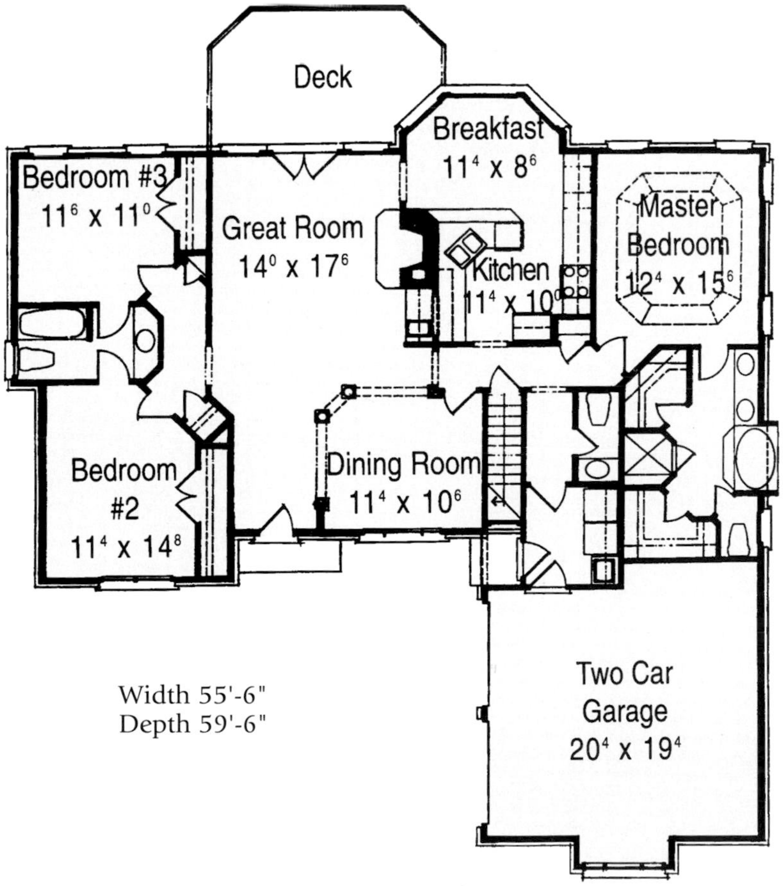
Deck
Breakfast
11⁴ x 8⁶
Bedroom #3
11⁶ x 11⁰
Great Room
14⁰ x 17⁶
Kitchen
11⁴ x 10⁰
Master
Bedroom
12⁴ x 15⁶
Dining Room
11⁴ x 10⁶
Bedroom
#2
11⁴ x 14⁸
Two Car
Garage
20⁴ x 19⁴

Width 55'-6"
Depth 59'-6"

Design T207

Square Footage: 1,733
Bedrooms: 3
Bathrooms: 2½

A brick facade and central gable with an arched window accent begin this Early American presentation. The foyer opens to a large great room, which has French doors that lead to a back deck for a warm, inviting feeling. The kitchen opens to a bright breakfast bay and easily serves the nearby formal dining room. The luxurious master suite, positioned quietly to the right rear of the home, offers comfort and a peaceful retreat with a garden tub, a separate shower and two lavatories. A two-car garage offers additional storage space as well as a sunny, box-bay window.

An inviting entry and bay window with copper flashing lend particular charm to this comfortable home. Gables and a multiple-level roof create a casual look that complements its stately brick facade.

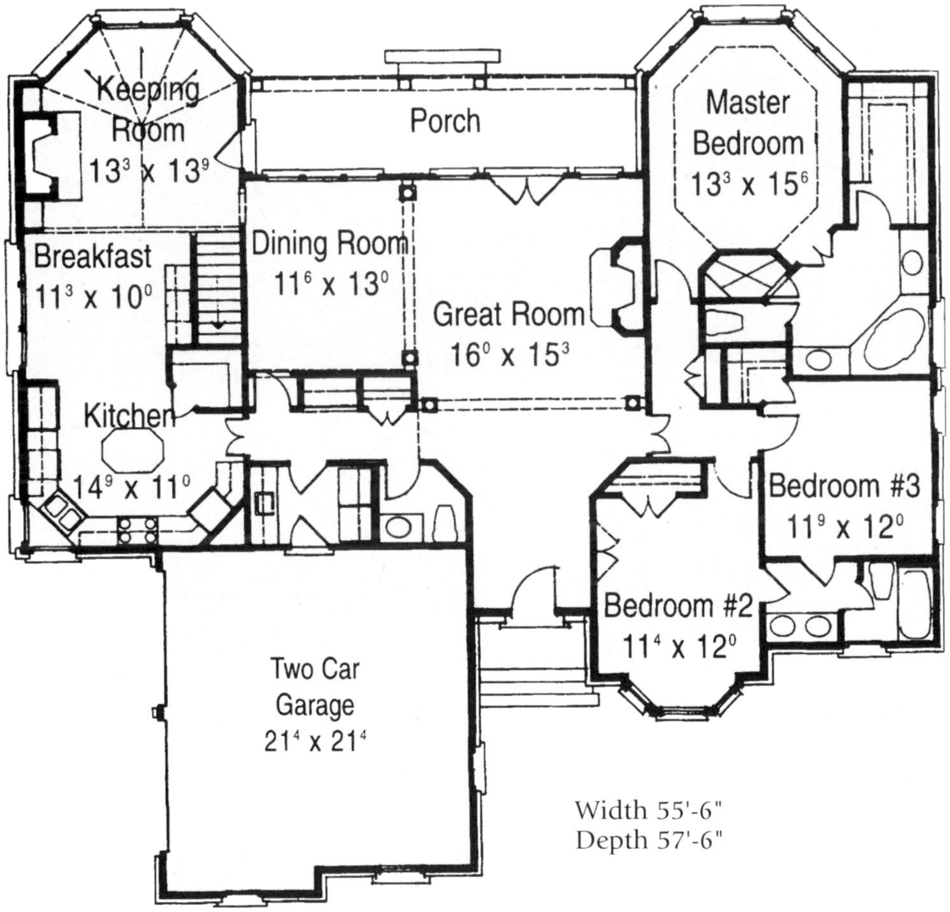

Width 55'-6"
Depth 57'-6"

RIVERS EDGE

Design T213

Square Footage: 1,738

Bedrooms: 3

Bathrooms: 2½

Classical details and a stately brick exterior accentuate the timeless elegance of this traditional home. A spacious floor plan offers an open great room and dining room, defined by decorative columns and set off by French doors, a triple window and a warming fireplace. The kitchen provides a large work island with a neighboring breakfast area and a keeping room with its own hearth. Bay windows brighten both the keeping room and the master suite, which features separate vanities, a walk-in closet and a garden tub. A covered porch expands the back of the house, providing an extra avenue for outdoor enjoyment.

ELLSWORTH MANOR

Design T090

Square Footage: 1,733
Bedrooms: 3
Bathrooms: 2½

Delightfully different, this brick one-story home has everything for the active family. The foyer opens to a formal dining room accented with decorative columns, and to a great room with a warming fireplace and lovely French doors to the rear deck. The efficient kitchen has an adjoining, light-filled breakfast nook. A split bedroom plan offers a secluded master suite with a coffered ceiling, His and Hers walk-in closets, a double-bowl vanity and a garden tub. Two family bedrooms, or one and a study, have separate access to a full bath on the left side of the plan.

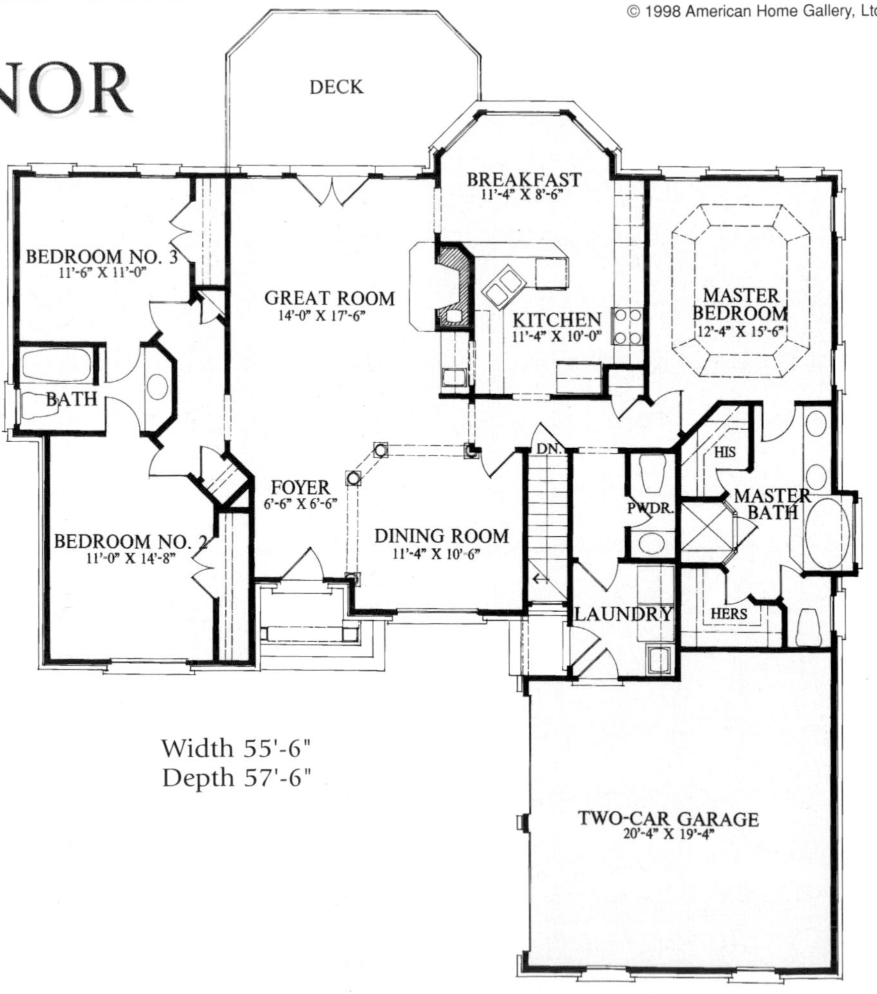

YORKTOWN GEORGIAN

Design T091

Square Footage: 1,850
Bedrooms: 3
Bathrooms: 2½

This stately brick home features a side-loading garage, which helps to maintain a beautiful facade. The elegant entry leads to a central hallway, connecting living areas and sleeping quarters, and opens to a formal dining room on the left. Plenty of natural light and views of the rear yard show off the great room, which includes a handsome fireplace and built-in bookcases. The spacious kitchen shares sunlight from the bayed breakfast nook. A splendid master suite with coffered ceiling offers a pleasant bath with a garden tub, a glass-enclosed shower, a dressing area and a walk-in closet. Two secondary bedrooms to the left of the plan share a full bath.

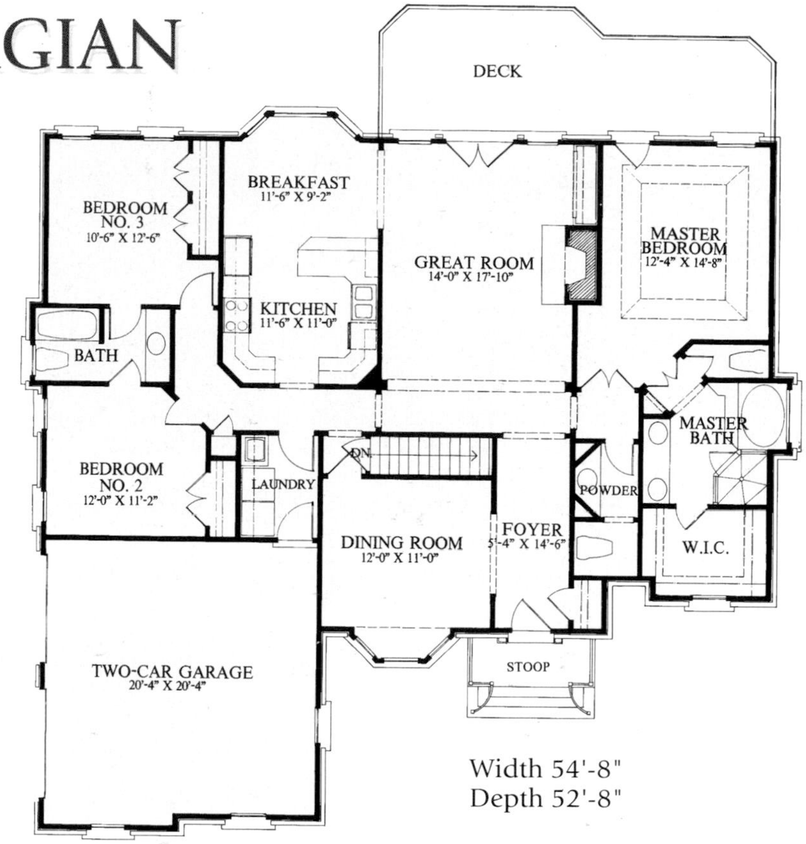
DECK
BREAKFAST
11'-6" X 9'-2"
BEDROOM
NO. 3
10'-6" X 12'-6"
KITCHEN
11'-6" X 11'-0"
GREAT ROOM
14'-0" X 17'-10"
MASTER
BEDROOM
12'-4" X 14'-8"
BATH
MASTER
BATH
BEDROOM
NO. 2
12'-0" X 11'-2"
LAUNDRY
DN
POWDER
FOYER
5'-4" X 14'-6"
DINING ROOM
12'-0" X 11'-0"
W.I.C.
STOOP
TWO-CAR GARAGE
20'-4" X 20'-4"

Width 54'-8"
Depth 52'-8"

SEDDON FALLS

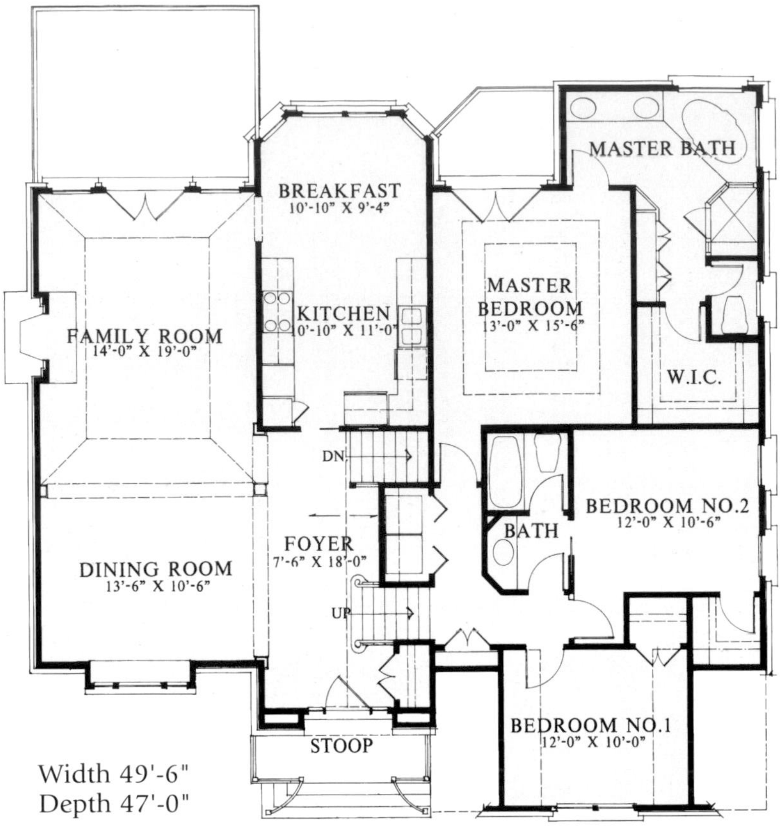

BREAKFAST
10'-10" X 9'-4"
MASTER BATH
MASTER BEDROOM
13'-0" X 15'-6"
KITCHEN
10'-10" X 11'-0"
FAMILY ROOM
14'-0" X 19'-0"
W.I.C.
DN
BEDROOM NO.2
12'-0" X 10'-6"
BATH
FOYER
7'-6" X 18'-0"
DINING ROOM
13'-6" X 10'-6"
UP
BEDROOM NO.1
12'-0" X 10'-0"
STOOP

Width 49'-6"
Depth 47'-0"

This lovely traditional home begins with a recessed entry that's set off by a graceful arch topped by a keystone. The foyer opens to a formal dining room, which adjoins the family room, replete with amenities such as a tray ceiling, a centered fireplace and a set of lovely French doors. A bayed breakfast nook enjoys expansive rear views and easy service from the kitchen. The master suite falls to the rear of the plan, and offers a compartmented toilet, a walk-in closet, a double-bowl vanity and an angled whirlpool tub. Bedroom 1 has a raised ceiling, while Bedroom 2 enjoys easy access to the compartmented hall bath.

Design T112

Square Footage: 1,770

Bedrooms: 3

Bathrooms: 2

TAPPING REEVE RETREAT

Graceful arches accent this traditional facade and announce a floor plan that's just a little different than the rest. The foyer and formal dining room along with an expansive family room with a centered fireplace are open to one another through columned archways. To the right of this central living area is a master suite with a coffered ceiling and a plush bath with dressing area, as well as a private den that offers a handsome fireplace. On the opposite side of the living area, a superb arrangement of the gourmet kitchen, the breakfast room with views of the side courtyard and a spectacular sun room create a casual place for family and guests to gather. Two family bedrooms and a full bath are connected by a hall just off the sun room.

Design T080

Square Footage: 2,120

Bedrooms: 3

Bathrooms: 3

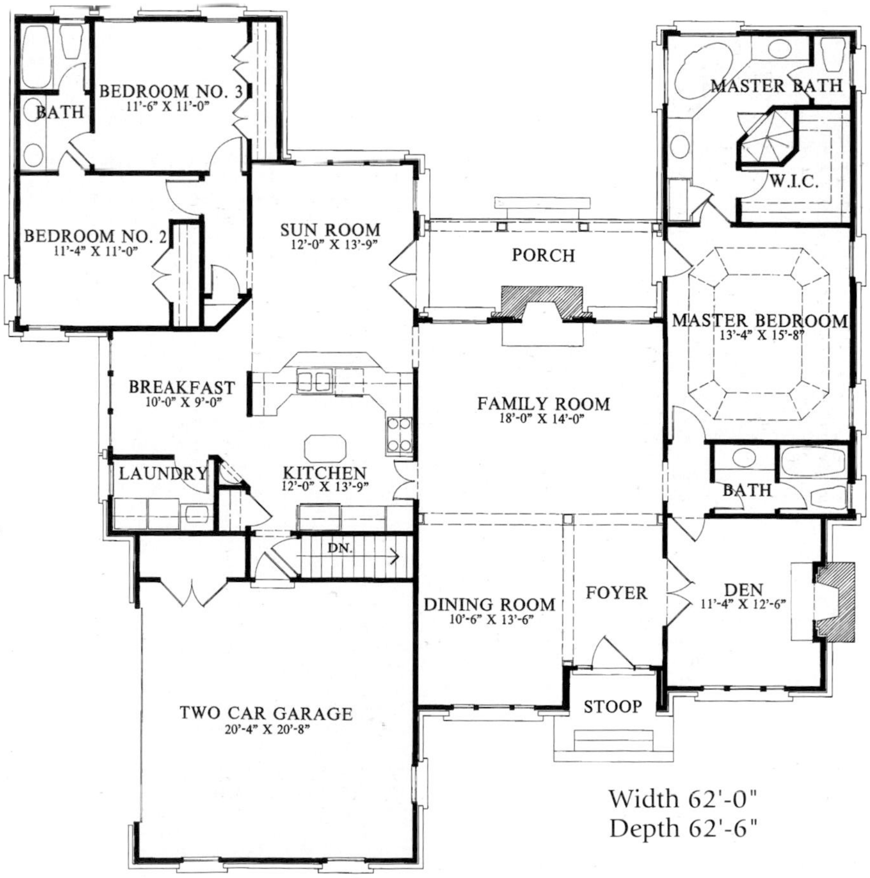

Width 62'-0"
Depth 62'-6"

A flared eave, multi-pane windows and graceful arches decorate the casual European-style facade and introduce an elegant interior theme that offers just a little more. The arch-top window sets off the stately motif with a touch of whimsy.

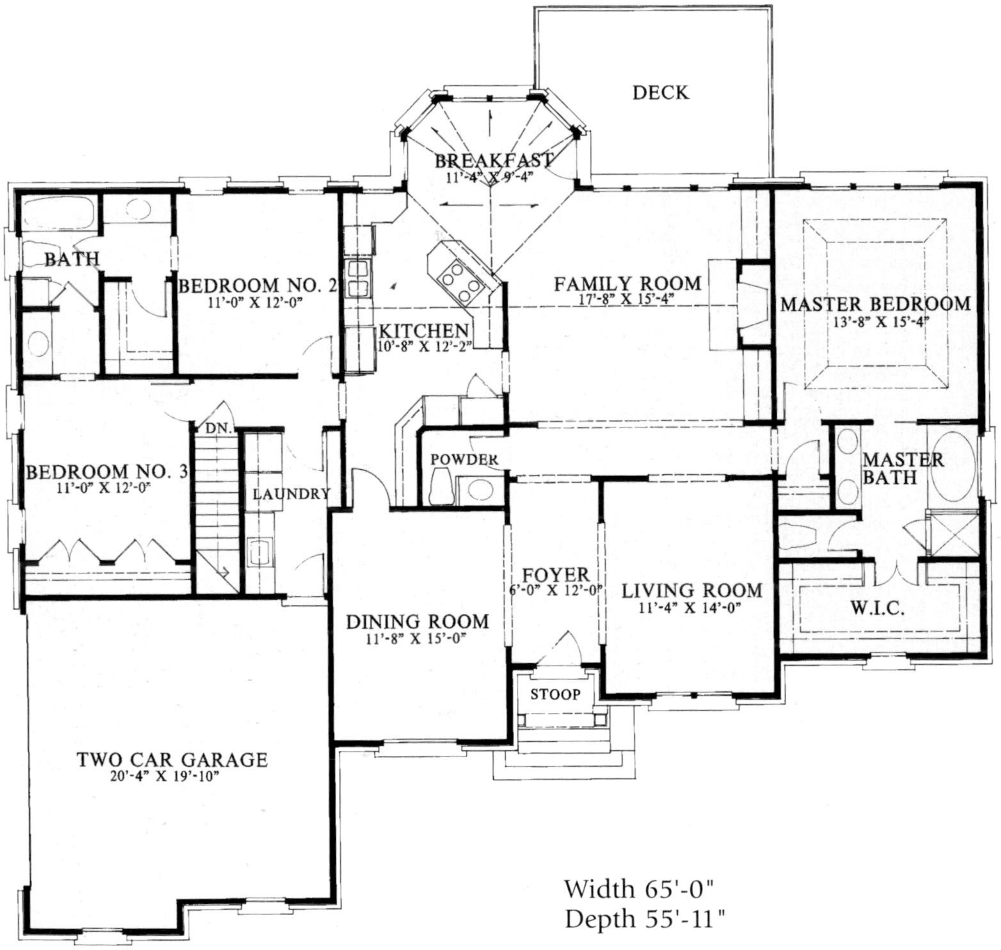
DECK
BREAKFAST
11'-4" X 9'-4"
BATH
BEDROOM NO. 2
11'-0" X 12'-0"
KITCHEN
10'-8" X 12'-2"
FAMILY ROOM
17'-8" X 15'-4"
MASTER BEDROOM
13'-8" X 15'-4"
DN.
BEDROOM NO. 3
11'-0" X 12'-0"
LAUNDRY
POWDER
MASTER
BATH
FOYER
6'-0" X 12'-0"
LIVING ROOM
11'-4" X 14'-0"
W.I.C.
DINING ROOM
11'-8" X 15'-0"
STOOP
TWO CAR GARAGE
20'-4" X 19'-10"

Width 65'-0"
Depth 55'-11"

CROPSEY FLARED COLONIAL

Design T073

Square Footage: 2,095

Bedrooms: 3

Bathrooms: 2½

Traditional and established, the look of this comfortable home is gently flavored with European elements. The foyer opens to the formal rooms and leads to casual living space, which opens to the entertainment deck. This versatile area offers a cozy fireplace with an extended hearth, built-in bookcases and wide views. The bayed breakfast nook opens to a spacious kitchen with a peninsula cooktop counter. A privacy door leads to the formal dining room which enjoys natural light from an arch-top window. Sleeping quarters include a master suite with a garden tub and two family bedrooms that share a full bath with separate vanities.

Ten Broeck Manor

Design T081

Square Footage: 2,295
Bedrooms: 3
Bathrooms: 2

One-story living takes a lovely traditional turn in this brick home. The entry foyer opens to the formal dining room and the great room through graceful columned archways. The open gourmet kitchen, bayed breakfast nook and keeping room with fireplace will be a magnet for family activity. French doors open to a spacious deck—an inviting place to enjoy the outdoors. Sleeping quarters include two family bedrooms and a hall bath, and a rambling master suite with a bayed sitting area and a deluxe bath. A two-car garage boasts a box-bay window and offers a convenient service entrance which leads to the kitchen.

DECK
SITTING AREA
12'-0" X 12'-0"
MASTER SUITE
13'-0" X 17'-6"
M.BATH
M.CLOSET
GREAT ROOM
20'-6" X 19'-0"
KITCHEN
10'-0" X 18'-0"
BREAKFAST
11'-4" X 10'-0"
KEEPING ROOM
11'-4" X 11'-0"
PNTRY
DN.
LAUNDRY
CLO.
CLO.
BATH
LIN.
COAT
BEDROOM NO. 3
12'-0" X 11'-8"
BEDROOM NO. 2
13'-10" X 12'-6"
FOYER
8'-0" X 14'-4"
DINING ROOM
12'-0" X 14'-4"
TWO CAR GARAGE
21'-4" X 21'-5"
STOOP

Width 69'-0"
Depth 49'-6"

Hip roofs, gentle arches and two dormers call up a sense of Ranch-style homes, circa 1950, to this charming cottage. The quoins and classical detailing of the columns add a more sophisticated appeal.

© 1998 American Home Gallery, Ltd.

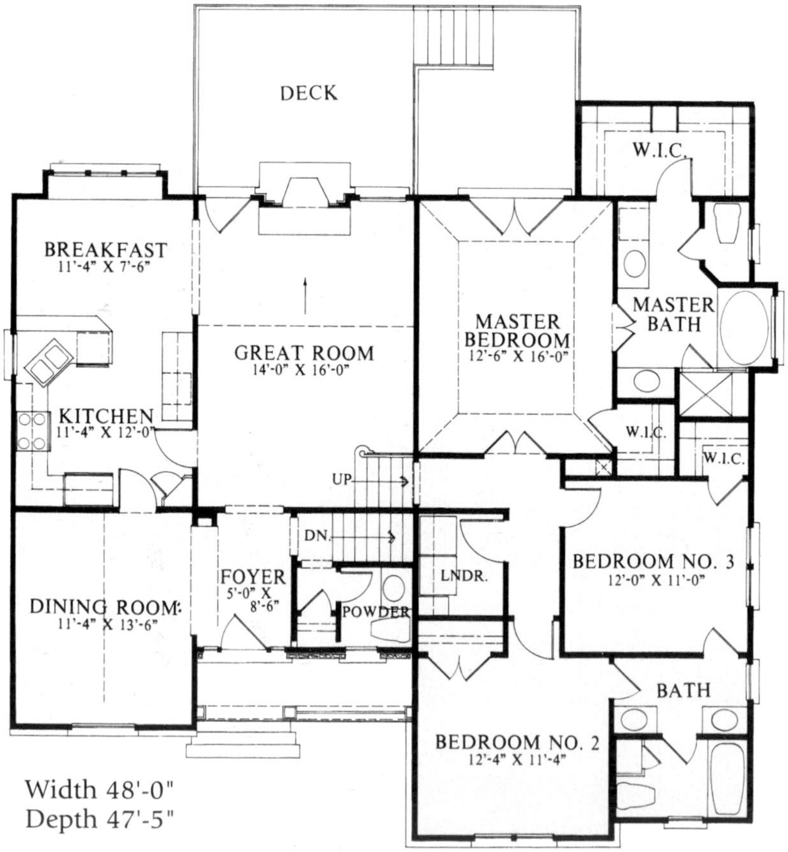
DECK
W.I.C.
BREAKFAST
11'-4" X 7'-6"
GREAT ROOM
14'-0" X 16'-0"
MASTER
BEDROOM
12'-6" X 16'-0"
MASTER
BATH
KITCHEN
11'-4" X 12'-0"
W.I.C.
W.I.C.
UP
DN.
FOYER
5'-0" X
8'-6"
LNDR.
BEDROOM NO. 3
12'-0" X 11'-0"
DINING ROOM
11'-4" X 13'-6"
POWDER
BATH
BEDROOM NO. 2
12'-4" X 11'-4"

Width 48'-0"
Depth 47'-5"

Markham Hill

Design T137

Square Footage: 1,770
Bedrooms: 3
Bathrooms: 2½

Gentle arches extend a warm welcome to this comfortable home, while a well-tailored foyer leads to both formal and casual areas. The dining room is easily served by the kitchen, which features wrapping counters and a breakfast room with a box-bay window. A fireplace in the great room is framed by a tall window and a French door, which leads to the rear deck. The sleeping wing includes a master suite with two walk-in closets, separate vanities and a garden tub. Two additional bedrooms, one with its own walk-in closet, share a bath with a compartmented lavatory.

PORCH
BREAKFAST
10'-0" X 10'-0"
GREAT ROOM
16'-0" X 18'-0"
MASTER BEDROOM
15'-0" X 14'-0"
W.I.C.
MASTER BATH
POWDER
KITCHEN
14'-0" X 11'-4"
DINING ROOM
10'-6" X 13'-0"
FOYER
5'-0" X 9'-0"
BEDROOM NO. 3
10'-6" X 10'-0"
BEDROOM NO. 2
11'-2" X 11'-0"
BATH
LAUND
5'-2" X 10'-6"
DN.
TWO CAR GARAGE
20'-4" X 19'-4"

Width 60'-0"
Depth 60'-6"

TILLMAN FALLS

A thoughtful blend of traditional and casual are brought together in this fundamentally simple design. With zoned living at the core of this floor plan, livability takes a convenient turn. The formal dining room is open to the central hallway and foyer, and features graceful columned archways to define its space. The great room has angled corners and a magnificent central fireplace and offers ample views to the rear grounds. Steps away is a well-lit breakfast room and an adjoining U-shaped kitchen with wrapping counter space. Sleeping quarters are clustered around a private hallway which offers a powder room. The master suite includes a resplendent bath with a garden tub and a walk-in closet.

Design T110

Square Footage: 1,815

Bedrooms: 3

Bathrooms: 2½

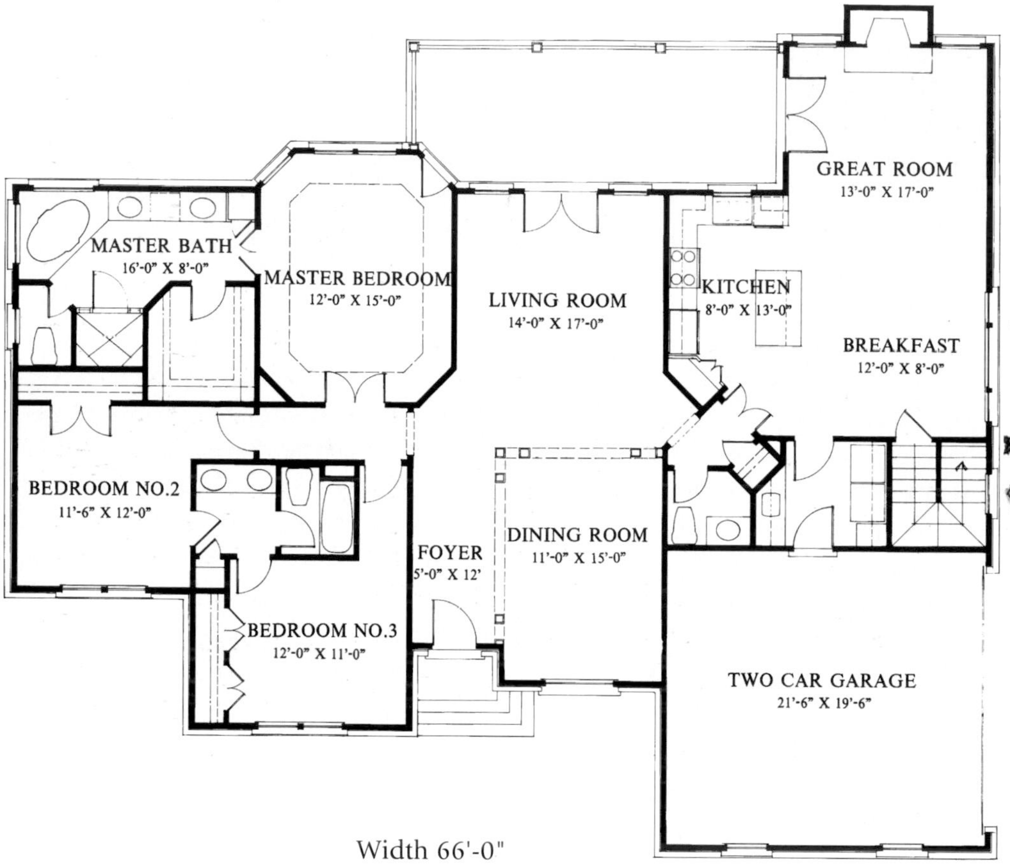

MASTER BATH
16'-0" X 8'-0"
MASTER BEDROOM
12'-0" X 15'-0"
LIVING ROOM
14'-0" X 17'-0"
KITCHEN
8'-0" X 13'-0"
GREAT ROOM
13'-0" X 17'-0"
BREAKFAST
12'-0" X 8'-0"
BEDROOM NO.2
11'-6" X 12'-0"
FOYER
5'-0" X 12'
DINING ROOM
11'-0" X 15'-0"
BEDROOM NO.3
12'-0" X 11'-0"
TWO CAR GARAGE
21'-6" X 19'-6"

Width 66'-0"
Depth 54'-0"

Stunning details cover the entry to this single-story American classic. Textures of brick and stucco are used to create an eclectic theme, softened by familiar accents such as fanlight transoms and paneled shutters.

VAUGHN HOMESTEAD

This American classic begins with a recessed entry that announces a modern interior designed for entertaining as well as relaxed gatherings. The foyer leads to the living room, which opens through French doors to the back property, and to a banquet-size dining room, defined by a splendid colonnade. The spacious kitchen has a work island and a sunlit breakfast area that shares the warmth of a hearth in the great room. French doors open to the master suite, which features a lovely bay window and a lavish bath. Two additional bedrooms, each with a spacious closet, share a bath with dual vanities.

Design T241

Square Footage: 2,077

Bedrooms: 3

Bathrooms: 2½

CAMBRIDGE CROSSING

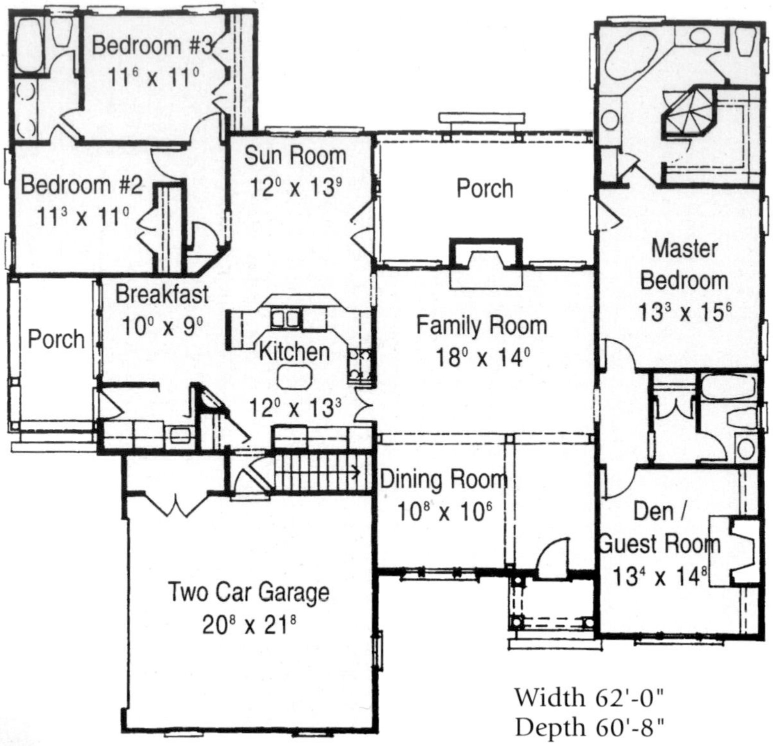

Decorative columns define the formal dining room of this lovely traditional home and announce a casual interior with plenty of space for family gatherings. The gourmet kitchen overlooks the sun room, which opens to the rear porch through French doors. A covered side porch invites morning meals outdoors, while the breakfast room offers a casual dining area inside. Split sleeping quarters allow the master suite a private wing which includes a den or guest room with its own fireplace. An angled, oversized shower and a corner whirlpool tub highlight the master bath. Each of the family bedrooms has private access to the shared bath, which offers a compartmented vanity.

Width 62'-0"
Depth 60'-8"

Design T212

Square Footage: 2,140

Bedrooms: 3

Bathrooms: 3

OAKRIDGE TRACE

Design T214

Square Footage: 2,150
Bedrooms: 3
Bathrooms: 3

This classic cottage with its brick exterior features a detailed porch and a box-bay window. Inside, the spacious dining room features column detailing and French doors that lead to the front porch. At the heart of the home, the family room features a hearth framed by windows that overlook the porch at the rear, providing an outstanding garden view. The master suite has direct access to the outdoors. The master bath has a large walk-in closet and separate vanities. Privately located, adjacent to the foyer, is a den with a built-in window seat and warming hearth. A full bath is right next to the den and is perfectly located to accommodate a guest.

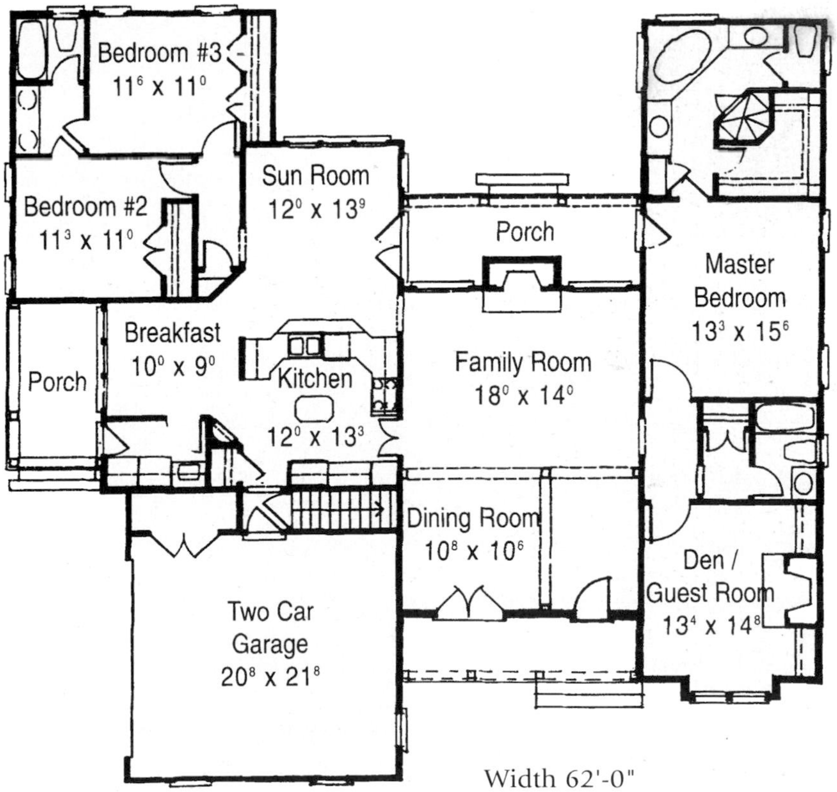

Width 62'-0"
Depth 59'-8"

Hampshire Bay Colonial

Design T079

First Floor: 1,140 square feet
Second Floor: 1,360 square feet
Total: 2,500 square feet

Bedrooms: 4
Bathrooms: 3½

Rich, traditional styling of brick and wood create a classy tone for this two-story home. The recessed entry opens to formal living and dining rooms. Sets of lovely windows in both areas allow an abundance of natural light. The kitchen features wide wrapping counters and easily serves the dining room as well as a breakfast area, which is graced with a bay window. A centered fireplace in the great room shares its warmth with the casual eating nook. On the second floor, two family bedrooms share a full bath with two lavatories. An additional bedroom has its own bath, plenty of wardrobe space and a private study. The master suite features a garden tub and separate shower, a walk-in closet and an angled vanity.

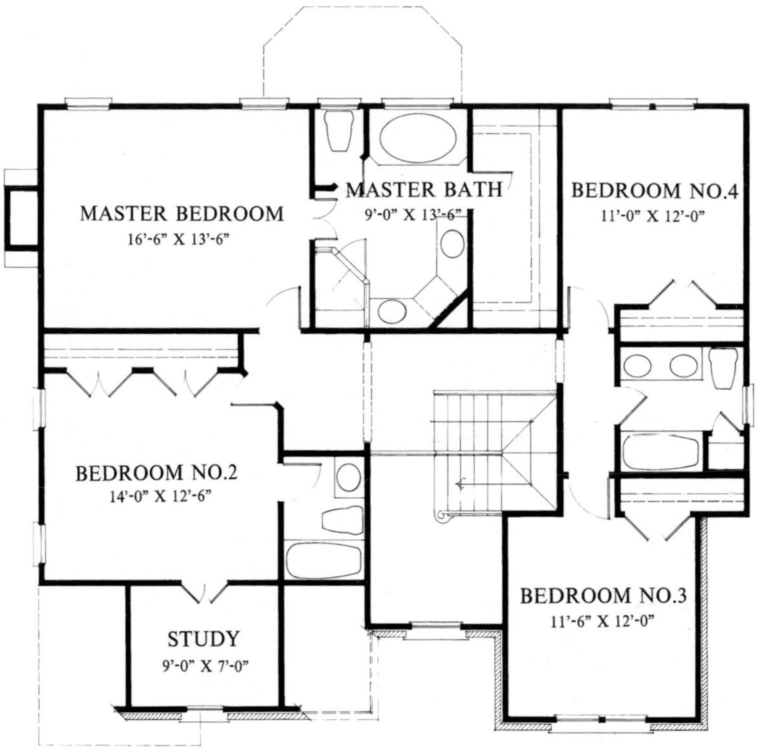
MASTER BEDROOM
16'-6" X 13'-6"
MASTER BATH
9'-0" X 13'-6"
BEDROOM NO.4
11'-0" X 12'-0"
BEDROOM NO.2
14'-0" X 12'-6"
BEDROOM NO.3
11'-6" X 12'-0"
STUDY
9'-0" X 7'-0"

Width 43'-6"
Depth 45'-0"

Second Floor

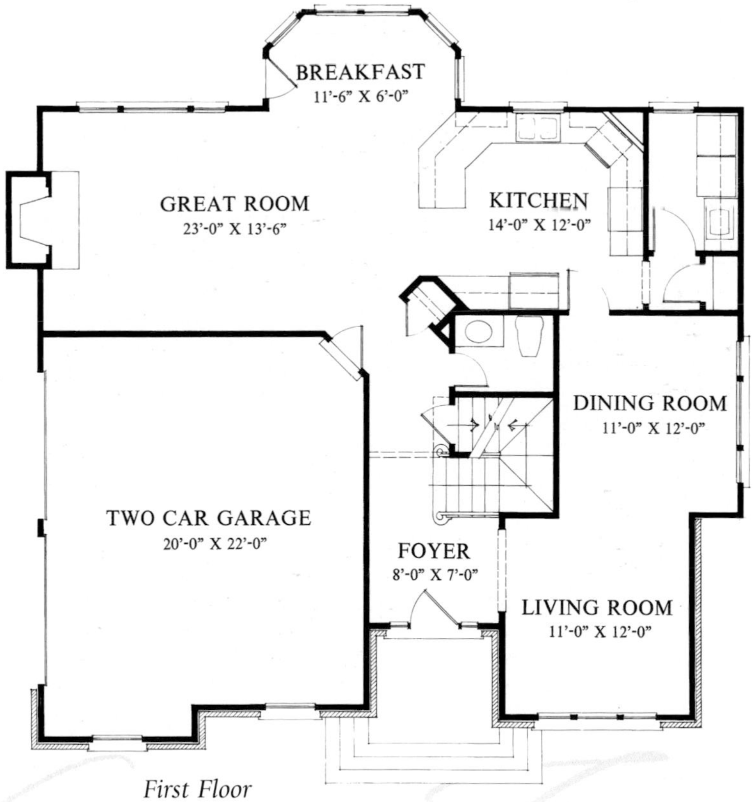
BREAKFAST
11'-6" X 6'-0"
GREAT ROOM
23'-0" X 13'-6"
KITCHEN
14'-0" X 12'-0"
DINING ROOM
11'-0" X 12'-0"
TWO CAR GARAGE
20'-0" X 22'-0"
FOYER
8'-0" X 7'-0"
LIVING ROOM
11'-0" X 12'-0"

First Floor

The garage is hidden to make the curb elevation seem larger than the home actually is. The front of the home is enhanced with a series of nested gables on a simple hipped rectangle. What seems to be a complicated home is really very simple to build.

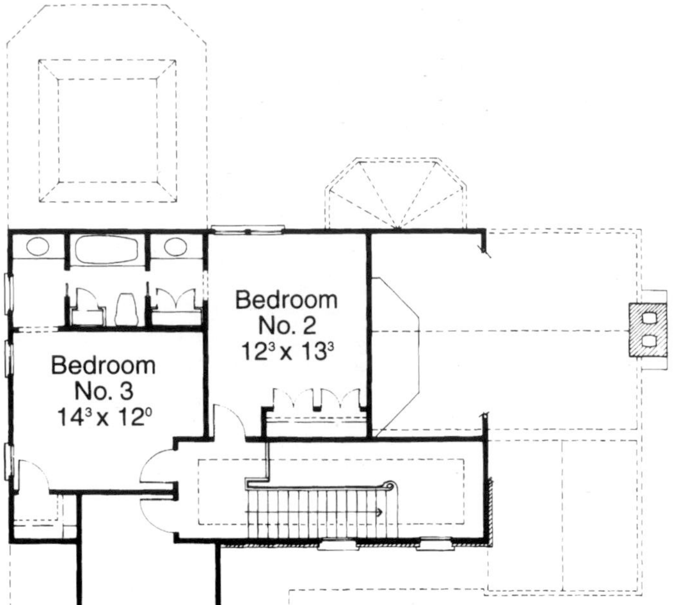

Second Floor

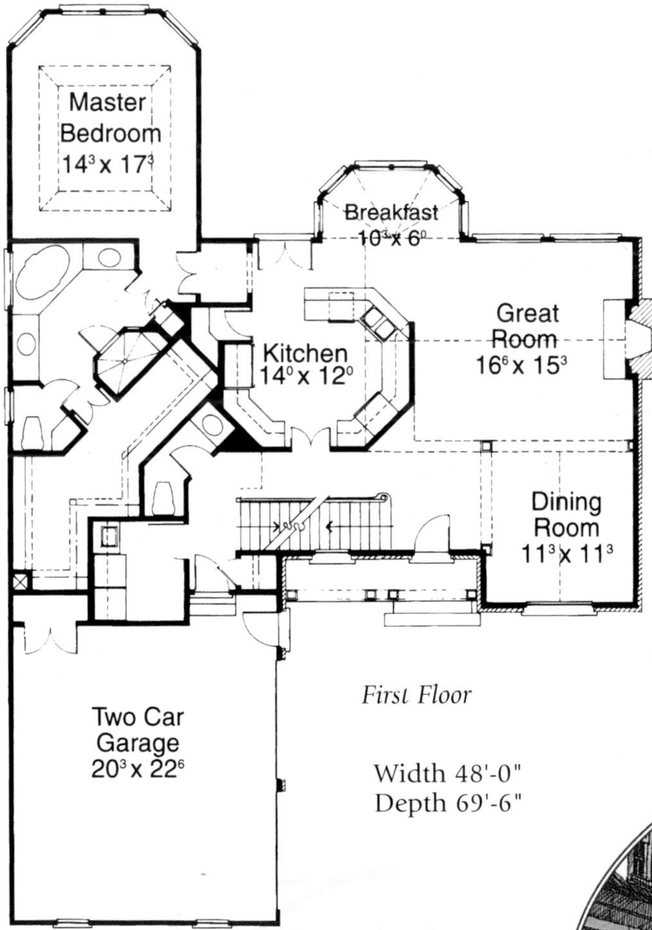

First Floor

Width 48'-0"
Depth 69'-6"

Here's a very casual and comfortable looking home. The detailing of the porch, garage doors and special windows are borrowed from homes seen in older neighborhoods of the 1930s and 1940s.

AZALEA HILL

Today's tastes are more eclectic and household arrangements come in new flavors, so a flexible floor plan is key. Traditional formality asks for well-defined rooms, while the demands of sophisticated lifestyles call for wide open spaces that bend to patterns of living. This plan marries the best of both casual and elegant elements for a home that breathes with individual style. The formal dining room opens through decorative pillars to the two-story great room, which features a fireplace. French doors lead from the a private vestibule to the deluxe master suite, a retreat which has a lavish bath with an angled whirlpool tub, a glass-enclosed shower, twin vanities and a rambling walk-in closet. Two family bedrooms share a bath upstairs.

Design T203

First Floor: 1,580 square feet
Second Floor: 595 square feet
Total: 2,175 square feet

Bedrooms: 3
Bathrooms: 2½

This sophisticated, classic home shows three parts: an entrance section, a living section and a garage carriage wing. The three sections marry nicely, with the front door having more importance than the garage.

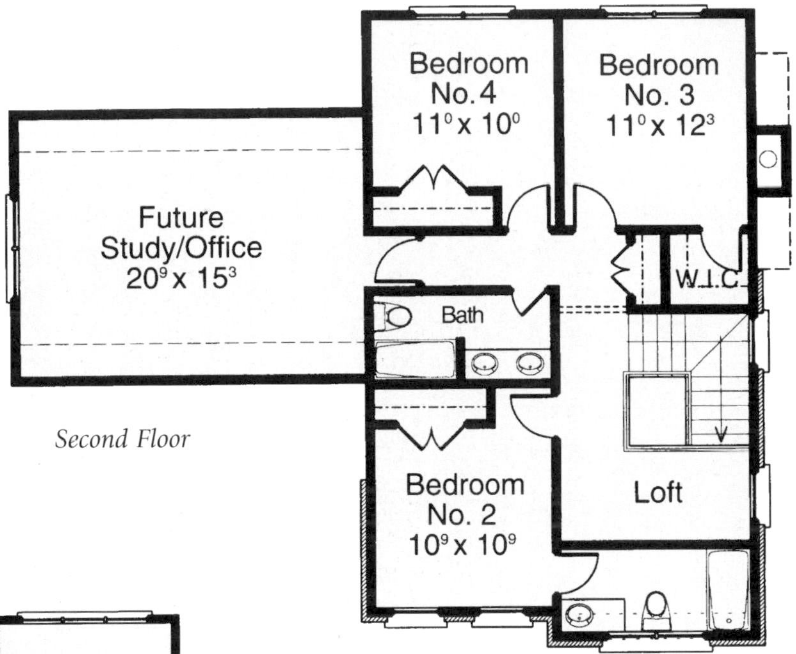

Second Floor

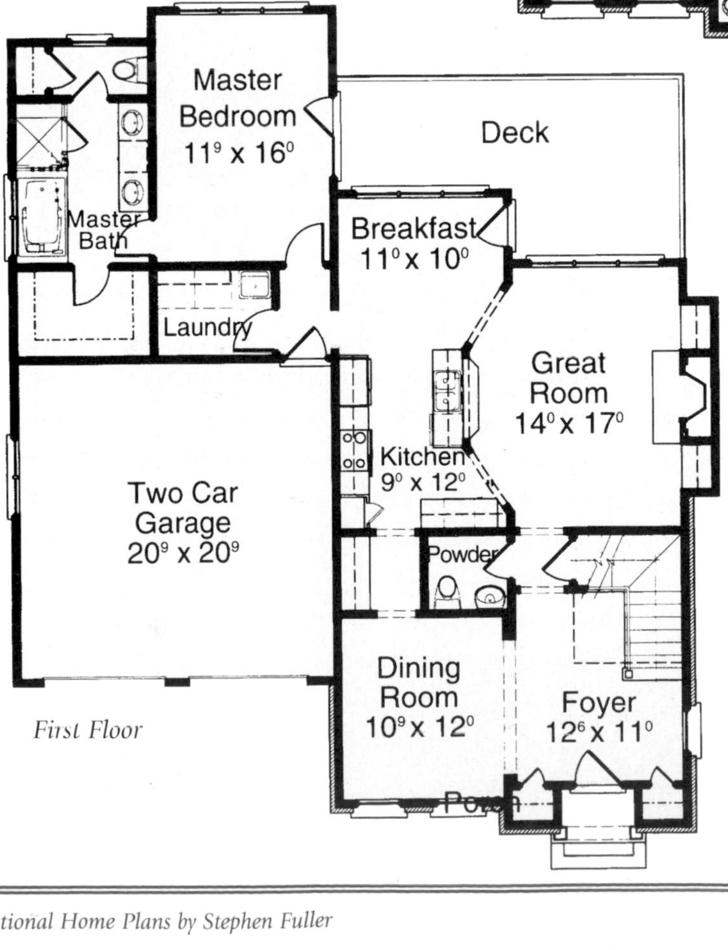

First Floor

Width 57'-6"
Depth 51'-6"

BRENTWOOD

Welcoming and graceful, this home is perfect for those who entertain and enjoy the company of friends and guests. The front steps lead to a recessed entry, enhanced with pilasters and a classical cornice detail. The foyer opens to the formal dining room, which is served by a well-organized kitchen through a butler's pantry. A centered fireplace warms the spacious great room, which has a lovely triple window. The nearby breakfast area leads out to the rear deck, also accessed from the master suite. Upstairs, two family bedrooms share a full bath while a fourth bedroom has a private bath. A loft area offers space for computers.

Design T229

First Floor: 1,355 square feet
Second Floor: 760 square feet
Total: 2,115 square feet

Bedrooms: 4
Bathrooms: 3½

STUDY PKG. 630
4 SET BLDG PKG 695
8 SET " " 735

GARRETT HOMESTEAD

Design T098

First Floor: 1,270 square feet
Second Floor: 1,070 square feet
Total: 2,340 square feet

Bedrooms: 4
Bathrooms: 3½

6:30 STUDY
675 4SET
730 8SET

Grand and welcoming, the columned entry to this traditional home manages a look that's both stylish and comfortable. Formal rooms frame the foyer, which leads to casual living space. A dramatic breakfast nook adjoins the family room and provides a highlight for the spacious interior. Open planning allows the warmth of the fireplace in the family room to enhance the eating area and kitchen as well. Natural light fills the casual living space through an abundance of windows. A secluded guest suite is convenient to the laundry and to the service entrance from the two-car garage. A coffered ceiling, two walk-in closets and separate vanities add both style and comfort to the second-floor master suite.

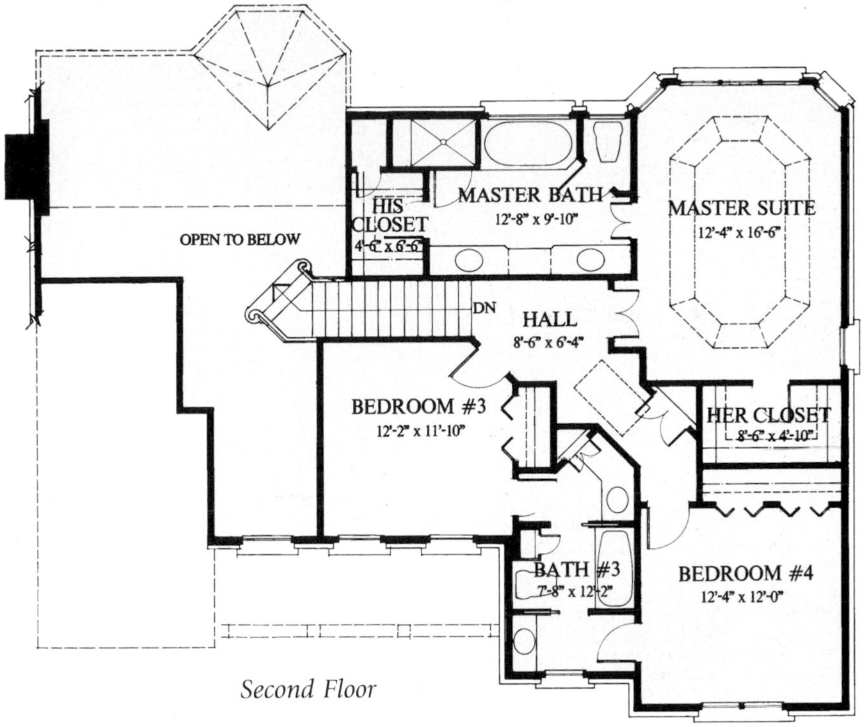

OPEN TO BELOW
HIS CLOSET
4'-6" x 6'-6"
MASTER BATH
12'-8" x 9'-10"
MASTER SUITE
12'-4" x 16'-6"
DN
HALL
8'-6" x 6'-4"
BEDROOM #3
12'-2" x 11'-10"
HER CLOSET
8'-6" x 4'-10"
BATH #3
7'-8" x 12'-2"
BEDROOM #4
12'-4" x 12'-0"

Second Floor

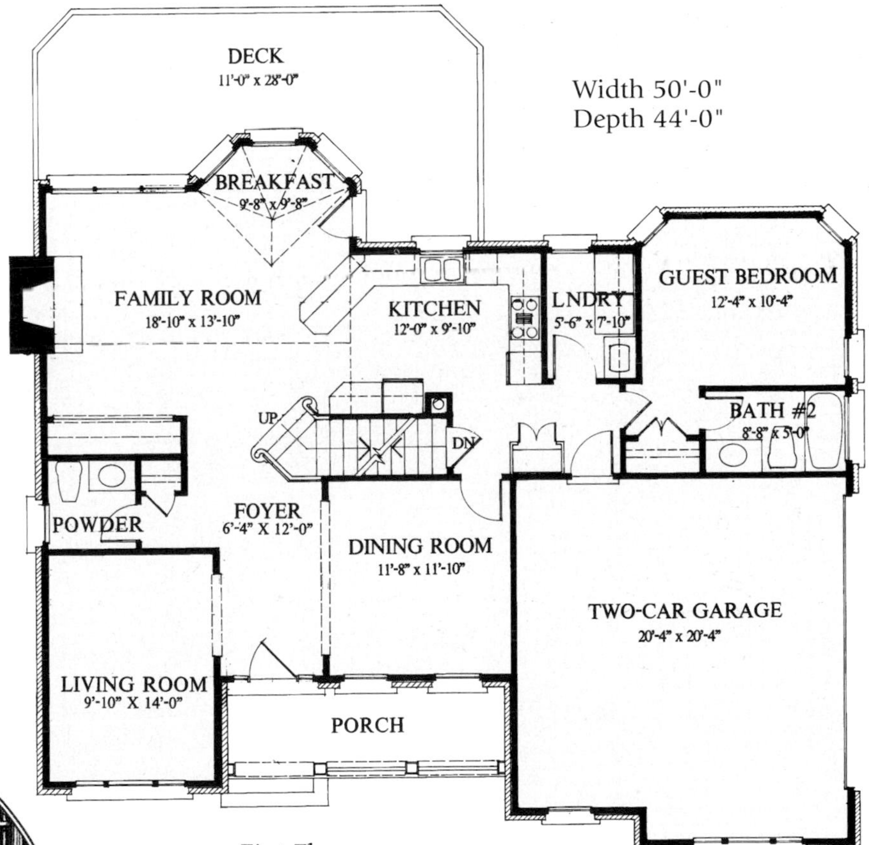

DECK
11'-0" x 28'-0"
Width 50'-0"
Depth 44'-0"
BREAKFAST
9'-8" x 9'-8"
FAMILY ROOM
18'-10" x 13'-10"
KITCHEN
12'-0" x 9'-10"
LNDRY
5'-6" x 7'-10"
GUEST BEDROOM
12'-4" x 10'-4"
UP
DN
BATH #2
8'-8" x 5'-0"
POWDER
FOYER
6'-4" X 12'-0"
DINING ROOM
11'-8" x 11'-10"
TWO-CAR GARAGE
20'-4" x 20'-4"
LIVING ROOM
9'-10" X 14'-0"
PORCH

First Floor

Decorative columns, a glass-paneled entry and simple balusters add a gentle Colonial flavor to this traditional home. The quaint front porch makes an inviting, casual place to gather, while formal rooms off the foyer handle more traditional occasions.

MASTER SUITE
15'-6" x 15'-0"
BEDROOM No.2
11'-6" x 12'-6"
BEDROOM No.4
12'-6" x 10'-0"
DN
OPEN TO BELOW
M. BATH
BATH
BEDROOM No.3
15'-4" x 13'-0"
MASTER CLOSET

Second Floor

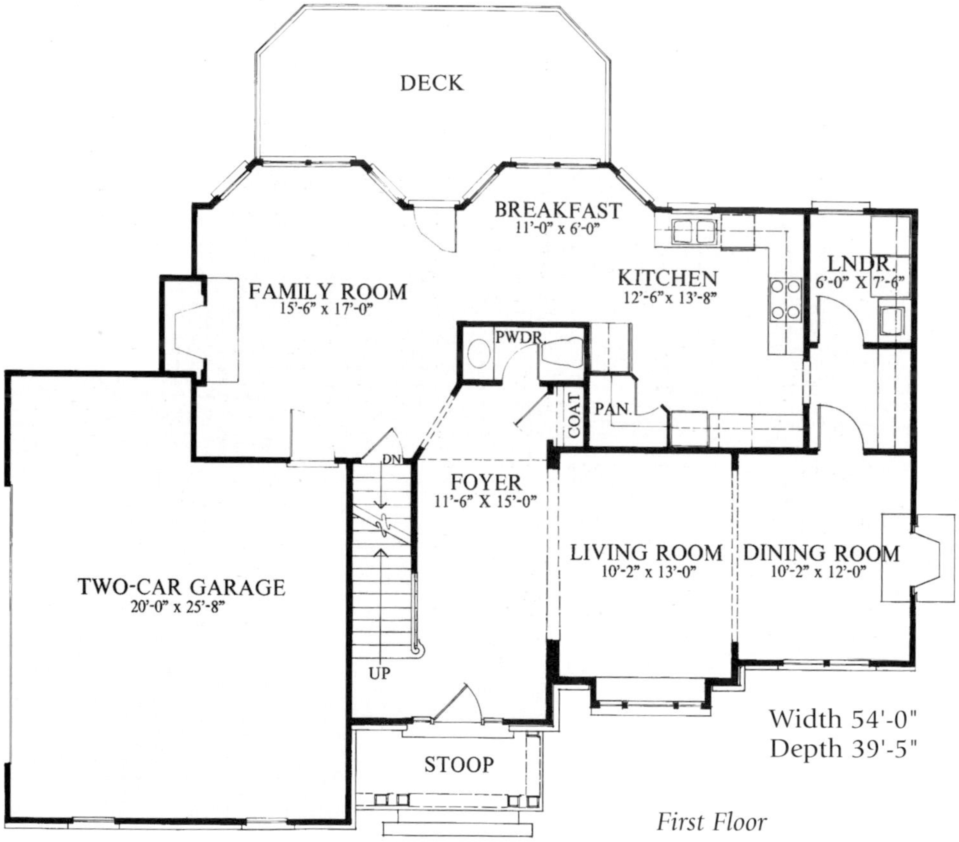
DECK
BREAKFAST
11'-0" x 6'-0"
FAMILY ROOM
15'-6" x 17'-0"
KITCHEN
12'-6"x 13'-8"
LNDR.
6'-0" X 7'-6"
PWDR
COAT
PAN.
DN
FOYER
11'-6" X 15'-0"
LIVING ROOM
10'-2" x 13'-0"
DINING ROOM
10'-2" x 12'-0"
TWO-CAR GARAGE
20'-0" x 25'-8"
UP
STOOP

Width 54'-0"
Depth 39'-5"

First Floor

This attractive, classic exterior introduces an open, sophisticated interior design. Flower boxes and a covered entrance flanked by columns enhance the brick-and-siding facade. Palladian and box-bay windows add smart elegance.

SIERRA

Design T056

First Floor: 1,156 square feet
Second Floor: 1,239 square feet
Total: 2,395 square feet

Bedrooms: 4
Bathrooms: 2½

At once sophisticated and casual, this appealing facade conceals an unrestrained floor plan, perfectly fit for family living as well as elegant entertaining. Formal rooms are thoughtfully placed to the right of the foyer, and provide a fireplace and two sets of lovely windows. A butler's pantry handles planned events and adjoins a well-organized kitchen with a breakfast area. Two large bay windows brighten the casual living space, which offers a door to the rear deck. The master suite, with its beautiful bay window, is located upstairs. The master bath has a luxurious tub, a separate shower and dual vanities. Three secondary bedrooms share a compartmented bath.

ORCHARD HILLS

Design T210

First Floor: 975 square feet
Second Floor: 1,320 square feet
Total: 2,295 square feet

Bedrooms: 4
Bathrooms: 2½

Many traditions come together handsomely in this picturesque home. A spacious foyer leads to the formal rooms, which are defined by a fireplace and arch-top windows. Bay windows brighten the breakfast area and the family room, which is warmed by a hearth. A French door opens to the rear deck—an inviting place to enjoy the outdoors. The kitchen features a corner pantry and wrapping counter space and serves the formal dining room through a convenient butler's pantry. Second-floor sleeping quarters include a generous master suite with two walk-in closets, separate vanities and a garden tub. Three additional bedrooms are connected by a gallery hall which leads to a full bath.

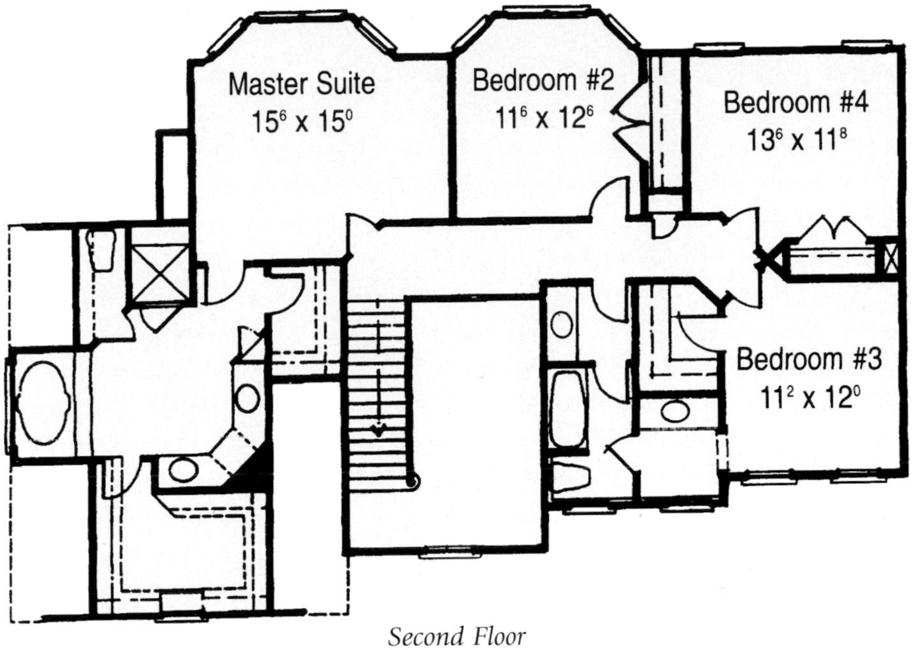

Second Floor

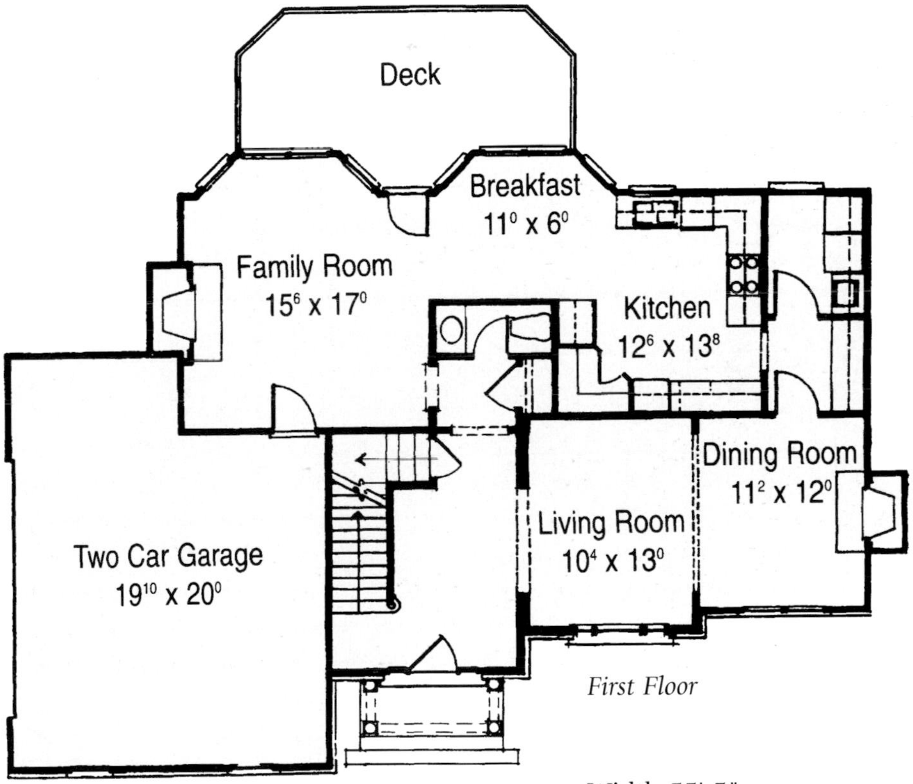

First Floor

Width 55'-5"
Depth 39'-0"

Traditional jack-arches artfully blended with arched transoms and asymmetrical gables create classic elegance on this lovely exterior. Glass panels surround the entry, complemented by pilasters and copper-seam flashing.

CHANTERELLE GLEN

Design T201

First Floor: 2,076 square feet
Second Floor: 843 square feet
Total: 2,919 square feet

Bedrooms: 4
Bathrooms: 3½

Elegant arches, rounded columns and a classic brick exterior resonate with a simple, natural theme: the pride of place. Inside, the foyer opens to a formal dining room, defined by decorative columns, and leads to a two-story great room with a fireplace and a bay window. The kitchen and breakfast area overlook this casual space and share its natural light. The master wing includes a spacious bedroom with a coffered ceiling, a sumptuous bath and a separate study with its own hearth. Two family bedrooms share the second floor with a loft that offers space for computers and books.

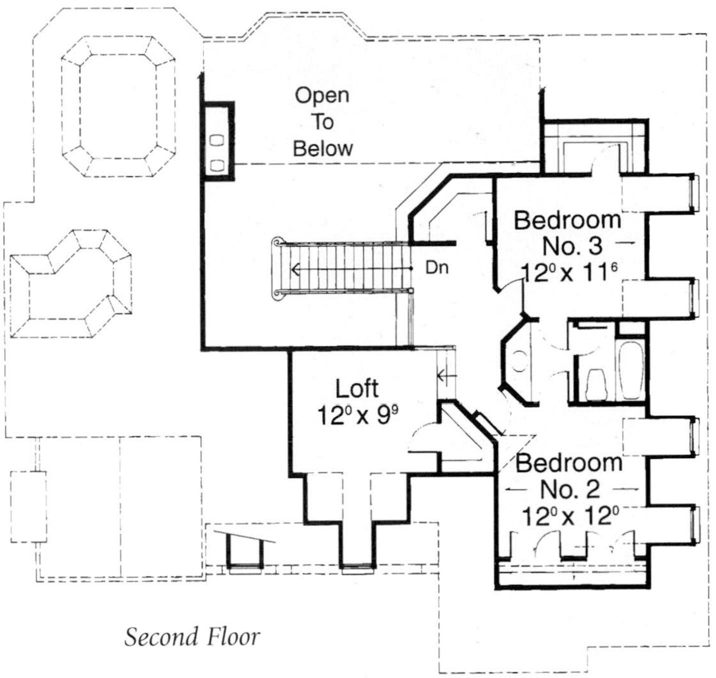

Second Floor

Width 57'-6"
Depth 51'-6"

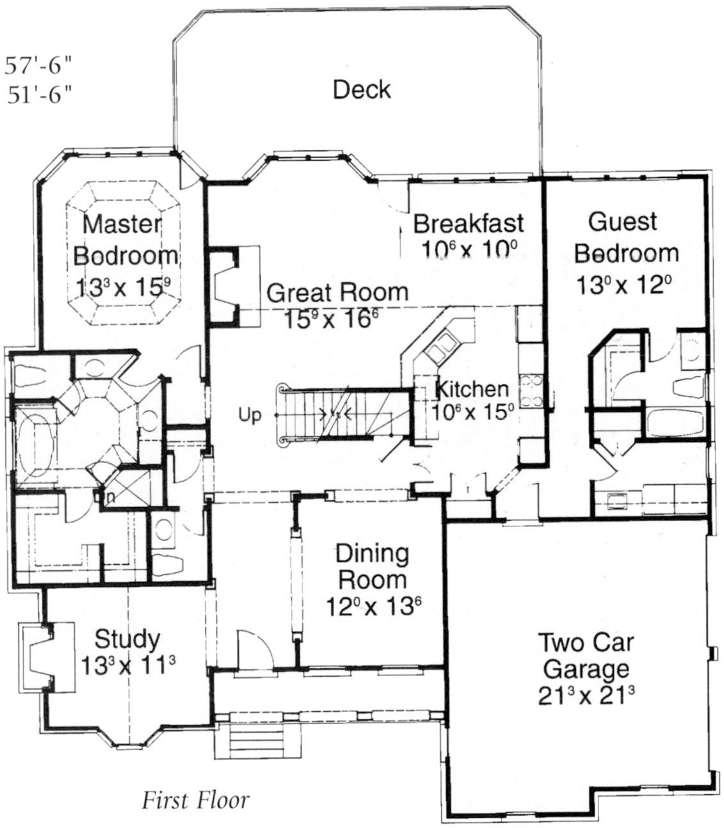

First Floor

A spiderweb fanlight and a box-paneled front door create a warm welcome, while a sitting porch adds an aura of hospitality. Muntin windows and sidelights add formality to this brick elevation.

A welcoming front porch signals the comfortable homey spaces within. Graceful arches and columns announce a modern style that retains the insouciant charm of an Early American country cottage.

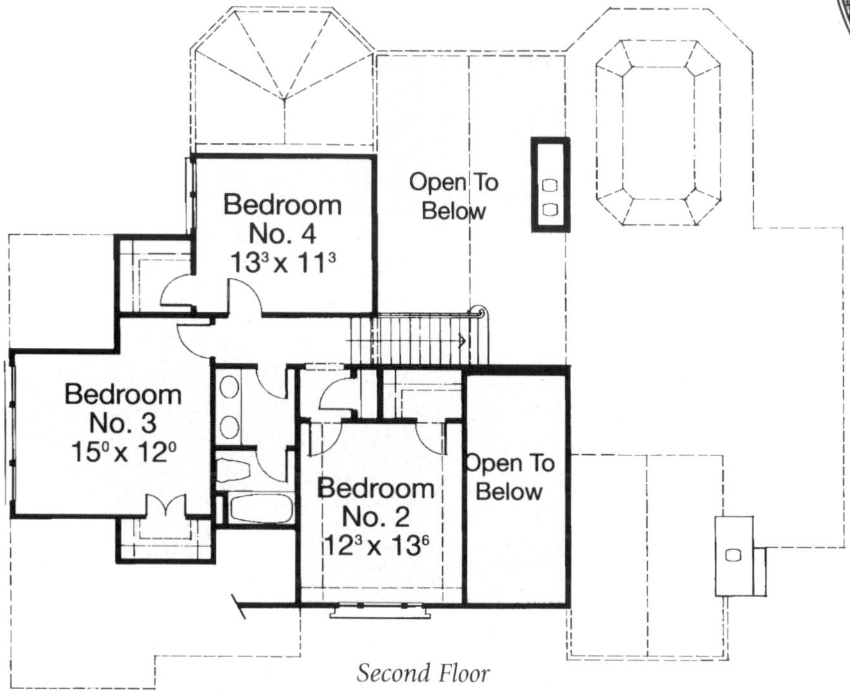

Second Floor

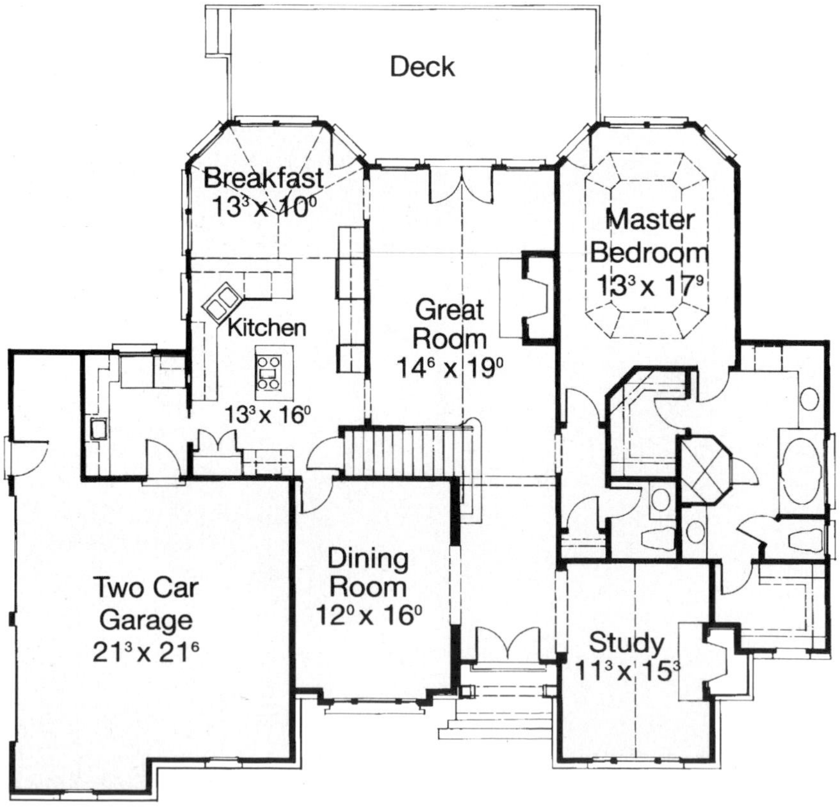

First Floor

Width 63'-0"
Depth 51'-6"

IVY GLEN

Design T189

First Floor: 1,932 square feet
Second Floor: 807 square feet
Total: 2,739 square feet

Bedrooms: 4 630 STUDY PK.
Bathrooms: 2½ 675 4 SET
735 8 PACKAGE

The brick-and-siding exterior of this Colonial adaptation is set off by a cozy, covered porch, just right for enjoying cool evenings outside. A two-story foyer opens to a quiet study with a centered fireplace, and to the formal dining room with views of the front property. The gourmet kitchen features an island cooktop counter and a charming breakfast nook. The great room soars two stories high but is made cozy by an extended-hearth fireplace. Two walk-in closets, a garden tub and a separate shower highlight the master bath, while a coffered ceiling decorates the homeowner's bedroom.

Design T198

First Floor: 1,621 square feet
Second Floor: 1,766 square feet
Total: 3,387 square feet

Bedrooms: 4
Bathrooms: 3½

STRATFORD PLACE

An all-American charm springs from the true Colonial style of this distinctive home. Formal rooms are set off from the foyer with decorative columns. At the heart of the home is a well-organized kitchen, which features an island cooktop counter, an ample pantry and counter space that's open to the breakfast and family rooms. A guest room is located behind the kitchen area, making it a perfect maid's quarters or guest room. The master suite has a private study, a fireplace and an amenity-laden bath with extended walk-in closet. Two additional bedrooms share a private, compartmented bath.

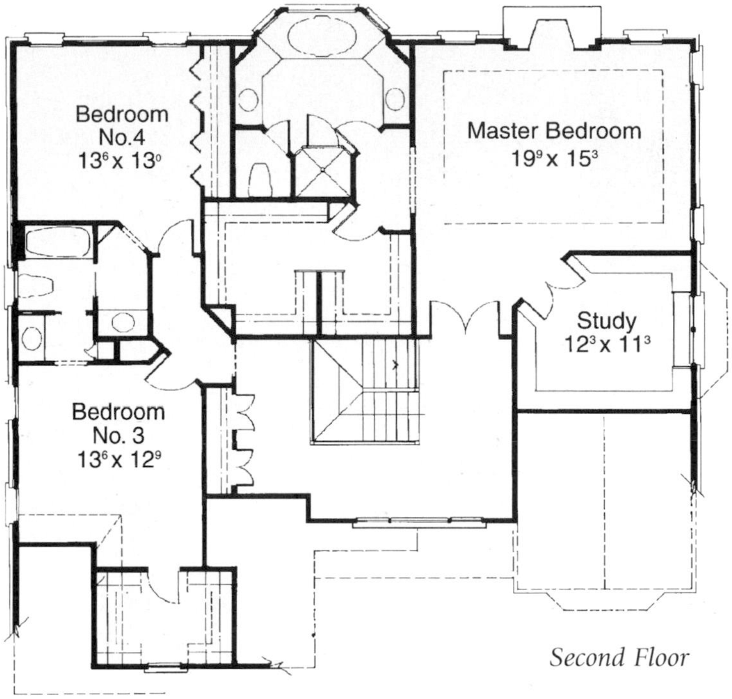

Second Floor

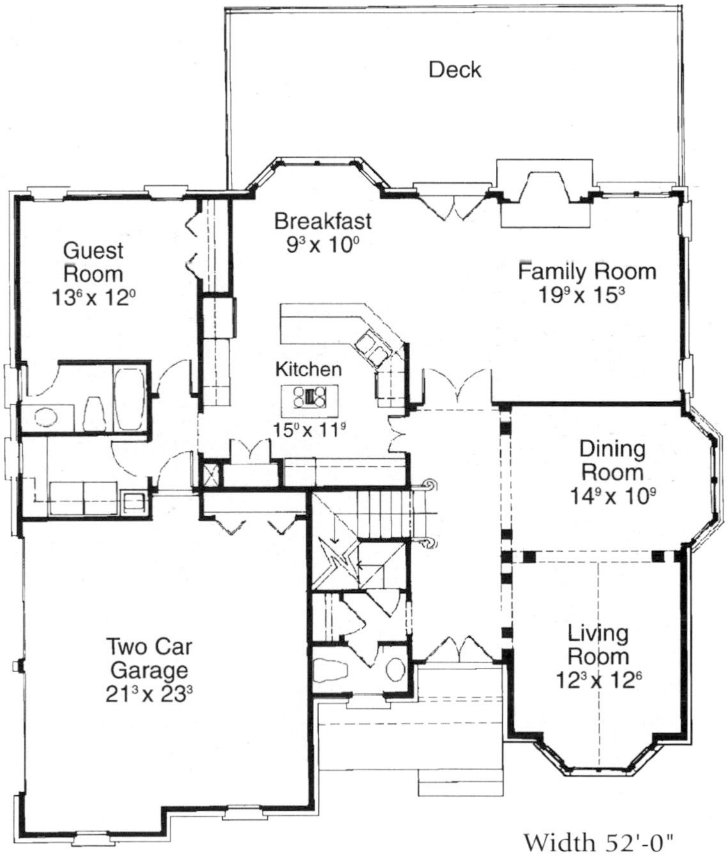

First Floor

Width 52'-0"
Depth 50'-6"

A Palladian window highlights this attractive classic exterior. Quoins and copper-seam flashing update an Old World look that offers a sense of gracious hospitality as well as stylish comfort.

This home is reminiscent of a country estate in Connecticut. A very informal layout has a traditional classical grand entry with a striking pediment attached to a porch with a colonnade.

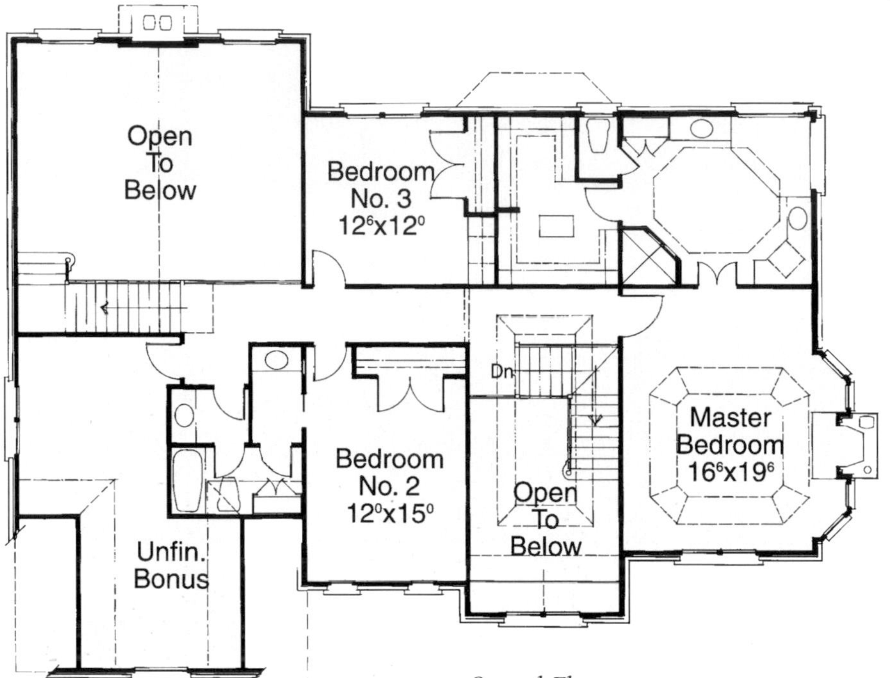

Second Floor

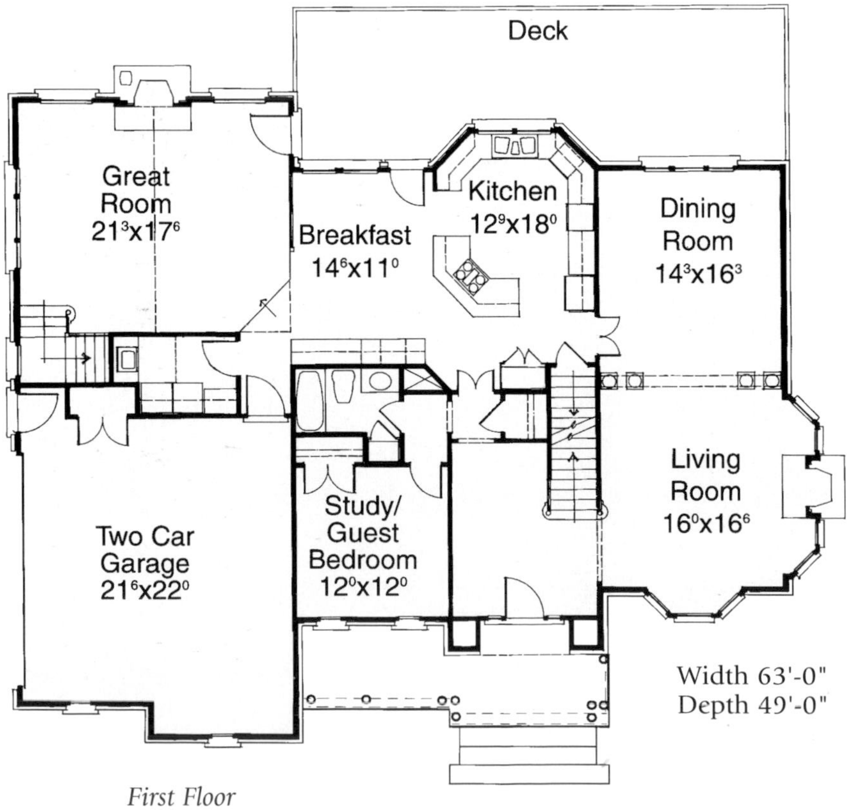

First Floor

HERITAGE VIEW

Design T192

First Floor: 1,888 square feet
Second Floor: 1,374 square feet
Total: 3,262 square feet

Bedrooms: 3 630 FOR A STUDY PKG.
Bathrooms: 3 675 FOR A 4 SET PKG.
730 FOR AN 8 SET PKG.

This graceful Colonial-style home speaks of a more gracious era with the first step of its lovely columned porch. A formal living room with a bay window detail and a cozy fireplace opens to the dining room. Conveniently located between formal and casual living areas is the gourmet kitchen, with a uniquely angled cooktop island and a breakfast area. The two-story great room is appointed with a lofty fireplace, a media corner and a rear staircase. Upstairs, tray ceilings highlight the master suite and lush bath while a romantic fireplace warms the bedroom. Two additional bedrooms and a full bath complete the sleeping quarters.

This is an elevation that never loses its appeal, with a center gable on a two-story main section flanked by one-story wings. It's a very classical shape, defined by the proportions of the lower and upper windows, and traditional quoin detailing, shown here in cast stone.

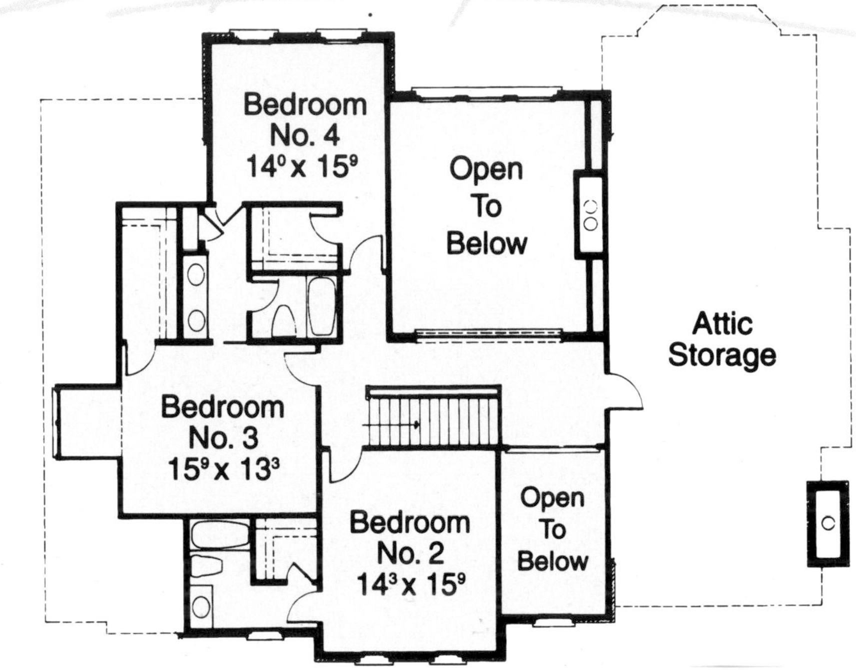

Bedroom No. 4 14^0 x 15^9
Open To Below
Attic Storage
Bedroom No. 3 15^9 x 13^3
Bedroom No. 2 14^3 x 15^9
Open To Below

Second Floor

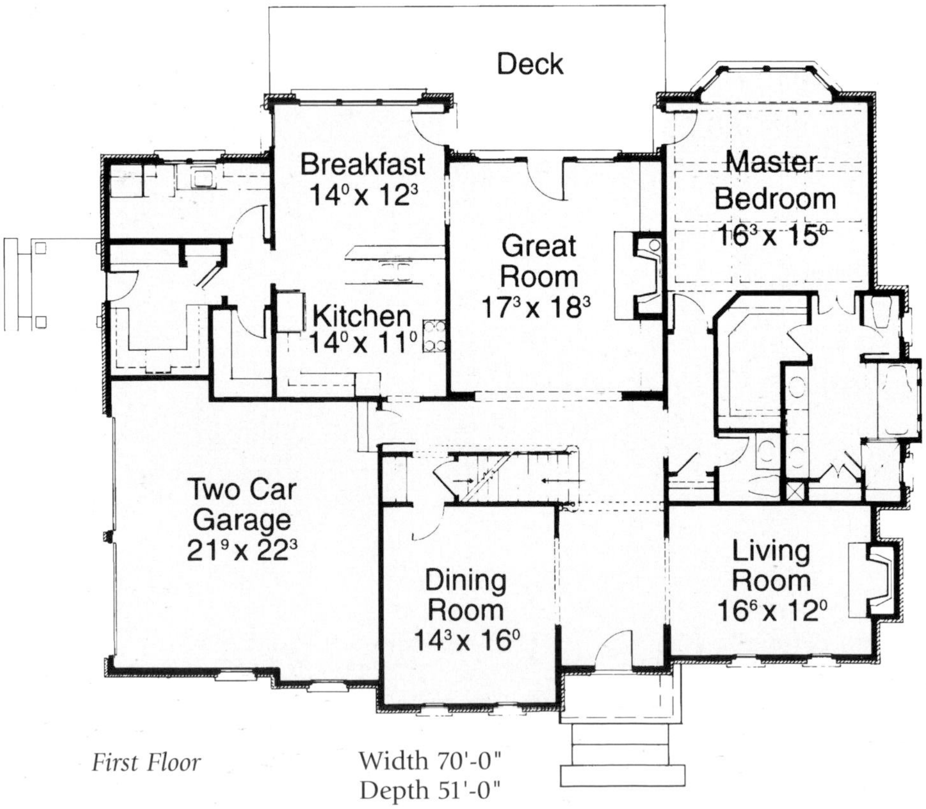

Deck
Breakfast 14^0 x 12^3
Master Bedroom 16^3 x 15^0
Great Room 17^3 x 18^3
Kitchen 14^0 x 11^0
Two Car Garage 21^9 x 22^3
Dining Room 14^3 x 16^0
Living Room 16^6 x 12^0

First Floor

Width 70'-0"
Depth 51'-0"

ROSEWOOD

Design T197

First Floor: 2,302 square feet
Second Floor: 1,177 square feet
Total: 3,479 square feet

Bedrooms: 4
Bathrooms: 2½

Classic quoins set off a stately pediment on this noble brick exterior, introducing a floor plan designed for 21st-Century living. The heart of this home is the great room, which offers a focal-point fireplace and a private door to the rear deck. The formal living room opens from the foyer and features its own hearth. A corner master suite boasts a lavish bath with a spa tub, as well as a bay window and a door to the rear deck. Upstairs, three additional bedrooms enjoy a balcony hall with overlooks to the foyer and to the great room, and share a full bath.

Design T178

First Floor: 3,065 square feet
Second Floor: 1,969 square feet
Total: 5,034 square feet

Bedrooms: 4
Bathrooms: 3½

630 FOR A STUDY PKG
675 FOR A 4 SET PKG
730 FOR AN 8 SET

MULBERRY PLACE

Elegance and luxury define this stately brick home. Creative design continues inside with a dramatic foyer that leads to the formal living and dining rooms. A convenient butler's pantry links the dining room and kitchen. Stunning amenities, such as a tray ceiling and a fireplace, dress the family room. The breakfast room enjoys natural light from a wall of windows and leads out to a solarium—perfect for morning meals. The master suite has a bay window and private access to the rear porch. Upstairs, two full baths, and a home office or fourth bedroom share a hall that leads to a sewing room.

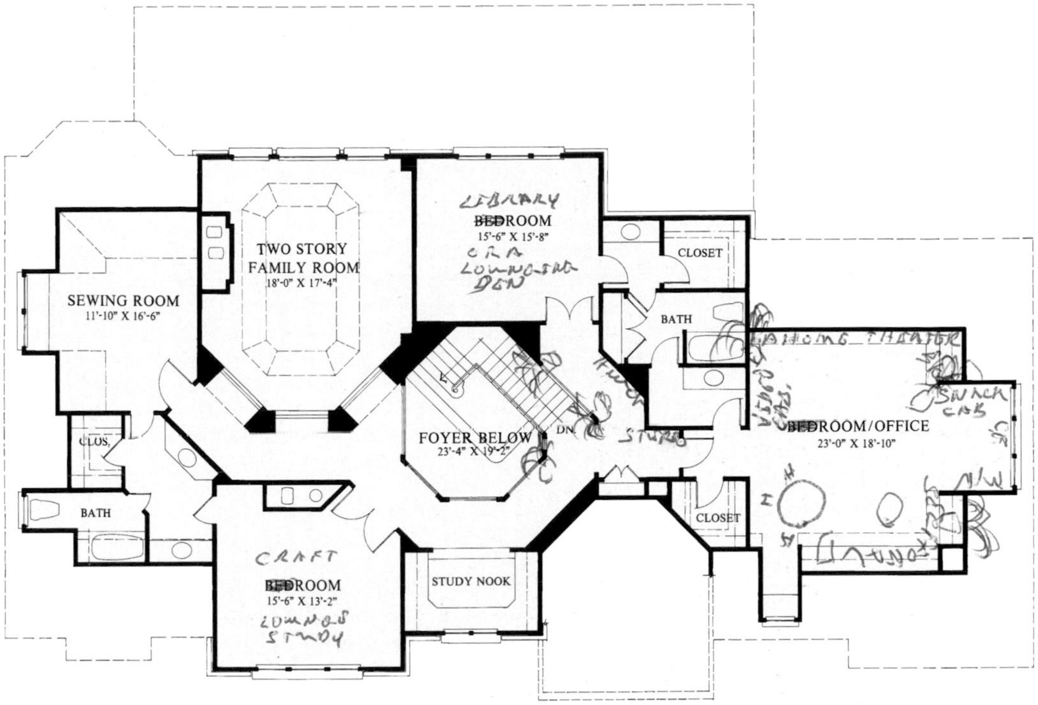
LIBRARY
BEDROOM
15'-6" X 15'-8"
CLOSET
TWO STORY
FAMILY ROOM
18'-0" X 17'-4"
SEWING ROOM
11'-10" X 16'-6"
BATH
FOYER BELOW
23'-4" X 19'-2"
DN
BEDROOM/OFFICE
23'-0" X 18'-10"
CLOS.
BATH
CLOSET
CRAFT
BEDROOM
15'-6" X 13'-2"
STUDY NOOK

Second Floor

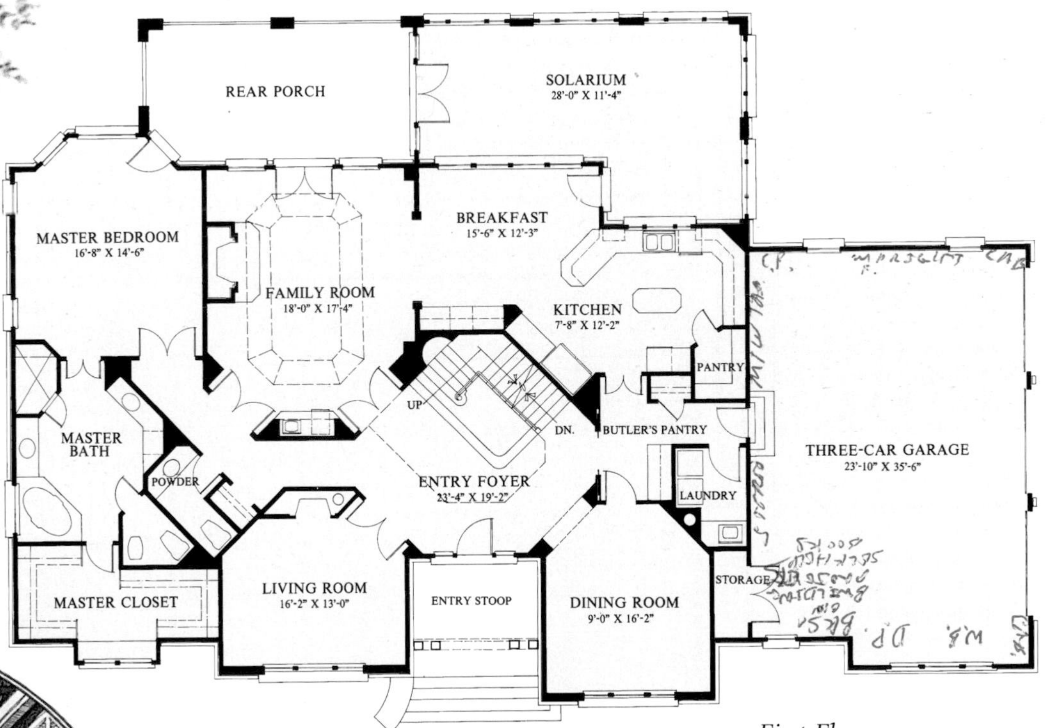
REAR PORCH
SOLARIUM
28'-0" X 11'-4"
MASTER BEDROOM
16'-8" X 14'-6"
BREAKFAST
15'-6" X 12'-3"
FAMILY ROOM
18'-0" X 17'-4"
KITCHEN
7'-8" X 12'-2"
PANTRY
UP
DN.
BUTLER'S PANTRY
THREE-CAR GARAGE
23'-10" X 35'-6"
MASTER BATH
POWDER
ENTRY FOYER
23'-4" X 19'-2"
LAUNDRY
STORAGE
MASTER CLOSET
LIVING ROOM
16'-2" X 13'-0"
ENTRY STOOP
DINING ROOM
9'-0" X 16'-2"

First Floor

Width 88'-6"
Depth 59'-3"

The dramatic brick exterior is enhanced by a recessed entry announced by twin sets of columns and a graceful arch. Asymmetrical gables with lovely stucco accents top a series of triple windows, which bring natural light into the open interior.

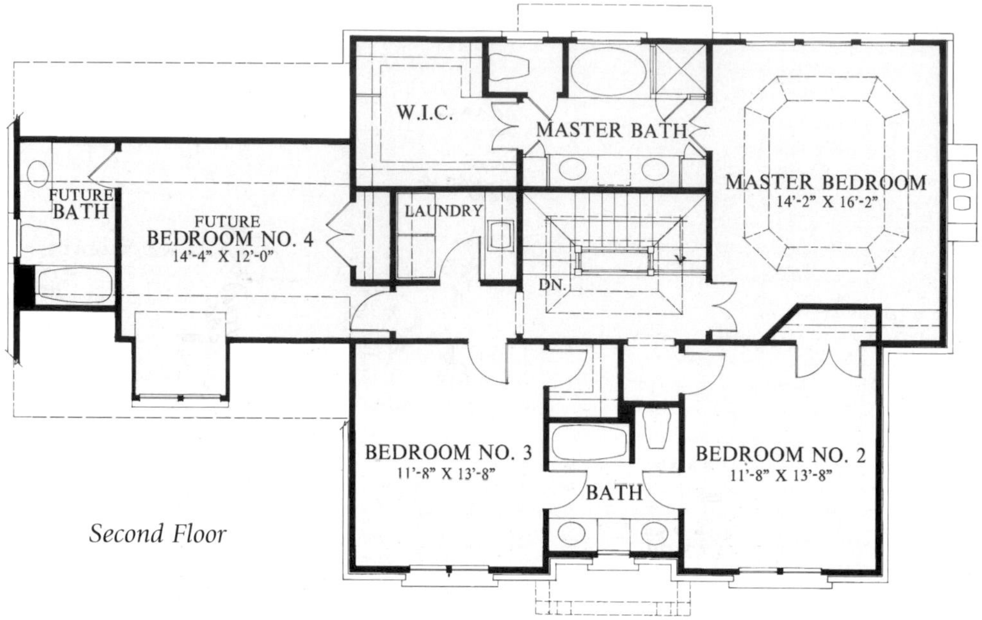
W.I.C.
MASTER BATH
MASTER BEDROOM
14'-2" X 16'-2"
LAUNDRY
FUTURE
BATH
FUTURE
BEDROOM NO. 4
14'-4" X 12'-0"
DN.
BEDROOM NO. 3
11'-8" X 13'-8"
BEDROOM NO. 2
11'-8" X 13'-8"
BATH

Second Floor

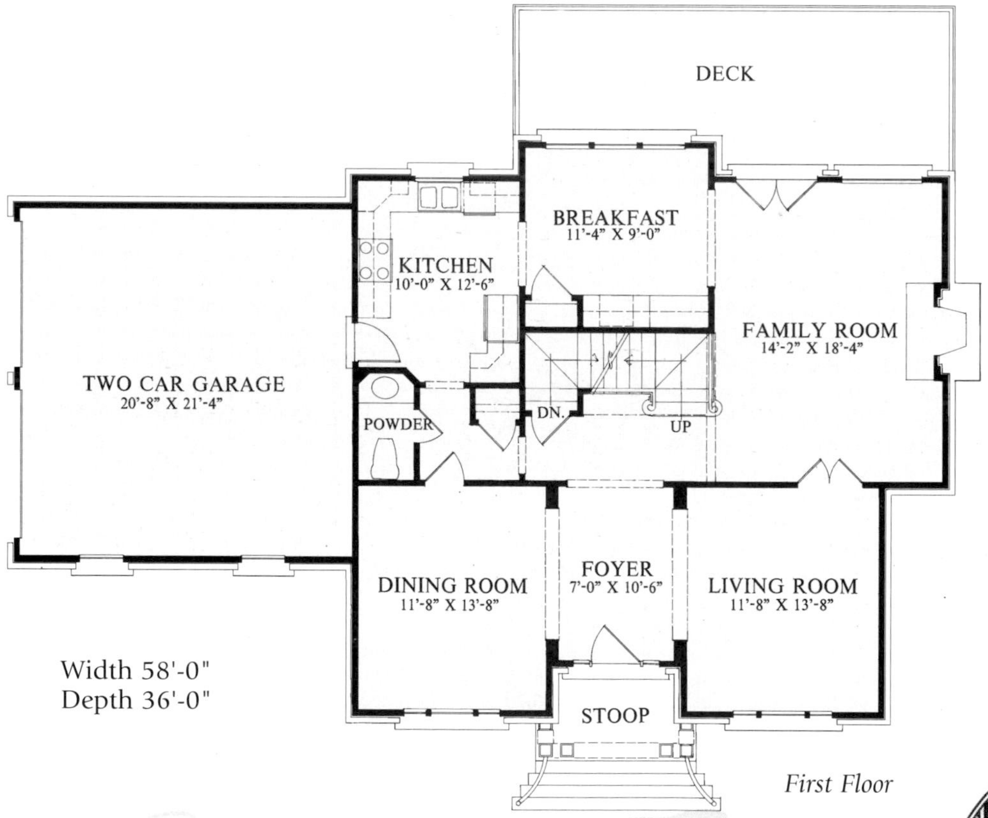
DECK
BREAKFAST
11'-4" X 9'-0"
KITCHEN
10'-0" X 12'-6"
FAMILY ROOM
14'-2" X 18'-4"
TWO CAR GARAGE
20'-8" X 21'-4"
POWDER
DN.
UP
DINING ROOM
11'-8" X 13'-8"
FOYER
7'-0" X 10'-6"
LIVING ROOM
11'-8" X 13'-8"
STOOP

Width 58'-0"
Depth 36'-0"

First Floor

The striking two-story double gable sections flank a very welcoming one-story porch, revealing a formality that's impressive but not overbearing. This is a popular elevation that has to be detailed correctly in order to lend a solid, substantial presence.

Westover Commons

Design T082

First Floor: 1,165 square feet
Second Floor: 1,050 square feet
Total: 2,215 square feet

Bedrooms: 3
Bathrooms: 2½

No detail is left to chance in this classically designed two-story home. A formal entry opens to the living and dining rooms through graceful arches. For casual gatherings, the family room provides ample space and features a warming fireplace and access to the rear deck. A roomy breakfast area is bathed in beautiful natural light from triple windows. The adjacent L-shaped kitchen handles any occasion with ease. Upstairs, the generous master suite includes a walk-in closet, a knee-space vanity, twin lavatories and a garden tub. A central hall leads to two family bedrooms and a full bath as well as bonus space, which offers the possibility of a fourth bedroom and bath.

Design T041

First Floor: 1,053 square feet
Second Floor: 1,053 square feet
Total: 2,106 square feet
Bedrooms: 4
Bathrooms: 3

STANTON GABLE

Brick takes a bold stand with this grand traditional design. From the front entry to rear deck, the floor plan offers flexible space for both formal and casual occasions in just over 2,000 square feet. The front study has a nearby full bath and would easily convert to a guest room. For planned entertaining, an elegant dining room is served by a gourmet kitchen with a walk-in pantry. Upstairs, a luxurious master suite opens from a balcony hall and features a coffered ceiling, a sitting area and a spacious bath with a garden tub and a walk-in closet.

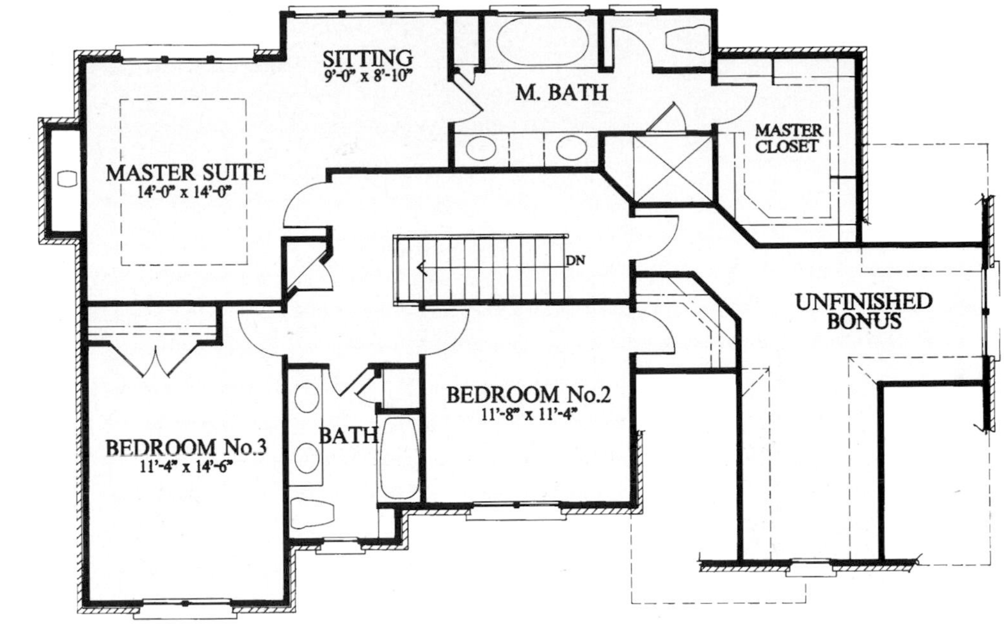
SITTING
9'-0" x 8'-10"
M. BATH
MASTER CLOSET
MASTER SUITE
14'-0" x 14'-0"
DN
UNFINISHED BONUS
BEDROOM No.2
11'-8" x 11'-4"
BEDROOM No.3
11'-4" x 14'-6"
BATH

Second Floor

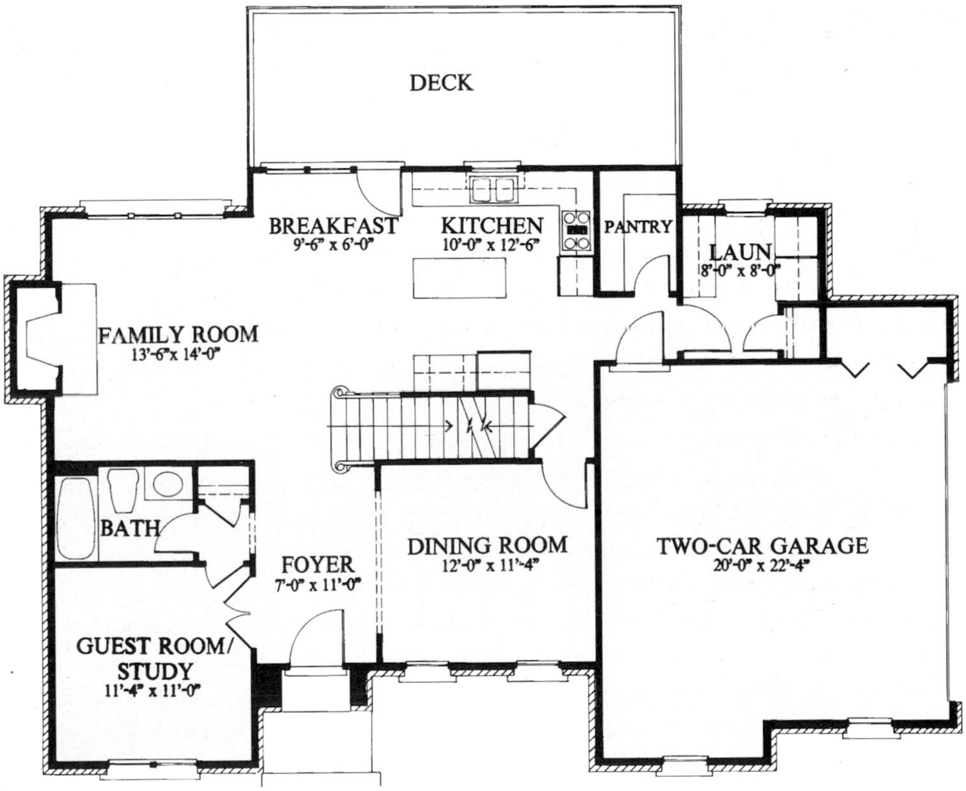
DECK
BREAKFAST
9'-6" x 6'-0"
KITCHEN
10'-0" x 12'-6"
PANTRY
LAUN
8'-0" x 8'-0"
FAMILY ROOM
13'-6"x 14'-0"
BATH
FOYER
7'-0" x 11'-0"
DINING ROOM
12'-0" x 11'-4"
TWO-CAR GARAGE
20'-0" x 22'-4"
GUEST ROOM/ STUDY
11'-4" x 11'-0"

Width 52'-0"
Depth 34'-0"

First Floor

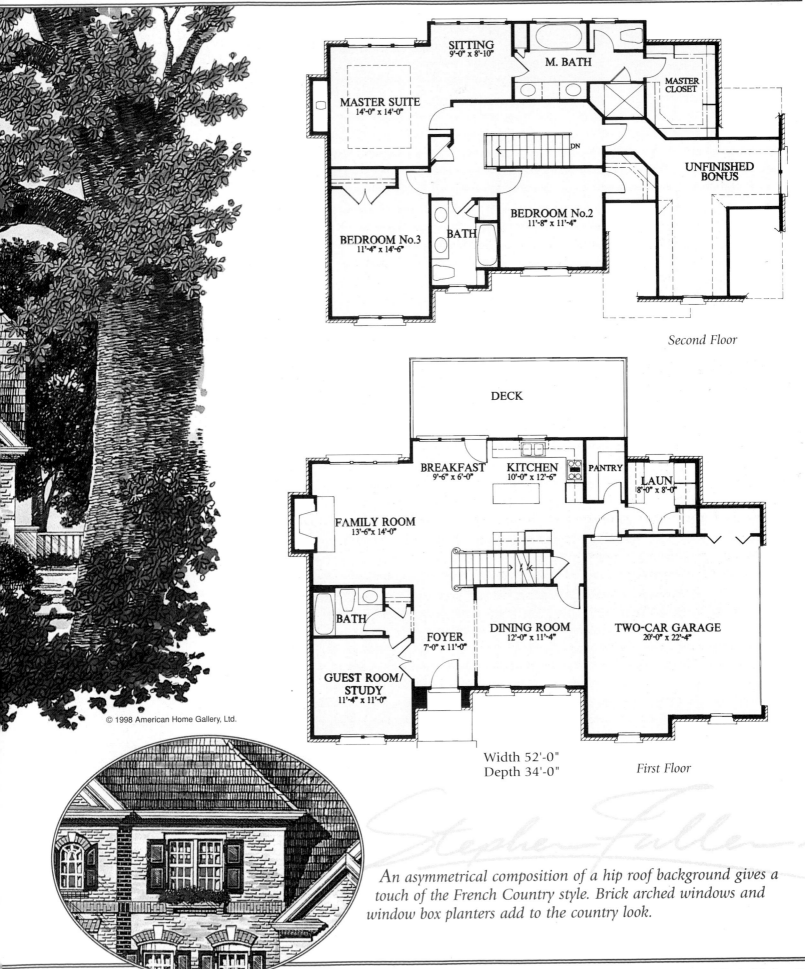

An asymmetrical composition of a hip roof background gives a touch of the French Country style. Brick arched windows and window box planters add to the country look.

Design T143

First Floor: 2,025 square feet
Second Floor: 688 square feet
Total: 2,713 square feet
Bedrooms: 3
Bathrooms: 2½

First Floor

Width 53'-9"
Depth 74'-3"

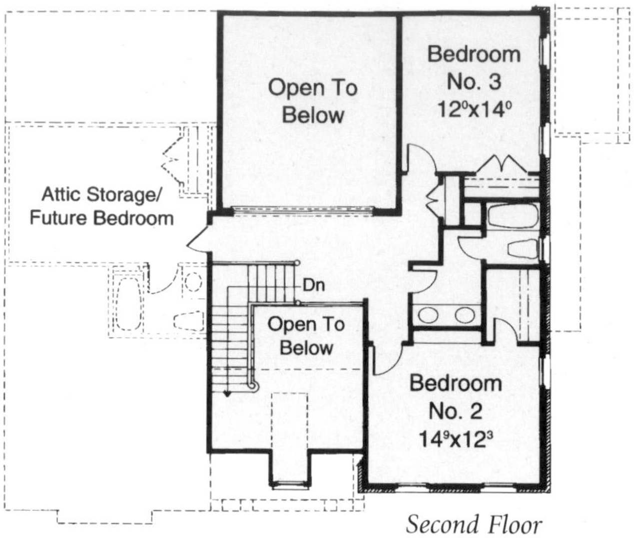

Second Floor

BRISCOE COMMONS

This 1½-story home reflects the Colonial architecture of the South, with a columned entry and paneled shutters. Inside, decorative columns open the foyer to the formal dining room, which opens through double doors to the gourmet kitchen. A cooktop counter overlooks the breakfast room, where a French door leads to a private porch. The central gallery hall connects the living area with a secluded master suite, highlighted by a dressing area, separate walk-in closets and a lavish bath designed for two. Upstairs, Bedrooms 2 and 3 share a full bath. Space for attic storage or a future bedroom and bath is furnished to develop as needed.

© 1998 American Home Gallery, Ltd.

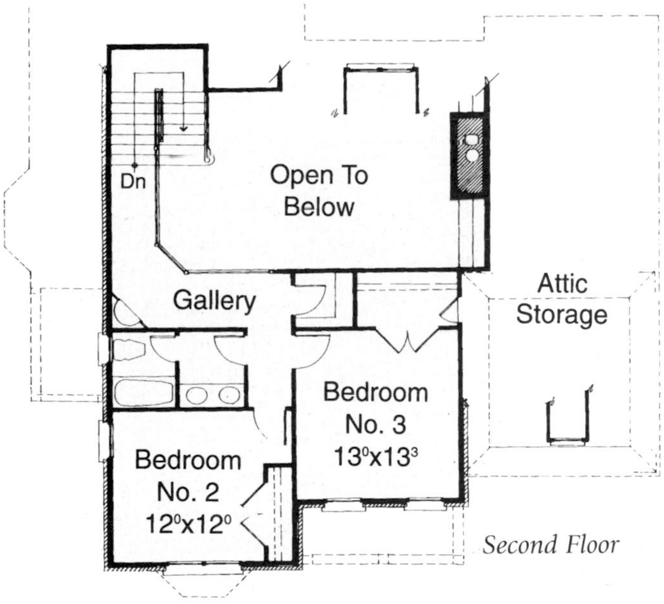

Dn
Open To Below
Gallery
Attic Storage
Bedroom No. 3 13⁰x13³
Bedroom No. 2 12⁰x12⁰

Second Floor

Design T152

First Floor: 1,824 square feet
Second Floor: 635 square feet
Total: 2,459 square feet

Bedrooms: 3
Bathrooms: 2½

Two Car Garage 21³x24³
Great Room 16³x18⁰
Dn
Up
Breakfast 12⁰x10⁰
Porch
Kitchen 14³x10⁶
Master Bedroom 15³x16⁰
Foyer
Dining Room 14³x12⁰
Porch

Width 52'-9"
Depth 68'-9"

First Floor

HARVEN ROW

An open great room is the heart of this Georgian-style home. The foyer leads through a central vestibule to the grand living area, which has a fireplace framed by built-in bookshelves and a French door that leads outside. The kitchen serves a breakfast room, enhanced with a bay window and a private morning porch. A tray ceiling adorns the master suite, and French doors lead through a dressing area with separate walk-in closets. Second-floor bedrooms share a gallery hall with walk-in storage and a balcony overlook.

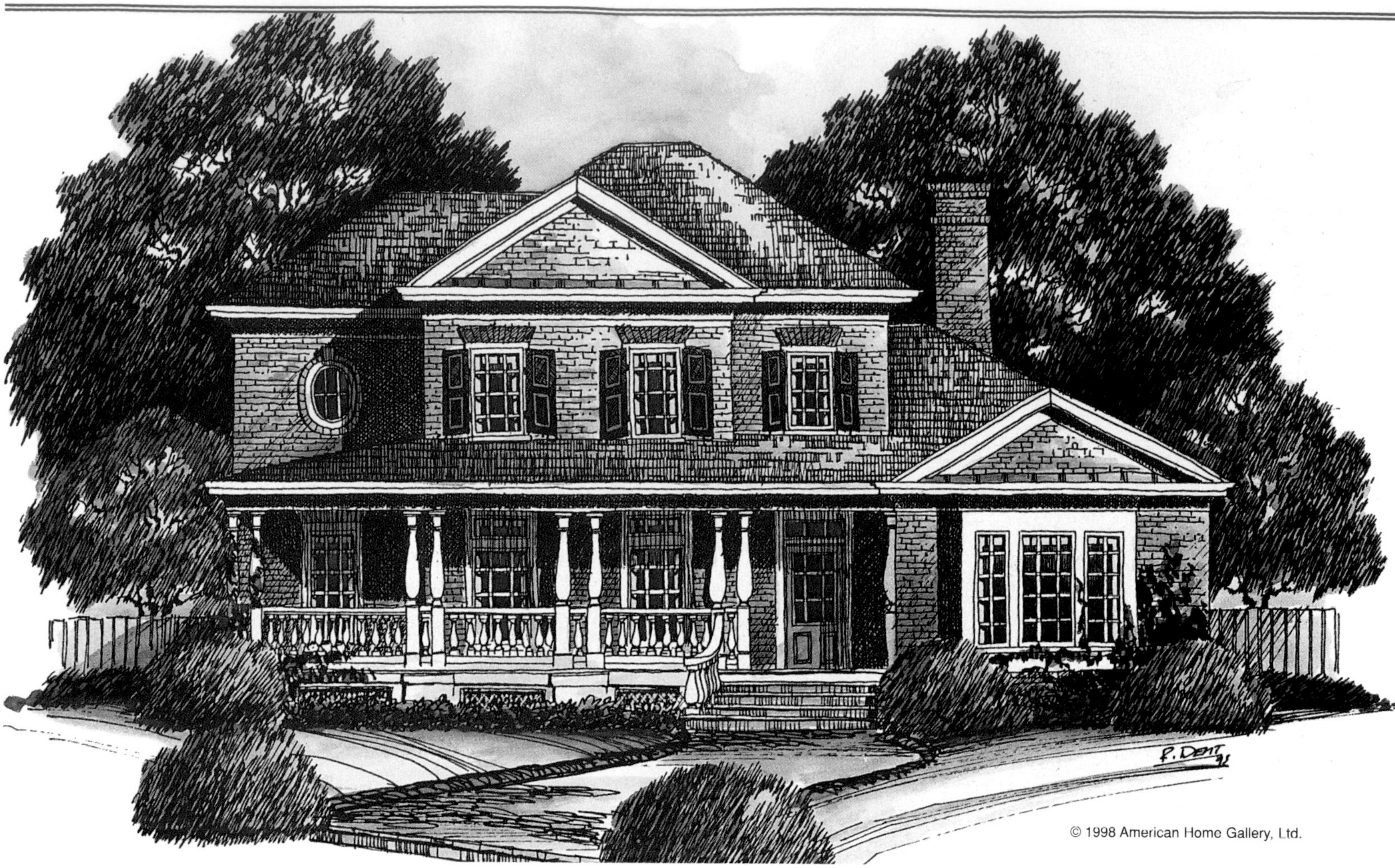

Design T144

First Floor: 1,787 square feet
Second Floor: 851 square feet
Total: 2,638 square feet

Bedrooms: 3
Bathrooms: 2½

Width 51'-3"
Depth 70'-6"

Two Car Garage 21³x21³
Deck
Great Room 16⁰x17⁰
Kitchen 13³x16⁶
Breakfast 12⁹x12⁹
Dn
Up
Dining Room 15⁰x12⁹
Foyer
Master Bedroom 15⁶x16³
Porch

First Floor

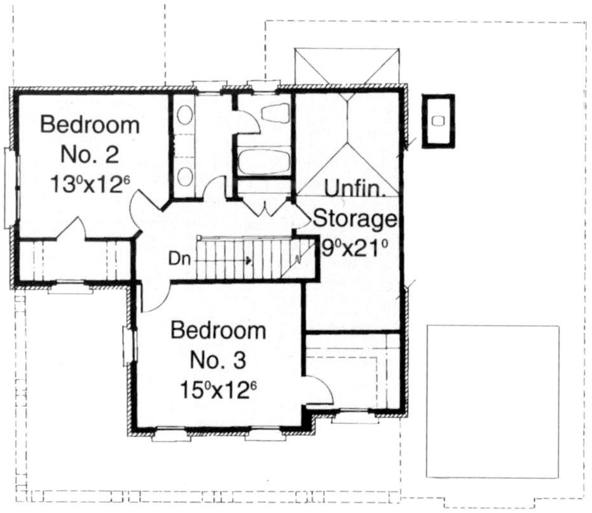
Bedroom No. 2 13⁰x12⁶
Unfin. Storage 9⁰x21⁰
Dn
Bedroom No. 3 15⁰x12⁶

Second Floor

FARNSWORTH LANE

Gently curved balusters and transom windows introduce a well-planned interior within this sterling Georgian design. A stunning coffered ceiling sets off the great room. The gourmet kitchen is open to the breakfast room and boasts an island cooktop counter. In the master suite, a lavish bath includes a whirlpool tub, a separate shower, twin vanities and a walk-in closet. Upstairs, two family bedrooms share a full bath and a hall that leads to unfinished bonus space, which may be developed into a hobby room or a home office.

Second Floor

ETHRIDGE POINTE

A graceful, arched transom sets off a clerestory window, complemented by a glass-paneled entry, rounded balusters and decorative columns on this traditional brick home. Inside, the foyer opens to the formal rooms as well as to casual living space. A fireplace warms the family room, enhanced by four lovely windows. To the rear of the plan, the gourmet kitchen has wide wrapping counters and a cooktop peninsula, which overlooks the bright breakfast room. On the second floor, a generous master suite has its own hearth.

Design T145

First Floor: 1,501 square feet
Second Floor: 1,252 square feet
Total: 2,753 square feet

Bedrooms: 3
Bathrooms: 2½

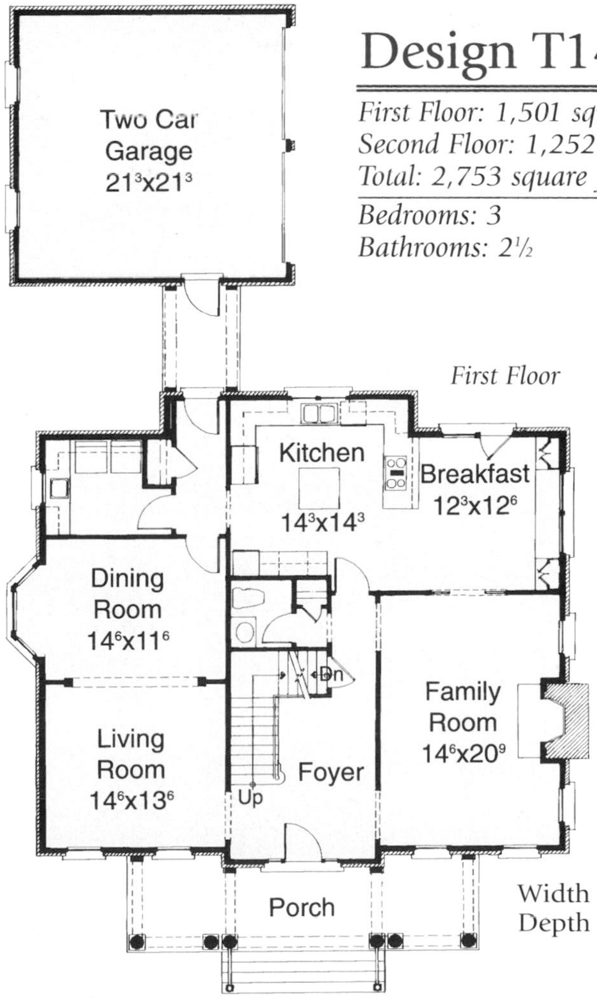

First Floor

Width 46'-3"
Depth 76'-9"

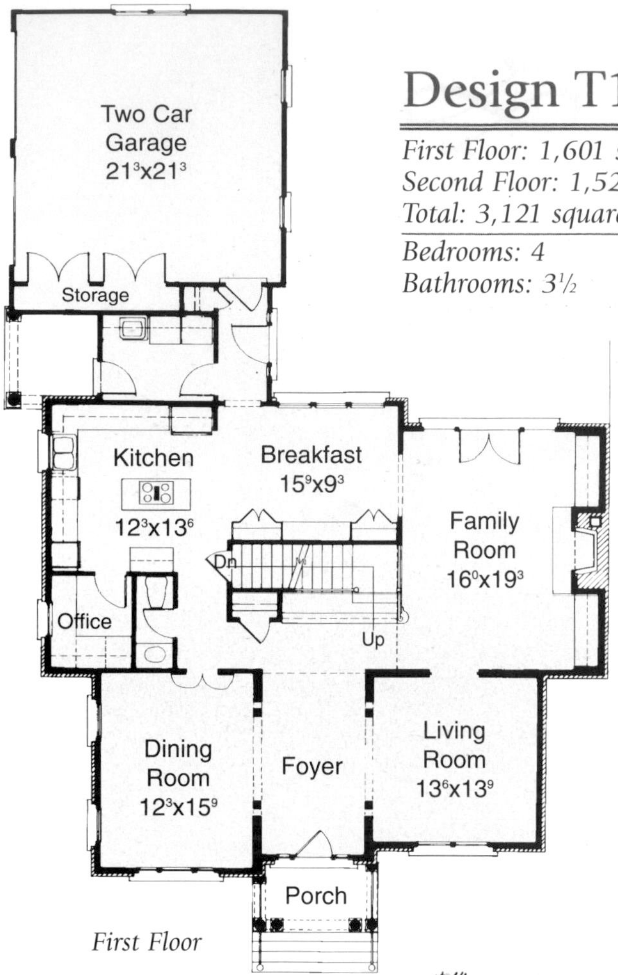

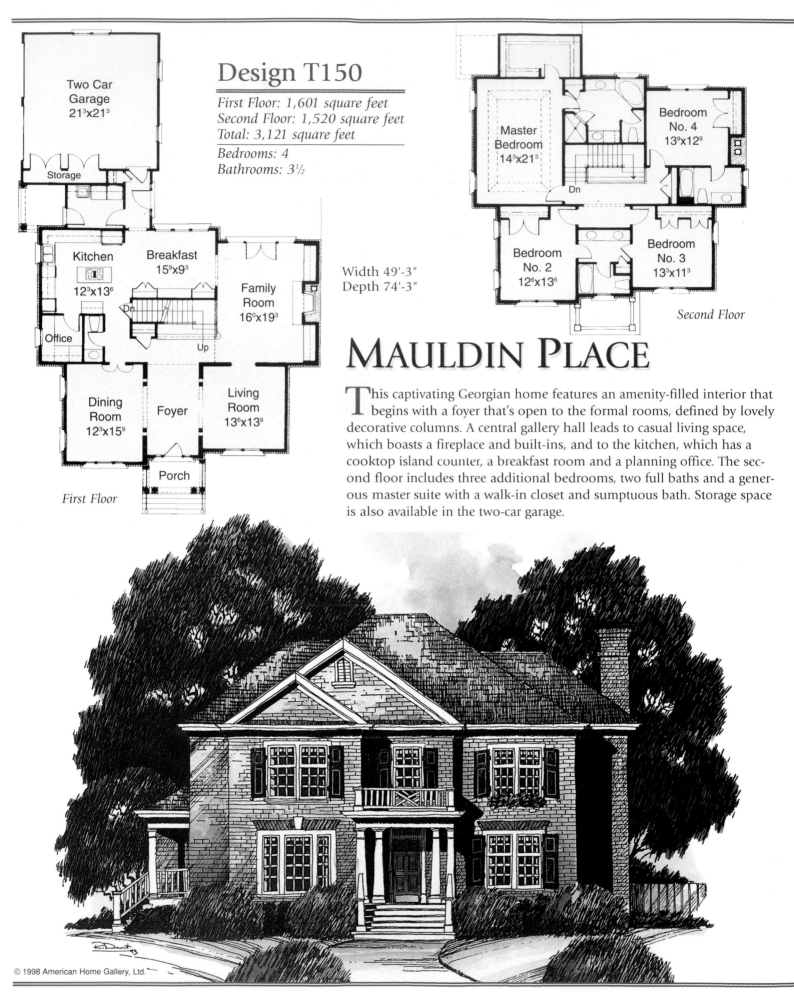

First Floor

Design T150

First Floor: 1,601 square feet
Second Floor: 1,520 square feet
Total: 3,121 square feet

Bedrooms: 4
Bathrooms: 3½

Width 49'-3"
Depth 74'-3"

Second Floor

MAULDIN PLACE

This captivating Georgian home features an amenity-filled interior that begins with a foyer that's open to the formal rooms, defined by lovely decorative columns. A central gallery hall leads to casual living space, which boasts a fireplace and built-ins, and to the kitchen, which has a cooktop island counter, a breakfast room and a planning office. The second floor includes three additional bedrooms, two full baths and a generous master suite with a walk-in closet and sumptuous bath. Storage space is also available in the two-car garage.

Design T146

First Floor: 1,609 square feet
Second Floor: 1,583 square feet
Total: 3,192 square feet
Bedrooms: 3
Bathrooms: 2½

LIBERTY WAY

Beautiful bay windows and a copper-seam roof complement two balustrades on this Colonial-style home. A gallery foyer opens to a formal living room or parlor on the left and, to the right, a family room warmed by a fireplace. French doors open to the rear porch, which is decked with square columns. The well-planned kitchen overlooks a breakfast area and easily serves the formal dining room through a convenient butler's pantry. Upstairs, two family bedrooms share a full bath, while the master bedroom leads to a dressing area framed by walk-in closets. A powder room, laundry and additional storage in the two-car garage complete the design.

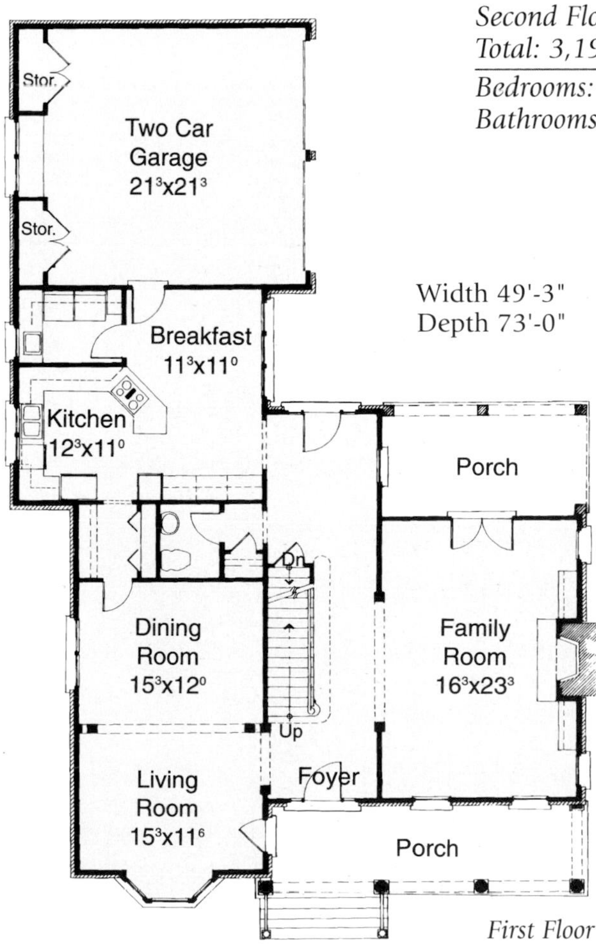

Width 49'-3"
Depth 73'-0"

First Floor

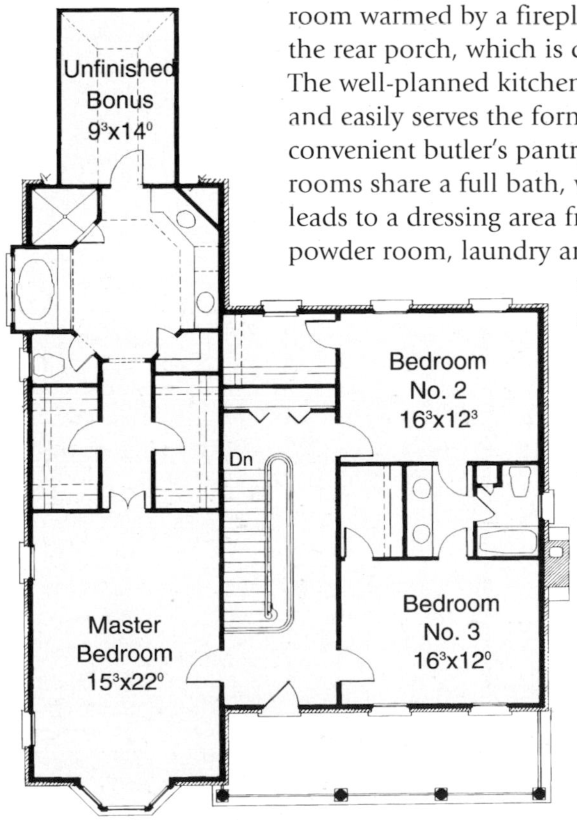

Second Floor

The simple elegance of this Georgian home is enhanced with formal details such as a Palladian window, panel shutters and a lovely arched entry. Brick accents and keystones add warmth and a comfortable scale.

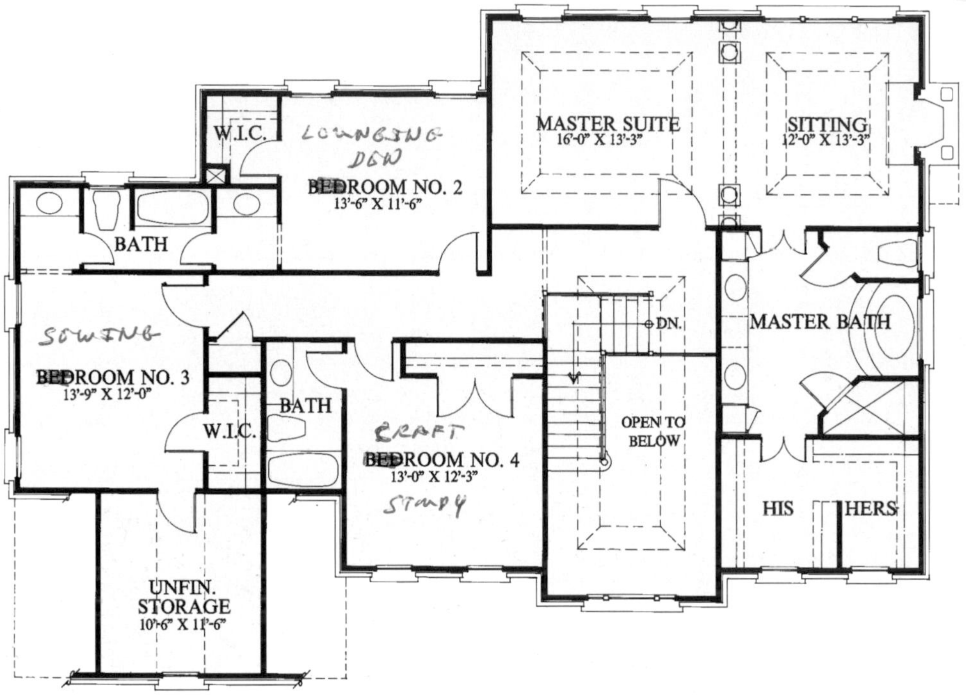

W.I.C.
BEDROOM NO. 2
13'-6" X 11'-6"
MASTER SUITE
16'-0" X 13'-3"
SITTING
12'-0" X 13'-3"
BATH
DN.
MASTER BATH
BEDROOM NO. 3
13'-9" X 12'-0"
BATH
W.I.C.
OPEN TO BELOW
BEDROOM NO. 4
13'-0" X 12'-3"
HIS
HERS
UNFIN. STORAGE
10'-6" X 11'-6"

Second Floor

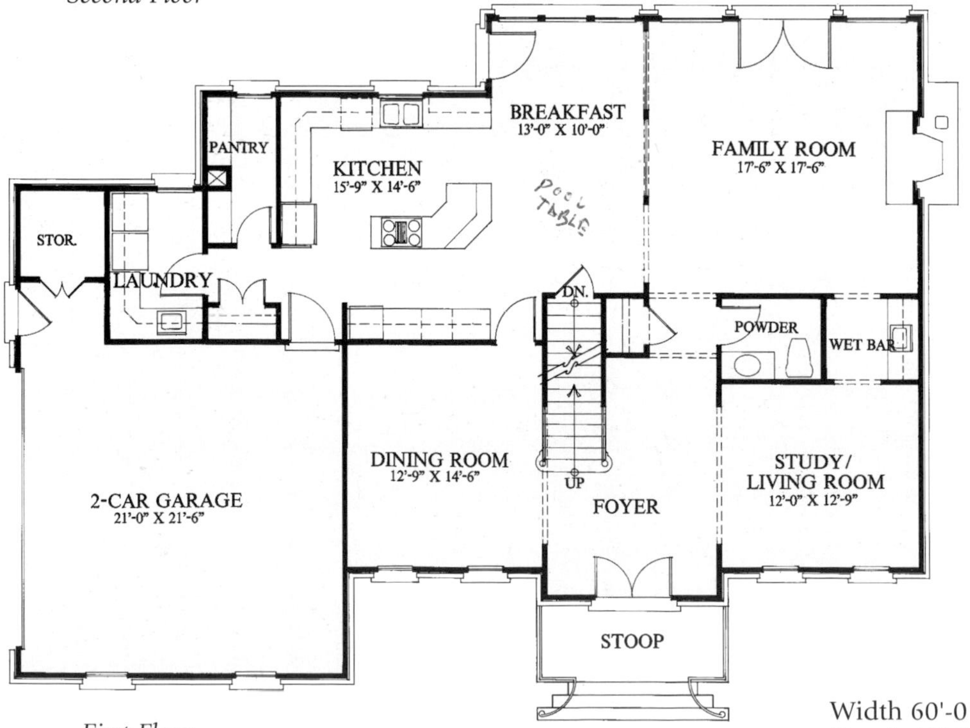

BREAKFAST
13'-0" X 10'-0"
PANTRY
KITCHEN
15'-9" X 14'-6"
FAMILY ROOM
17'-6" X 17'-6"
STOR.
LAUNDRY
DN.
POWDER
WET BAR
DINING ROOM
12'-9" X 14'-6"
UP
STUDY/ LIVING ROOM
12'-0" X 12'-9"
2-CAR GARAGE
21'-0" X 21'-6"
FOYER
STOOP

First Floor

Width 60'-0"
Depth 43'-0"

Dunwoody Classic

Design T066

First Floor: 1,554 square feet
Second Floor: 1,648 square feet
Total: 3,202 square feet

Bedrooms: 4
Bathrooms: 3½

The classic styling of this American traditional is defined by a double-door entrance with a transom and a Palladian window above. Inside, a grand foyer is flanked by a spacious dining room and a formal study or living room. A large family room with a fireplace and a full wall of glass opens conveniently to the kitchen and breakfast room. The master suite is on the second floor and features a sitting room with a fireplace announced by decorative columns. Two additional bedrooms share a bath while a fourth provides its own bath.

MAGNOLIA PLACE

Design T027

First Floor: 1,455 square feet
Second Floor: 1,649 square feet
Total: 3,104 square feet

Bedrooms: 4
Bathrooms: 3½

Stately and proud, this Georgian home features the elegant symmetry that has made the style so enduring. The two-story foyer is flanked by the spacious dining room and the formal living room, both of which contain fireplaces. A large family room with wide views of the outdoors opens to a sunlit breakfast bay and kitchen. The master suite features a tray ceiling and French doors that open onto a covered porch. A grand master bath with all the amenities, including a garden tub and a sizable double closet, completes the master suite. Two other bedrooms share a bath while another has its own private bath. The fourth bedroom also features a sunny nook for sitting or reading.

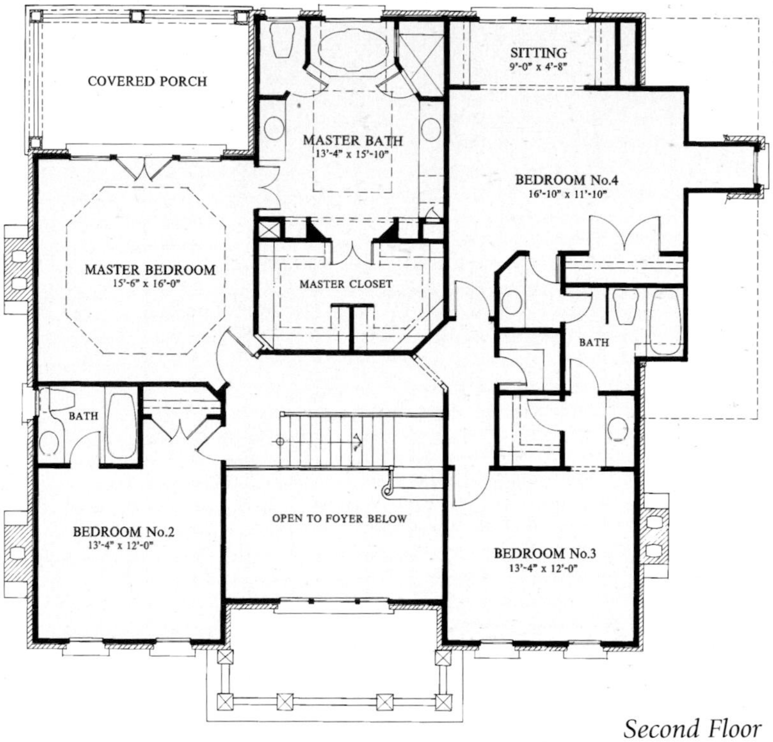
COVERED PORCH
SITTING
9'-0" x 4'-8"
MASTER BATH
13'-4" x 15'-10"
BEDROOM No.4
16'-10" x 11'-10"
MASTER BEDROOM
15'-6" x 16'-0"
MASTER CLOSET
BATH
BATH
BEDROOM No.2
13'-4" x 12'-0"
OPEN TO FOYER BELOW
BEDROOM No.3
13'-4" x 12'-0"

Second Floor

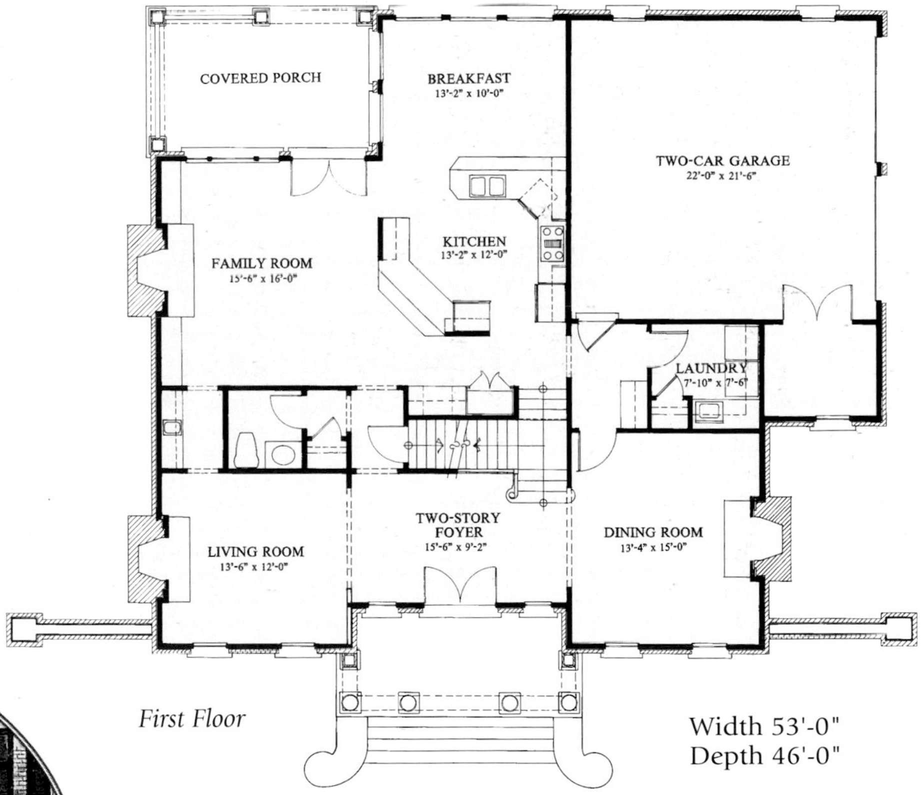
COVERED PORCH
BREAKFAST
13'-2" x 10'-0"
TWO-CAR GARAGE
22'-0" x 21'-6"
KITCHEN
13'-2" x 12'-0"
FAMILY ROOM
15'-6" x 16'-0"
LAUNDRY
7'-10" x 7'-6"
TWO-STORY
FOYER
15'-6" x 9'-2"
LIVING ROOM
13'-6" x 12'-0"
DINING ROOM
13'-4" x 15'-0"

First Floor

Width 53'-0"
Depth 46'-0"

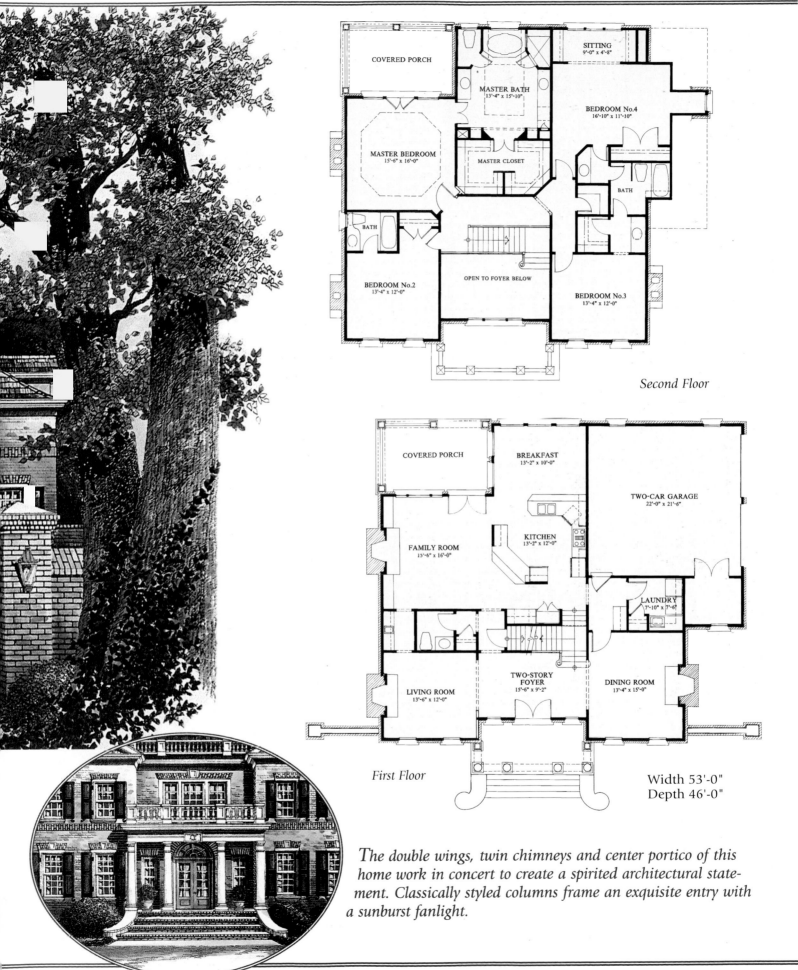

The double wings, twin chimneys and center portico of this home work in concert to create a spirited architectural statement. Classically styled columns frame an exquisite entry with a sunburst fanlight.

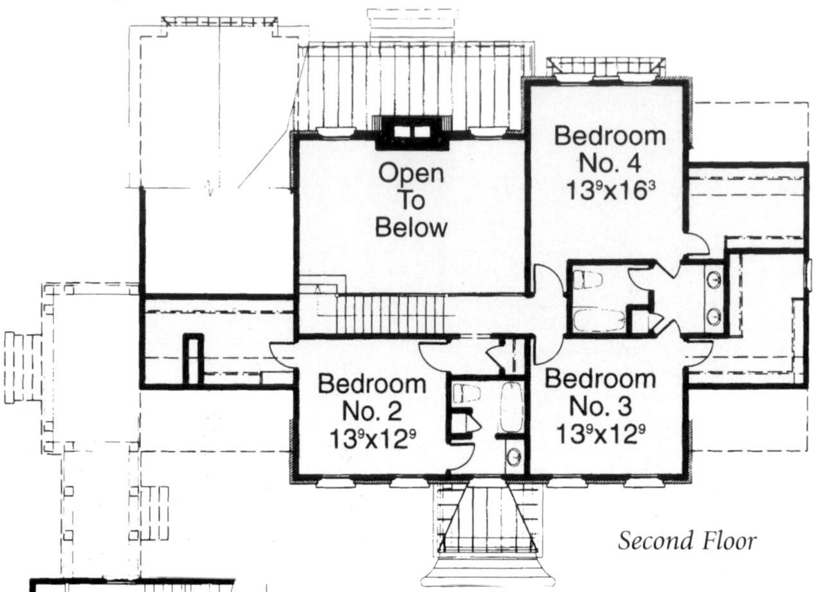

Second Floor

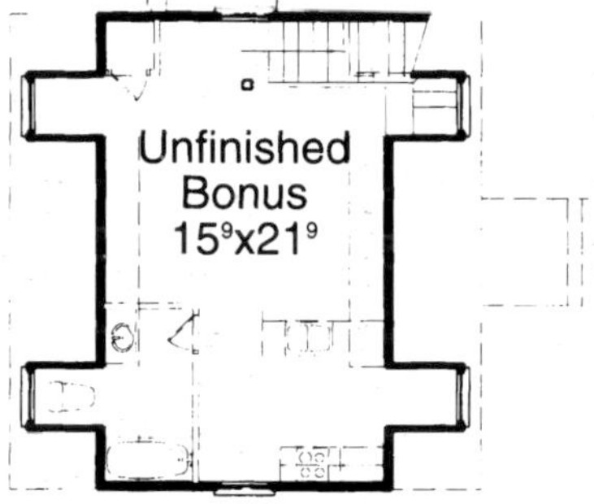

First Floor

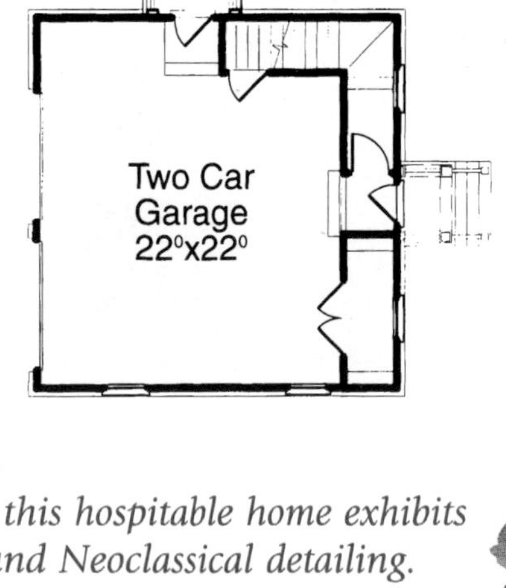

Width 76'-0"
Depth 77'-9"

The exterior of this hospitable home exhibits rich Georgian and Neoclassical detailing. Lap-sided wings call to mind carefully planned, comfortable additions.

Rear Elevation

© 1998 American Home Gallery, Ltd.

WHITFORD PLACE

A classically simple brick exterior and a columned entrance distinguish this gracious and comfortable home, inspired by the Federal-style residences of Colonial New England. Columns and pilasters capped by a pediment call up this architectural style, complemented by a porte cochere. Formal areas frame the foyer, which opens to the great room, with a centered fireplace and two sets of French doors. The master suite boasts a secluded bath and a private door to the rear porch. A bright breakfast area opens to the gourmet kitchen, which includes a spacious pantry and island cooktop.

Design T195

First Floor: 2,140 square feet
Second Floor: 1,219 square feet
Total: 3,359 square feet

Bedrooms: 4
Bathrooms: 3½

There is a hint of Jeffersonian classicism in the white Doric columns that set off the rear elevation of this Georgian adaptation. The porch added to one side serves to soften the formality of the elevation and bring the design more in line with today's lifestyles.

Rear Elevation

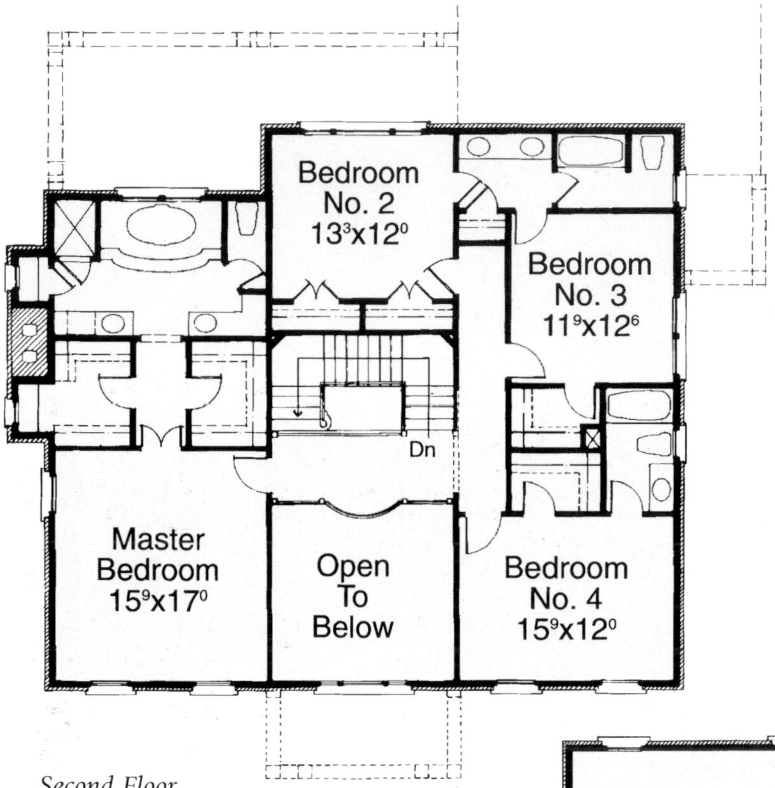

Second Floor

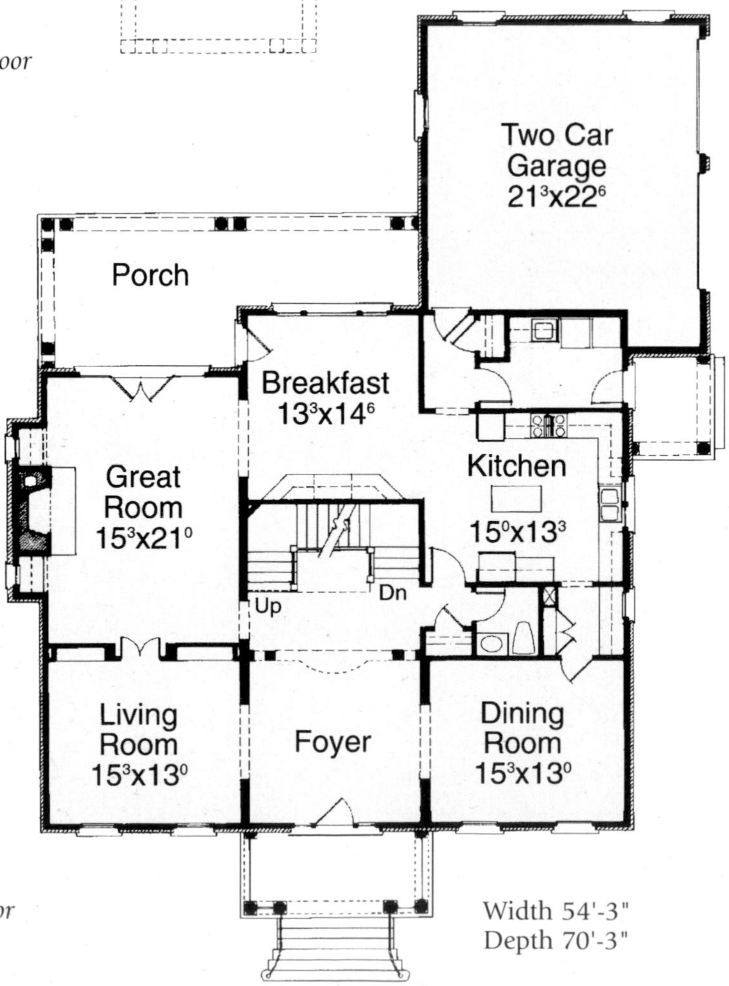

First Floor

Width 54'-3"
Depth 70'-3"

WESTBURY

Design T169

First Floor: 1,828 square feet
Second Floor: 1,552 square feet
Total: 3,380 square feet

Bedrooms: 4
Bathrooms: 3½

An excellent adaptation of the Georgian architecture that graces the Southern colonies, this handsome home is symmetrically balanced, polished and formal. Supported by Ionic columns, the elegant portico that dresses the facade features a standing-seam copper roof, while exquisite details like a spider-web fanlight and oval-shaped sidelights illuminate the spacious entryway. Casual elegance presides within, with the formal living room leading to a grand great room, made cozy by a focal-point fireplace. Upstairs, the sleeping quarters include a master suite with twin walk-in closets, a bedroom with its own bath and two additional bedrooms that share a bath.

Design T161

First Floor: 2,297 square feet
Second Floor: 1,383 square feet
Total: 3,680 square feet
Bedrooms: 4
Bathrooms: 3½

PRESTWOOD

Although not symmetrical in the classic Georgian sense, this stately facade shows a subtle sense of balance, with a Southern heritage—and hospitality. Doric pilasters support the entry pediment and are echoed in the pillars of the front porch. The cozy keeping room in this plan creates space filled with natural light, and draws it in closer with a hearth. Gatherings, large and small, may spill out onto the covered porch. The master suite enjoys a walk-through dressing area with a U-shaped wardrobe, as well as a private bath with a garden tub.

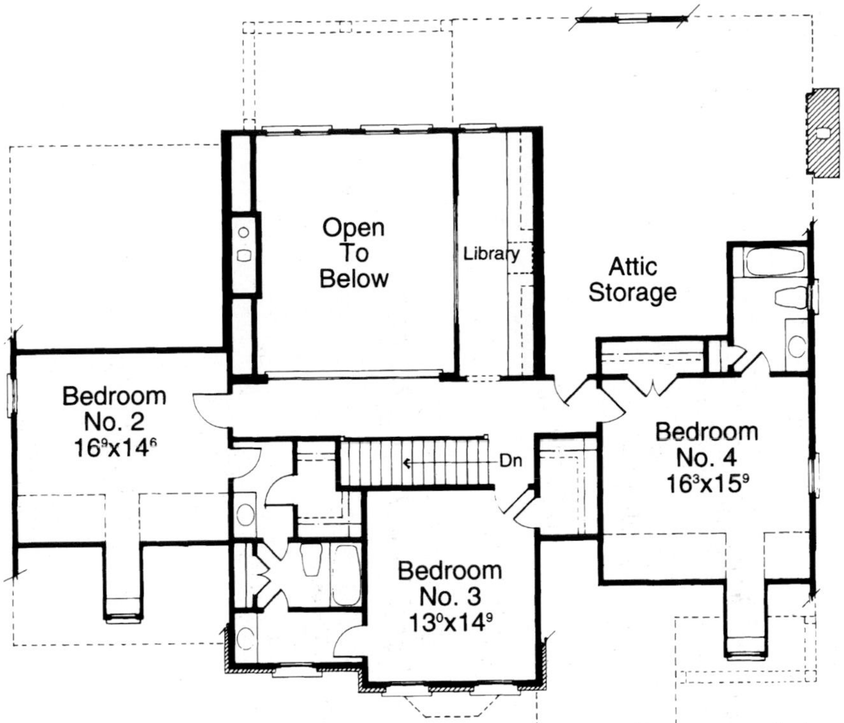

Second Floor

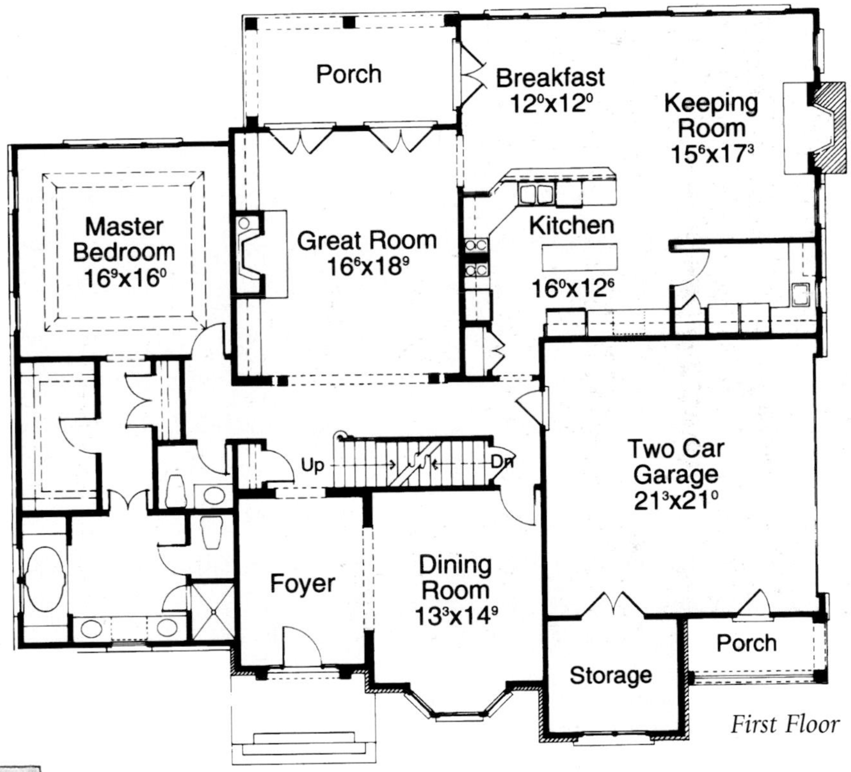

First Floor

Width 65'-0"
Depth 55'-6"

Rear Elevation

This brick-and-siding facade offers a look that's not stuffy or self-conscious but simply comfortable. A Georgian formality is modified by the asymmetrical design that makes the house more casual and more appropriate for living today.

WARRENTON

Design T166

First Floor: 1,615 square feet
Second Floor: 1,510 square feet
Total: 3,125 square feet

Bedrooms: 4
Bathrooms: 3½

Double-hung windows and shutters typify the Georgian Revival style, while an inset porch acknowledges more than a passing acquaintance with the Federal period in post-Revolutionary America. Columns create a charming entry to a well-cultivated and stylish interior design. The great room offers a focal-point fireplace and opens to a solarium with views of the rear property. Family and friends will gather in the bright breakfast area, open to the kitchen. The nearby deck poses an invitation to enjoy the outdoors. Upstairs, a generous master suite features a walk-through dressing area and a lavish bath.

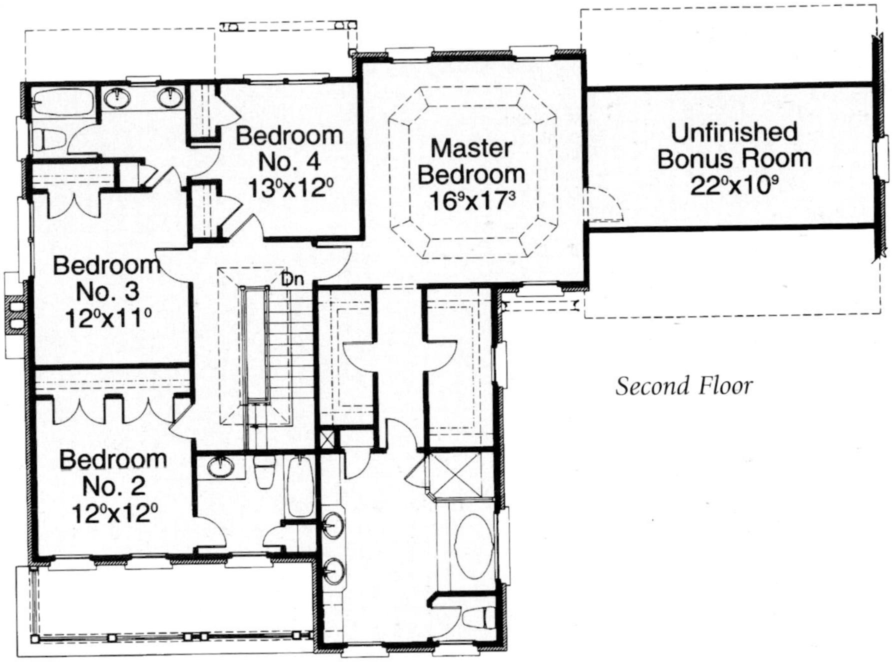

Second Floor

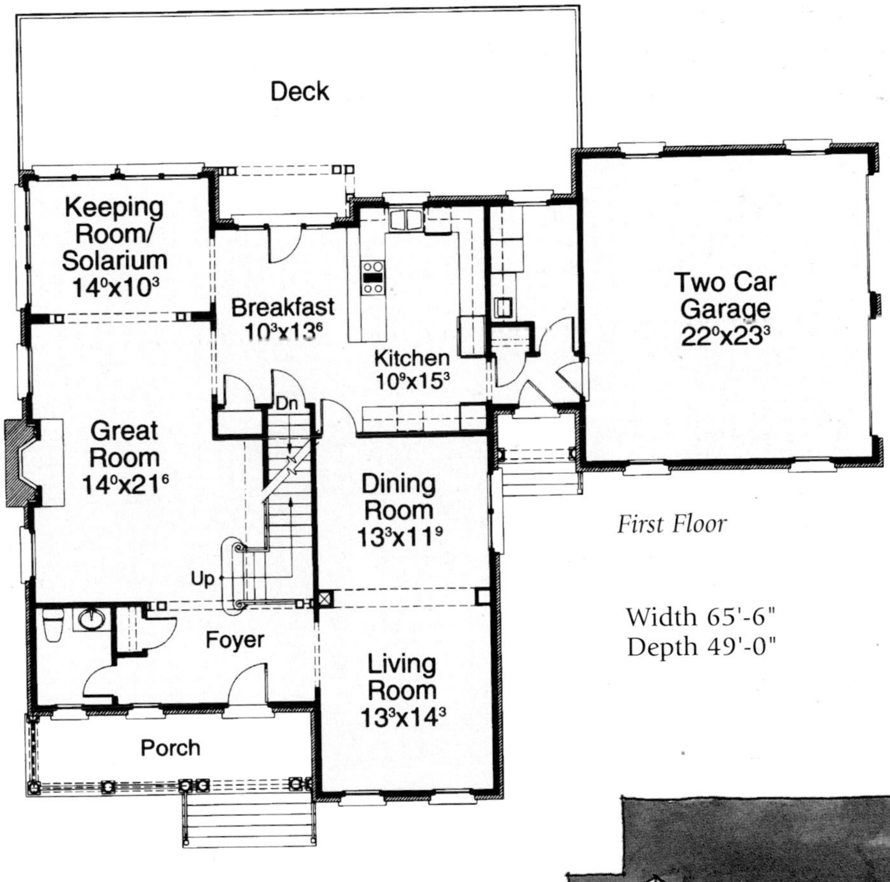

First Floor

Width 65'-6"
Depth 49'-0"

An amalgam of several architectural styles, this quintessentially American house is both classic and casual—as appropriate for planned entertaining as it is for family living. Formal without being formidable, casual without losing its sense of style, this Georgian Revival home is the perfect setting for families who take a similar approach to life.

Rear Elevation

WELLINGTON

Design T156

Square Footage: 2,998
Bedrooms: 3
Bathrooms: 2½

The idiom may be distinctly Georgian but this genteel home also speaks of other, less formal periods in classical American architecture. A lively counterbalance exists between the gracefully arched Palladian window and the welcoming curve of the stair balustrade. At the heart of this sophisticated floor plan lies a lighthearted spirit, with French doors in the great room to bring in a sense of nature. The master suite occupies the left wing of the house, while the right wing is given over to two additional bedrooms that share a bath.

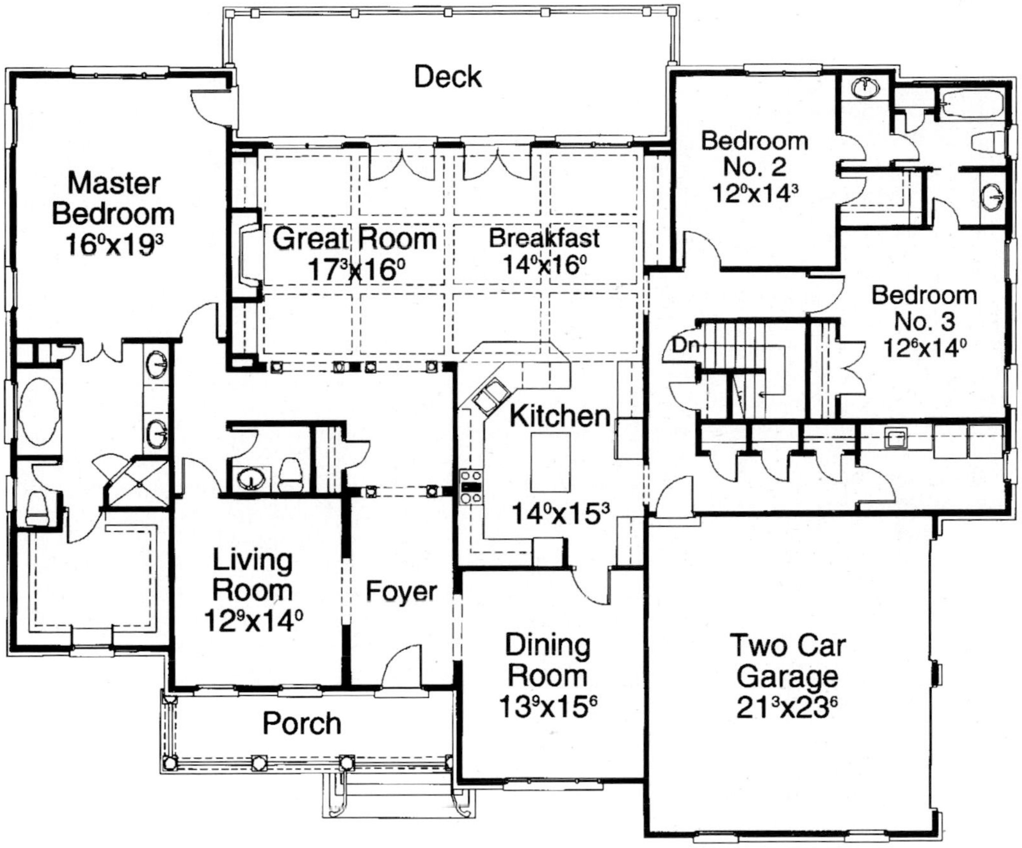

Width 75'-6"
Depth 57'-0"

This Colonial adaptation enjoys well-remembered details, such as transoms and fanlights, but insists on a distinctly contemporary interior. Classic and comfortable, sized and appointed for easy family living, it is also a home that entertains beautifully.

Rear Elevation

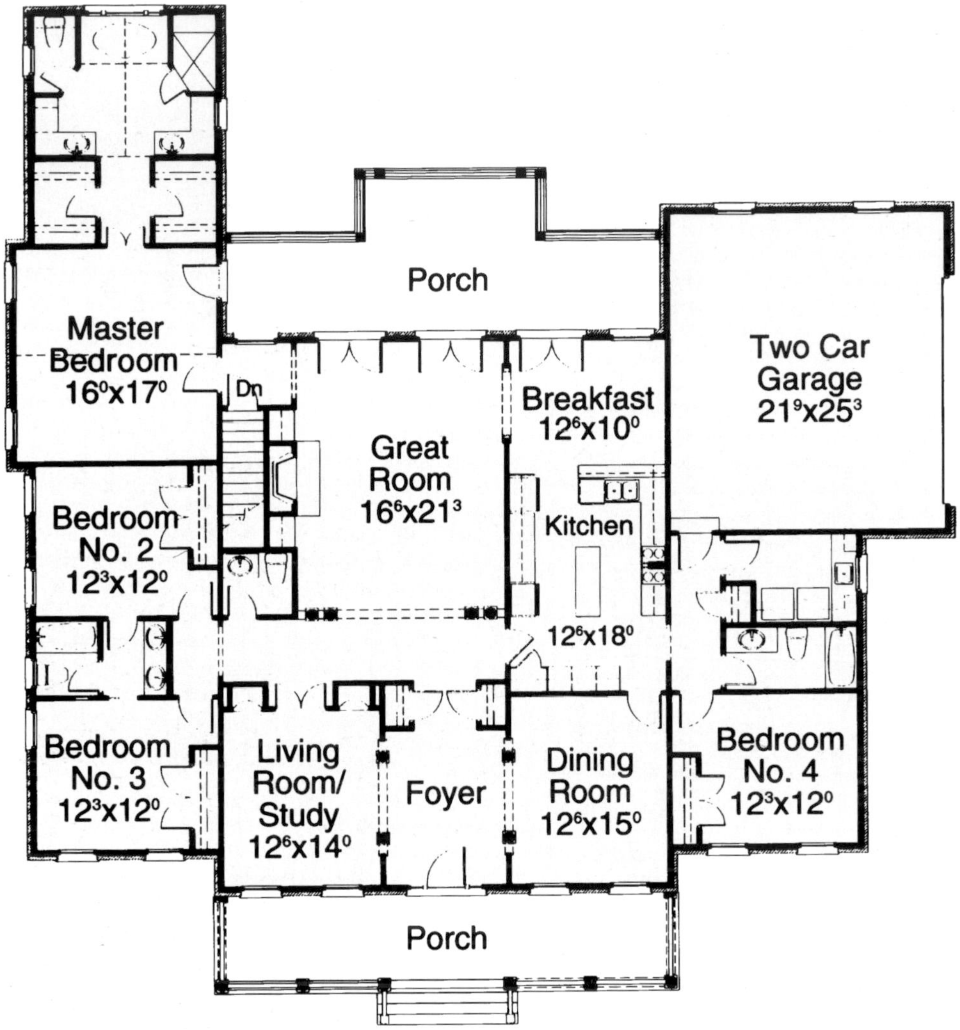
Porch
Master Bedroom 16⁰x17⁰
Dn
Great Room 16⁶x21³
Breakfast 12⁶x10⁰
Two Car Garage 21⁹x25³
Bedroom No. 2 12³x12⁰
Kitchen
12⁶x18⁰
Bedroom No. 3 12³x12⁰
Living Room/ Study 12⁶x14⁰
Foyer
Dining Room 12⁶x15⁰
Bedroom No. 4 12³x12⁰
Porch

Width 73'-0"
Depth 70'-6"

Rear Elevation

Two charming dormers complement a stately pediment, supported by two sets of columns, on the rear elevation of this lovely cottage. A wonderful home for families who value their time together, this enduring classic combines great warmth and unmistakable elegance.

ADDISON

Descended from the architecture that developed in America's Low Country, this spacious home retains the insouciant charm of a coastal cottage and offers an elegance that is appropriate for any setting or climate today. The broad stairway and deep porch say welcome in soft, Southern style, while the elliptical fanlight and circular sidelights that frame the door speak of Georgian-style refinements. Inside, a gallery opens to the great room, where two sets of French doors to the covered porch complement a focal-point fireplace. A gourmet kitchen with a centered food preparation island overlooks a spacious breakfast area with French doors to the rear porch.

Design T165

Square Footage: 3,066

Bedrooms: 4

Bathrooms: 3½

Randolph

Design T157

Square Footage: 2,987
Bedrooms: 3
Bathrooms: 2½

Post and beam construction and a gently curved balustrade give a nod to America's past, and introduce a distinctly modern floor plan. The entry portico, supported with columns, is a classic—beloved by no less a builder of both houses and nations than Thomas Jefferson, who adopted this motif for his own Monticello. Formal rooms include a study, or parlor, and a dining room just off the foyer, which leads to grand living space for casual gatherings. The great room opens to the rear deck through French doors, and offers an extended-hearth fireplace, while the U-shaped kitchen overlooks a spacious keeping room with its own hearth. Split sleeping quarters include a master suite with a whirlpool bath and two family bedrooms.

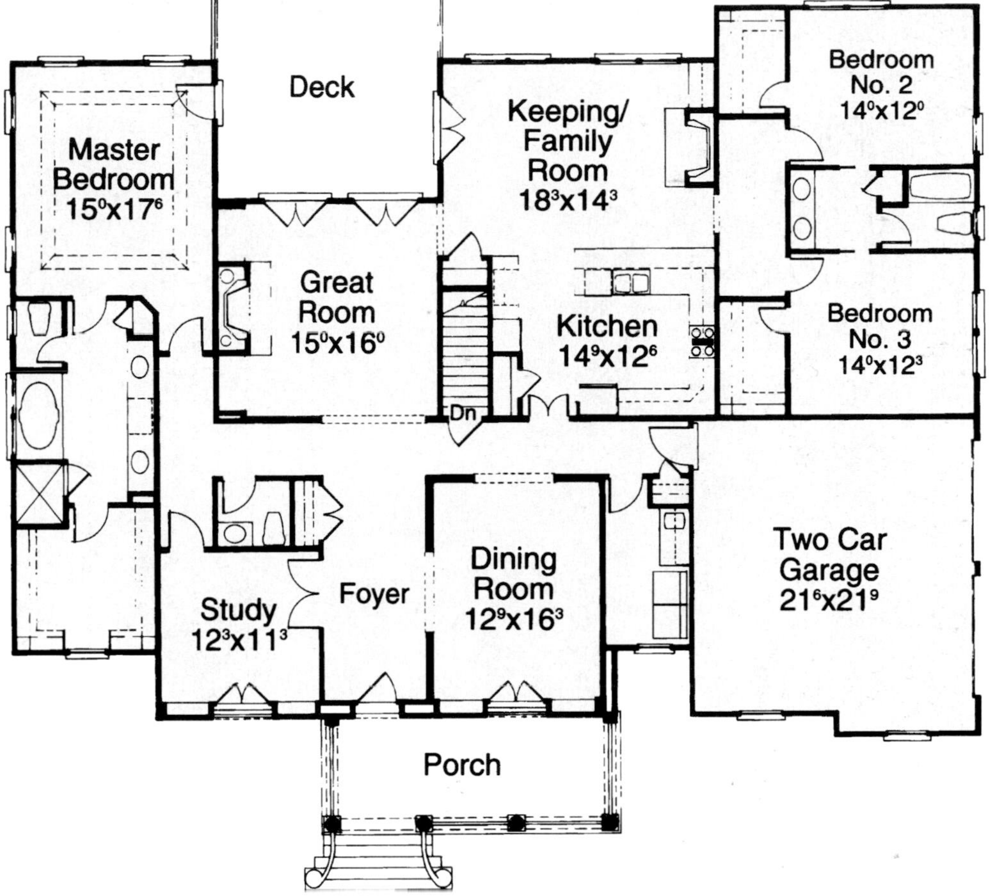
Deck
Master Bedroom 15⁰x17⁶
Keeping/ Family Room 18³x14³
Bedroom No. 2 14⁰x12⁰
Great Room 15⁰x16⁰
Kitchen 14⁹x12⁶
Bedroom No. 3 14⁰x12³
Dn
Study 12³x11³
Foyer
Dining Room 12⁹x16³
Two Car Garage 21⁶x21⁹
Porch

Width 74'-0"
Depth 62'-0"

Rear Elevation

With a design heritage distinguished through the centuries, the Early Classical style of this home is a study in contrasts. There's something of a cozy cottage feeling here but the house also makes a statement about gracious living and fine entertaining.

West Paces Estate

Design T007

Square Footage: 2,697

Bedrooms: 3 630 A STUDY PRG 675 4 SET PRG

Bathrooms: 2½ 730 8 SET PRG

Symmetrical architectural features, including twin chimneys and a double stairway, create a balanced statement on this Colonial-style home. A sunlit foyer leads straight into the spacious great room, where French doors and large side windows provide a generous view of the covered veranda in back. The great room features a tray ceiling and a fireplace, bordered by twin bookcases. Another great view is offered from the spacious kitchen, which has a breakfast bar and a roomy work island. The master suite provides a large balanced bath, a spacious closet and a glass sitting area with access to the veranda.

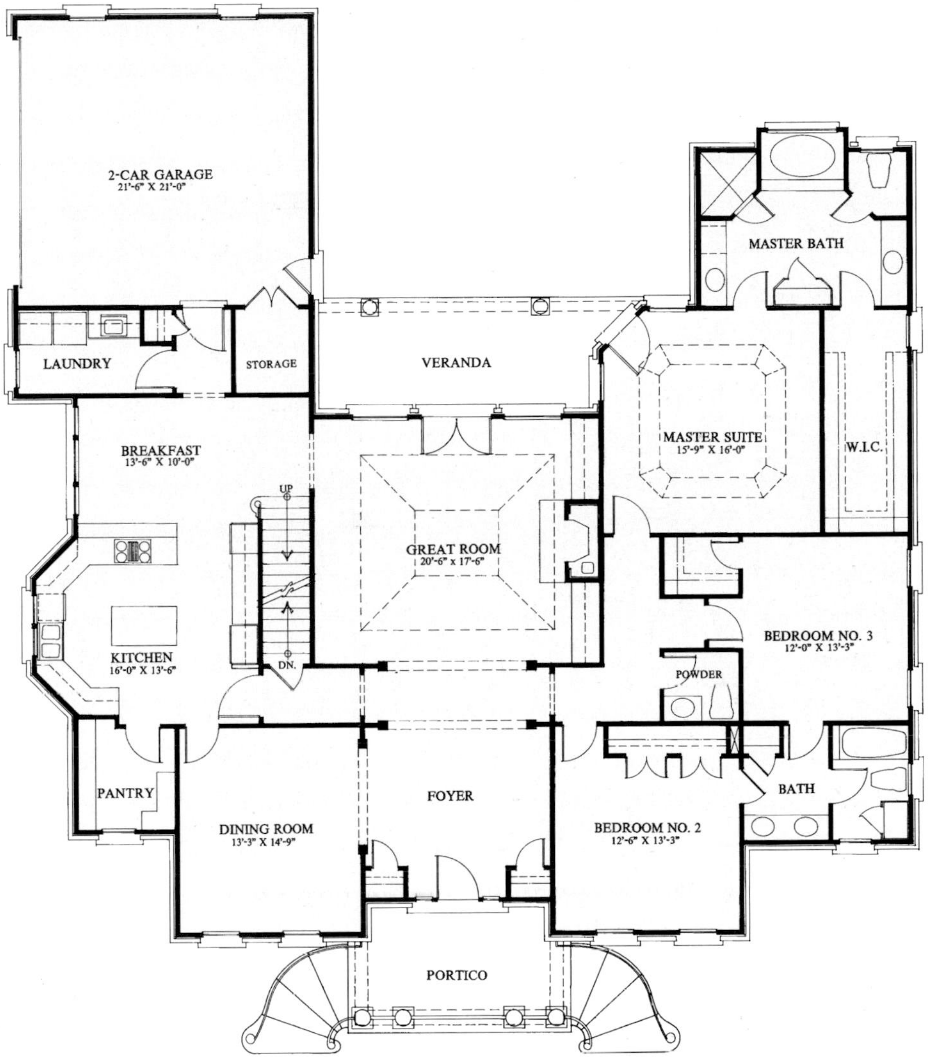
2-CAR GARAGE
21'-6" X 21'-0"
MASTER BATH
LAUNDRY
STORAGE
VERANDA
MASTER SUITE
15'-9" X 16'-0"
W.I.C.
BREAKFAST
13'-6" X 10'-0"
UP
GREAT ROOM
20'-6" x 17'-6"
BEDROOM NO. 3
12'-0" X 13'-3"
KITCHEN
16'-0" X 13'-6"
DN.
POWDER
PANTRY
FOYER
BATH
DINING ROOM
13'-3" X 14'-9"
BEDROOM NO. 2
12'-6" X 13'-3"
PORTICO

Width 65'-3"
Depth 67'-3"

This Neo-Classical one-story home has a temple portico entry porch centered in the main body of the exterior, that's capped by a high hip roof. Other Neo-Classical details include the dentil molding at the eaves and gable, and the fanlight over the door with two sidelights.

WINDSOR PLACE

Design T119

First Floor: 2,530 square feet
Second Floor: 1,969 square feet
Total: 4,499 square feet

Bedrooms: 3
Bathrooms: 3½

630 FOREST STUDY PKG
675 4 SDT PKG.
730 8 SFT PKG.

Width 75'-10"
Depth 58'-4"

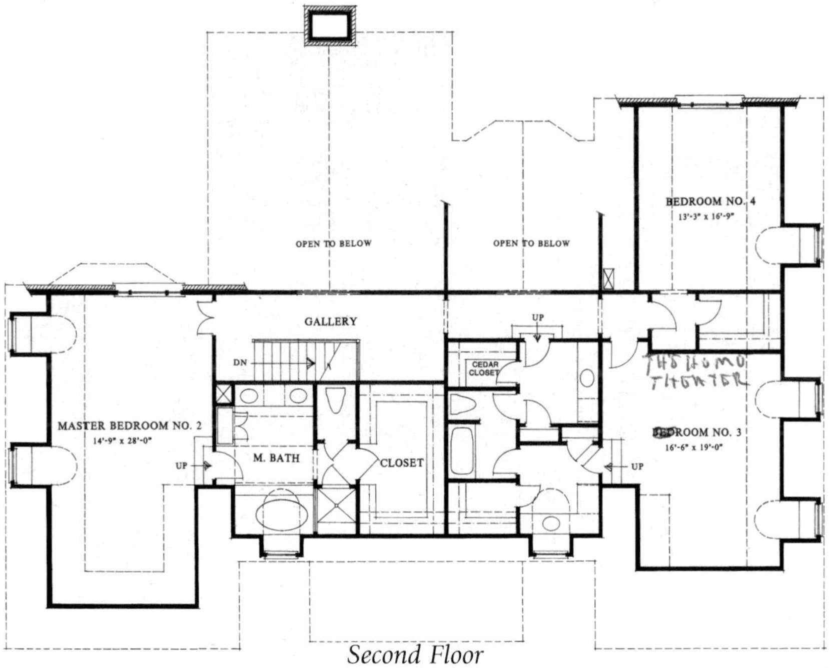

Second Floor

First Floor

The entry to this classic home is introduced by a grand double staircase, enhanced by wrought iron railings, that leads past rounded columns to a stylish portico. Beyond the foyer, the vaulted great room, with its immense central fireplace, provides convenient access to the remainder of the house. Both the breakfast room and the great room are open to the second floor gallery. The functional master suite provides easy passage to all areas of the home yet maintains a private retreat with a view to the back property.

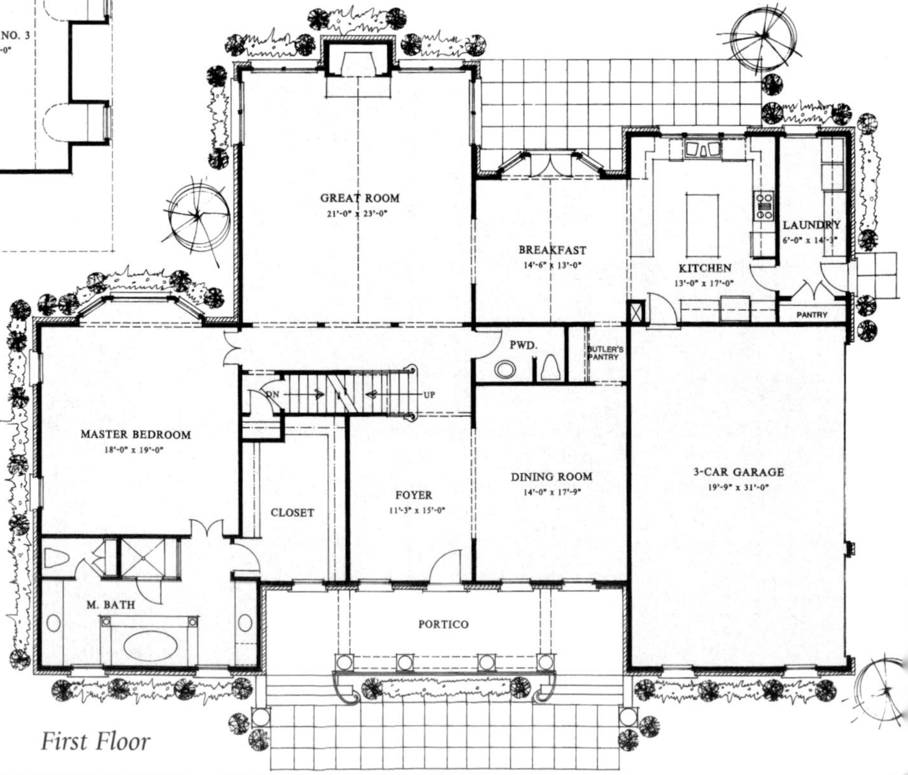

BUCKINGHAM COURT

Design T116

First Floor: 3,509 square feet
Second Floor: 1,564 square feet
Total: 5,073 square feet
Bedrooms: 4
Bathrooms: 4½ + ½

Classic symmetry sets off this graceful exterior, with two sets of double columns framed by tall windows and topped with a detailed pediment. The central gallery hall connects casual living areas with the master wing. A delightful dressing area with a split vanity and a bay window introduces a lavish master bath and leads to a walk-in closet. The homeowner's bedroom features a bumped-out glass sitting area, a tray ceiling and a through-fireplace that it shares with the great room. The gourmet kitchen has a food prep island with a double sink, and a lovely breakfast bay.

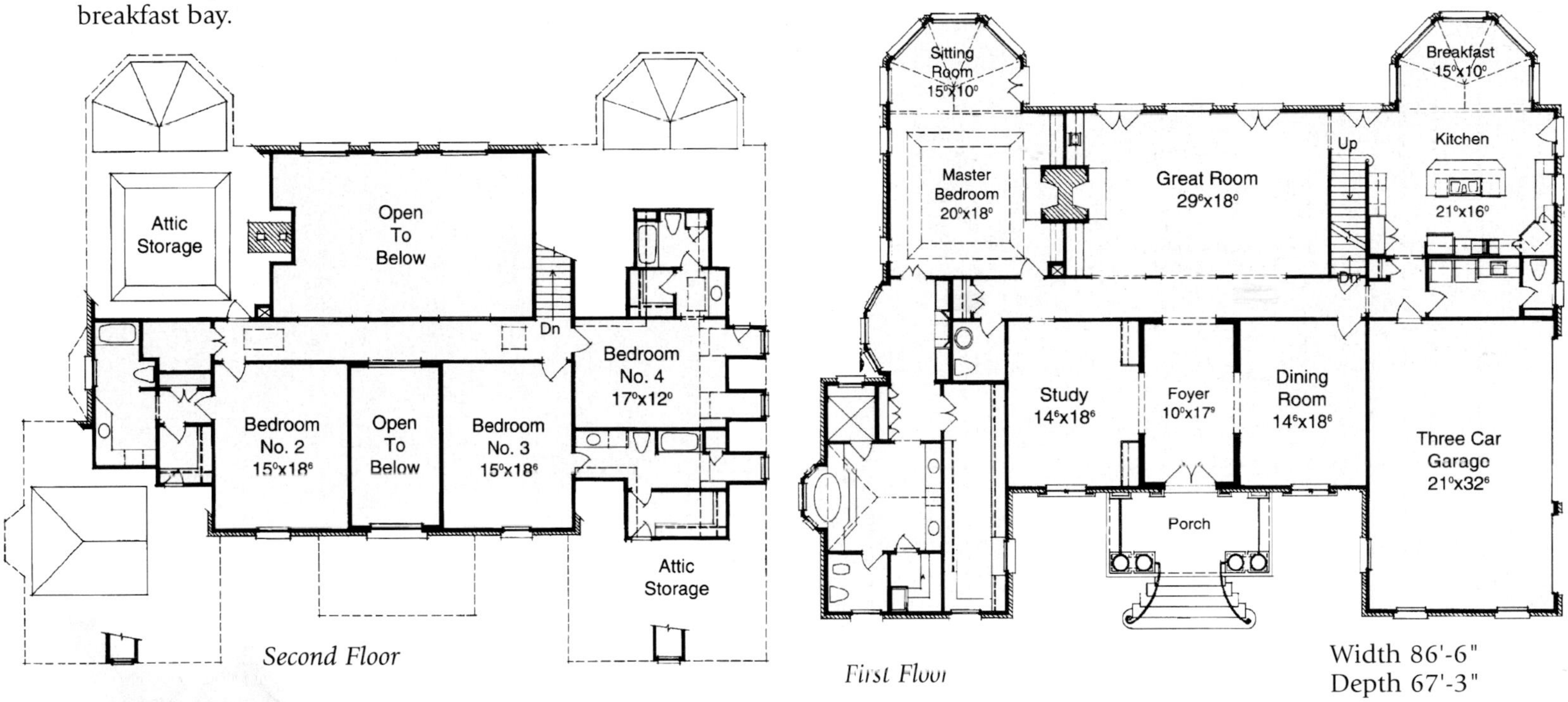

Attic Storage
Open To Below
Dn
Bedroom No. 4 17⁰x12⁰
Bedroom No. 2 15⁰x18⁶
Open To Below
Bedroom No. 3 15⁰x18⁶
Attic Storage
Second Floor
Sitting Room 15⁶x10⁰
Breakfast 15⁰x10⁰
Master Bedroom 20⁰x18⁰
Great Room 29⁶x18⁰
Up
Kitchen 21⁰x16⁰
Dn
Study 14⁶x18⁶
Foyer 10⁰x17⁹
Dining Room 14⁶x18⁶
Three Car Garage 21⁰x32⁶
Porch
First Floor

Width 86'-6"
Depth 67'-3"

This grand design has many timeless architectural features that make it a classic. A double sweeping staircase leads to the symmetrical entry, which is framed by four large columns supporting the elegantly detailed pediment.

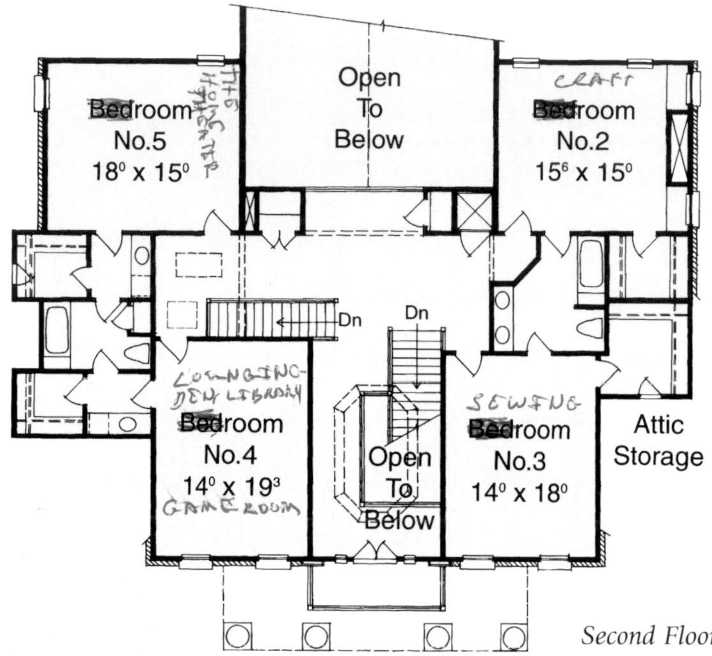

Second Floor

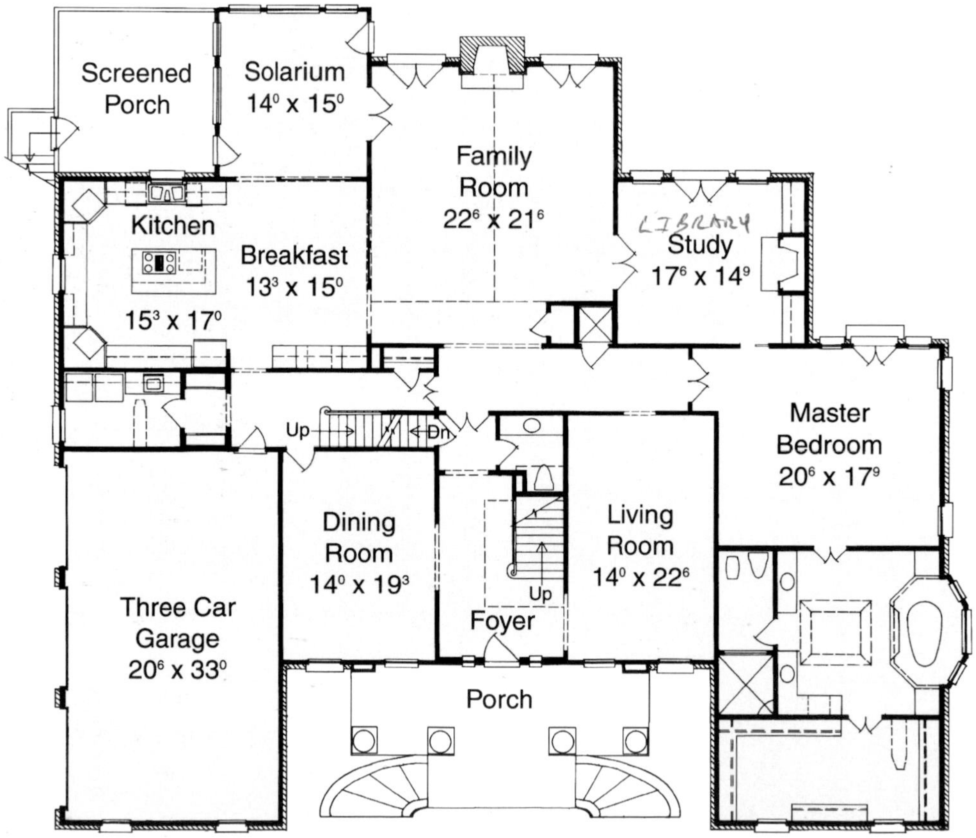

Width 85'-3"
Depth 74'-0"

First Floor

BRIDGEPORT PLANTATION

Design T126

First Floor: 3,902 square feet
Second Floor: 2,159 square feet
Total: 6,061 square feet

Bedrooms: 5
Bathrooms: 3½

638 FOR A STUDY PKG,
675 A 4 SET
730 AN 8 SET

A fine depiction of Southern elegance, this home displays some of the great architectural elements of Greek Revival style. Inside, the foyer is flanked by the formal living and dining rooms and leads impressively to the staircase, which ascends to the balcony porch above. Beyond the foyer, the vaulted family room, with a centered fireplace framed by windows, opens to the study and to the solarium. French doors lead out to the terrace, a perfect spot for morning meals or evening leisure. The master suite has its own bay window and a lavish bath, while two additional [redacted]rooms share a full bath with compartmented vanities.

OXFORD HALL

Design T117

First Floor: 3,365 square feet
Second Floor: 1,456 square feet
Total: 4,821 square feet

Bedrooms: 4
Bathrooms: 3½

The graceful lines of this formal Georgian brick manor are an inviting presence in any neighborhood. An open foyer enjoys views of the back property through the living room, which features a fireplace framed with built-in bookshelves. Dinner guests will want to linger on the rear terrace, which opens through French doors, from formal and casual areas. The gourmet kitchen has a cooktop island, a walk-in pantry and a breakfast area that's open to the bright family room. Homeowners will enjoy the master bedroom's private sitting area, which has two skylights, a fireplace and access to the terrace.

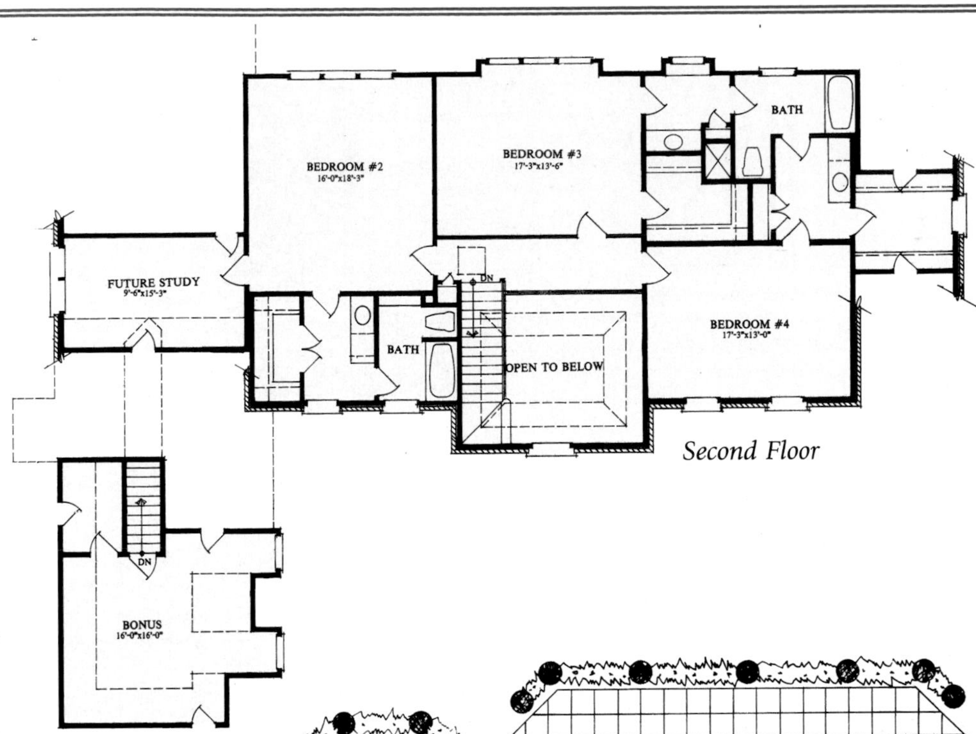

BEDROOM #2
16'-0"x18'-3"
BEDROOM #3
17'-3"x13'-6"
BATH
FUTURE STUDY
9'-6"x15'-3"
DN
BATH
OPEN TO BELOW
BEDROOM #4
17'-3"x13'-0"
DN
BONUS
16'-0"x16'-0"

Second Floor

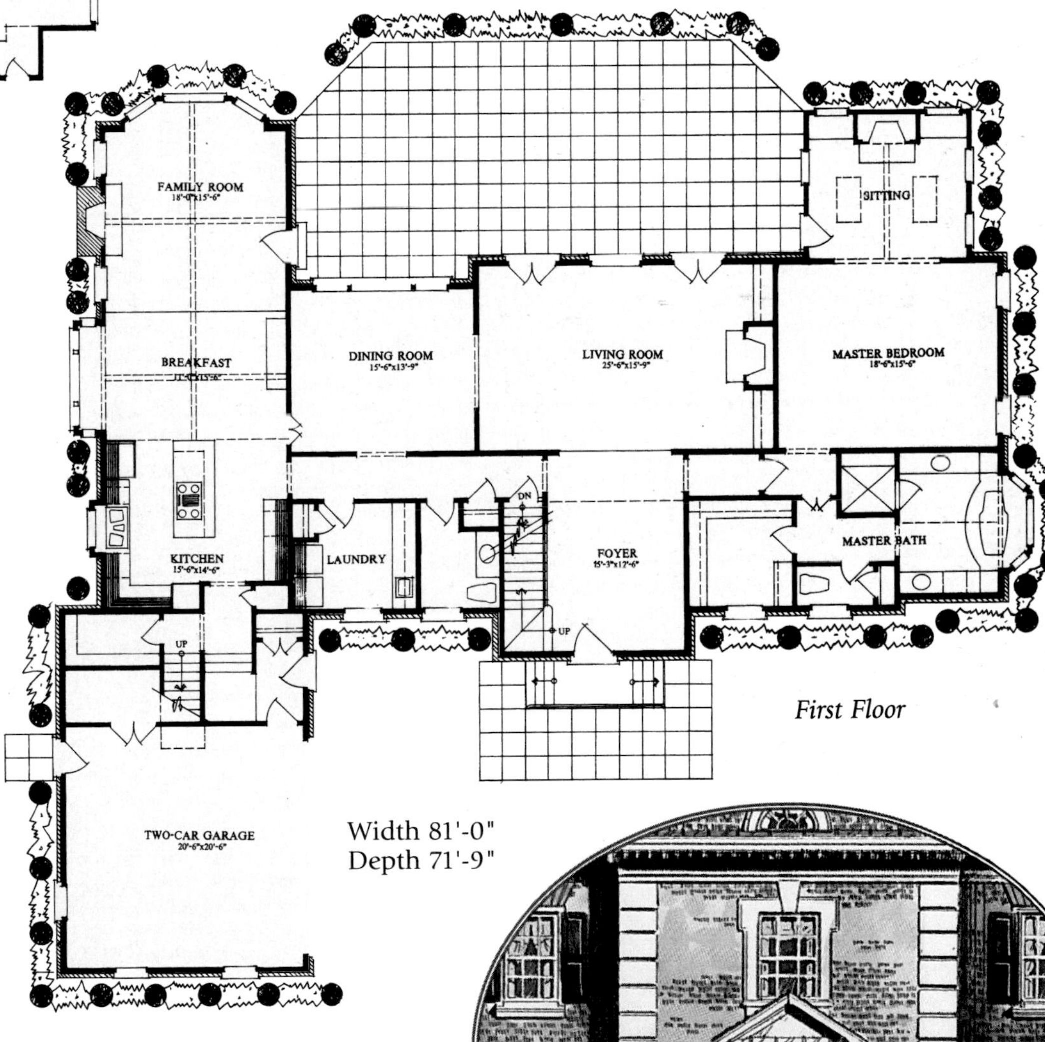

FAMILY ROOM
SITTING
BREAKFAST
DINING ROOM
15'-6"x13'-9"
LIVING ROOM
25'-6"x15'-9"
MASTER BEDROOM
18'-6"x15'-6"
KITCHEN
15'-6"x14'-6"
LAUNDRY
DN
FOYER
15'-3"x12'-6"
MASTER BATH
UP
UP
TWO-CAR GARAGE
20'-6"x20'-6"

First Floor

Width 81'-0"
Depth 71'-9"

Classical details enhance the historical and stately elegance of this beautiful Georgian home. A simple pediment, pilasters and an arched transom above the paneled entry provide a tasteful complement to quoins and jack-arches.

NORFOLK RIDGE

Design T125

Main Floor: 4,646 square feet
Lower Floor: 1,974 square feet
Total: 6,620 square feet

Bedrooms: 3
Bathrooms: 3½

630 FOR A STUDY PACKAGE
675 FOR A 4 SET PACKAGE

Timeless in every detail, this home displays a stately manner through classic symmetry and a perfect blend of style and comfort. The open foyer offers an ideal location for greeting guests and provides a double entrance to the living room. The well-planned kitchen is convenient to the formal dining room and to the breakfast area, which opens to a lovely octagonal den. A sumptuous master suite offers a vaulted bath, a separate walk-in closet with a dressing area, and private stair access to the exercise room and spa below. The lower floor also provides a recreation room with a fireplace, and bonus space that may be developed later.

HOME THEATER W/ SURROUND SOUND STEREO

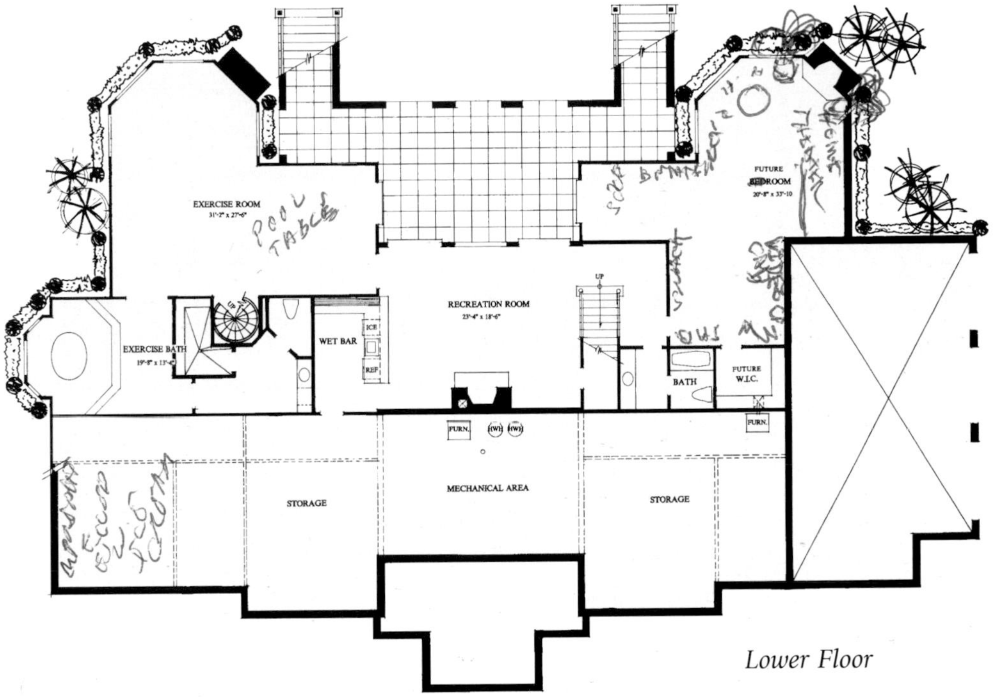

Lower Floor

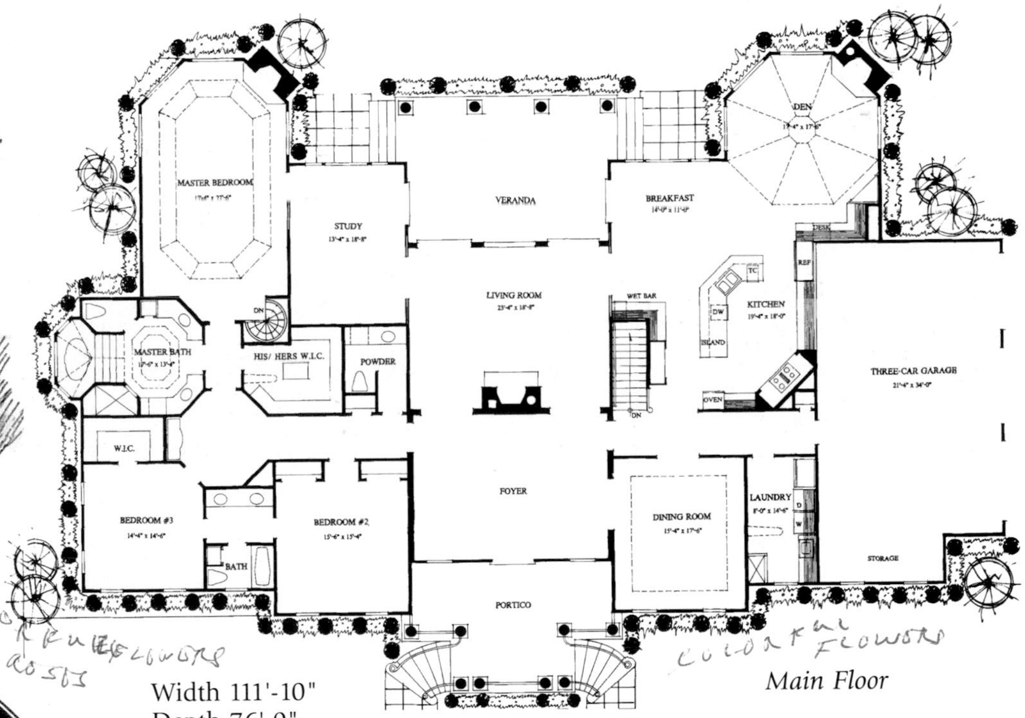

Width 111'-10"
Depth 76'-0"

Main Floor

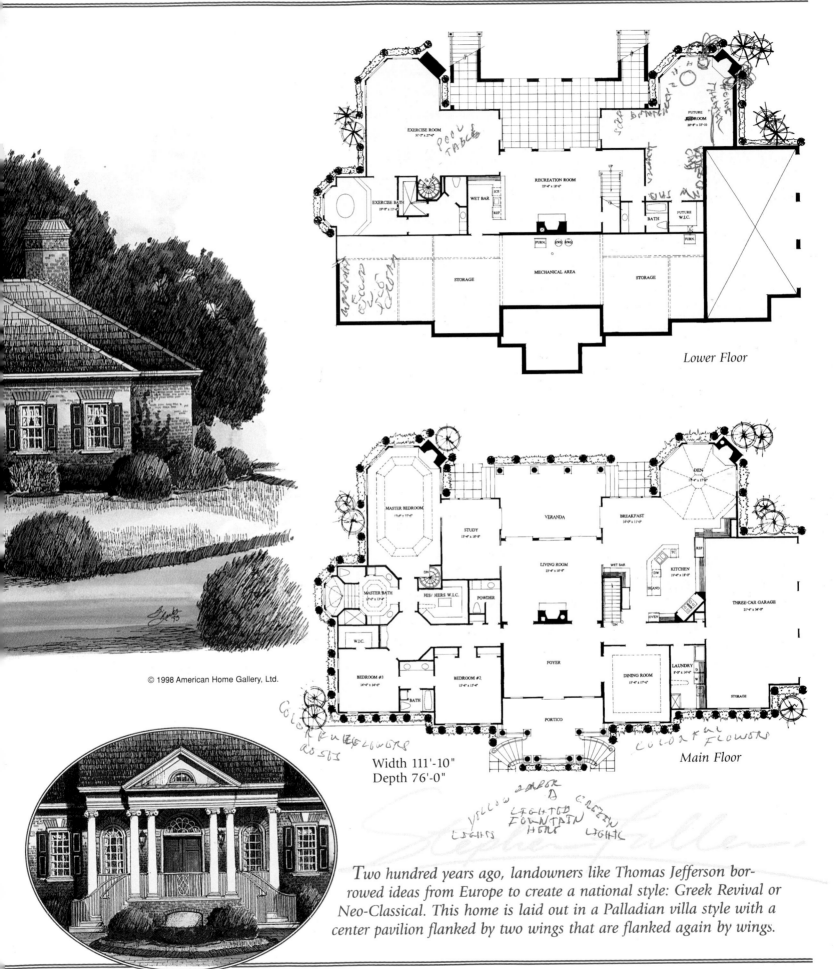

Two hundred years ago, landowners like Thomas Jefferson borrowed ideas from Europe to create a national style: Greek Revival or Neo-Classical. This home is laid out in a Palladian villa style with a center pavilion flanked by two wings that are flanked again by wings.

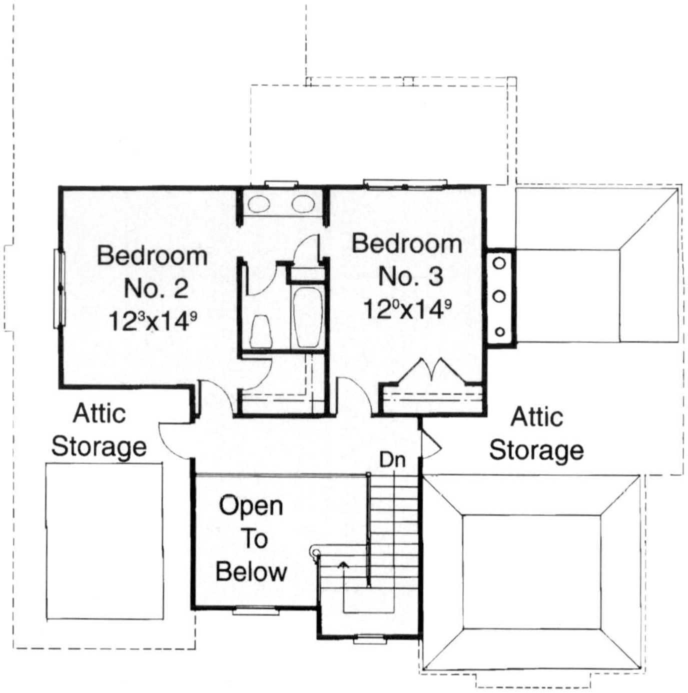

Second Floor

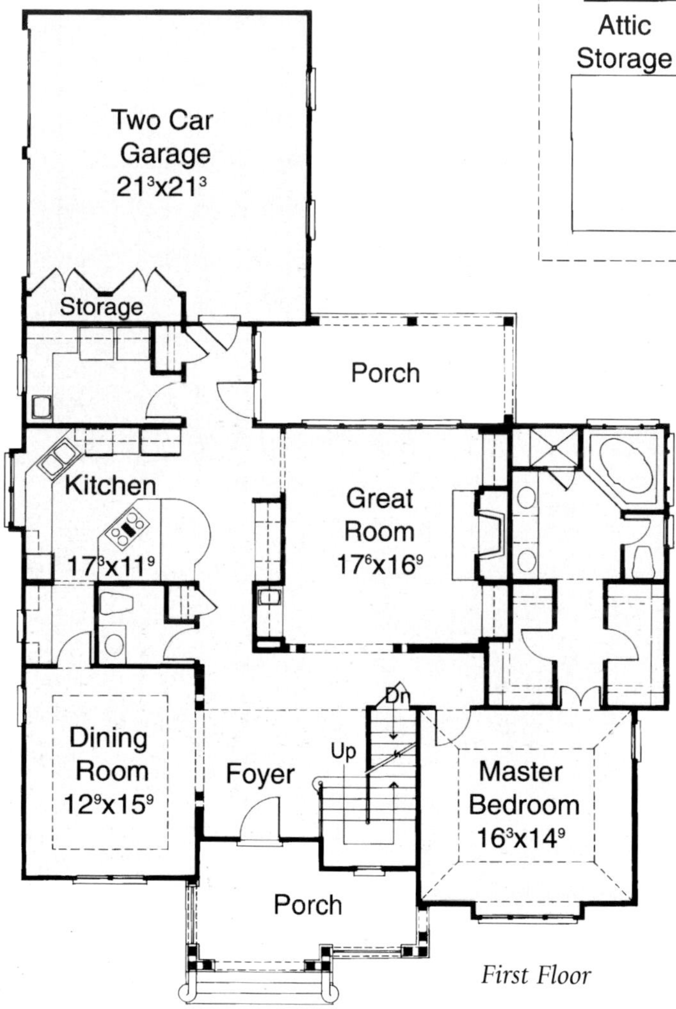

First Floor

Width 49'-9"
Depth 74'-3"

A modern blend of classic and casual fuse past and present on this Victorian Revival home. An outstanding facade features enduring elements such as a double pediment supported by twin sets of pilasters, while the glass-paneled entry leads to flexible interior space.

ANSLEY WALK

Design T139

First Floor: 1,859 square feet
Second Floor: 645 square feet
Total: 2,504 square feet

Bedrooms: 3
Bathrooms: 3½

Charming entry details complement copper seam flashing and lend a gentle Early American flavor to this traditional home. A well-planned interior starts with a spacious foyer, which opens to the formal dining room and leads to the great room. Planned events as well as "lose the shoes" gatherings are welcomed in this spacious living area, which has a centered fireplace and built-in bookshelves. An angled cooktop counter with a snack bar handles quick meals and invites impromptu family gatherings in the kitchen. The secluded master suite has a dressing area and two walk-in closets, a deluxe bath and a box-bay window.

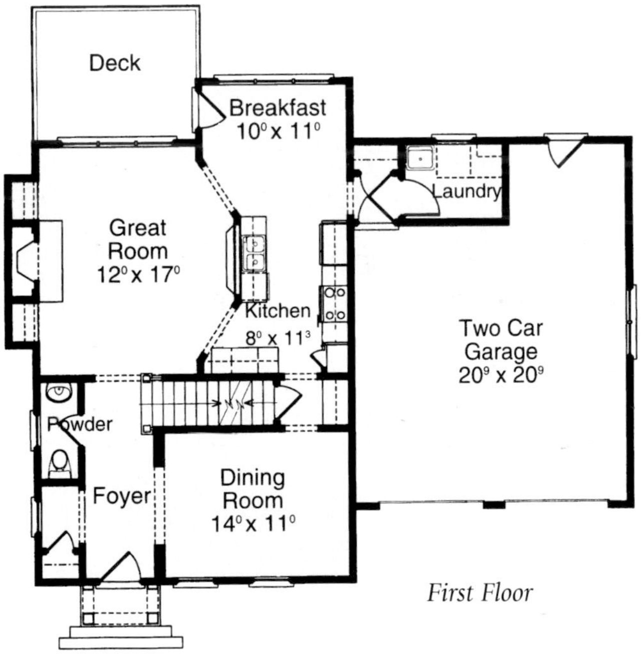

First Floor

AVALON

A rich heritage is demonstrated in the Early American details of this Colonial-style home. The entry pediment announces an interior rich with amenities, with a quiet formal area to the front of the plan and casual living space to the back. A well-organized kitchen has a bright breakfast room with access to the rear deck. The heart of the home is the great room, which has a fireplace and triple-window views of the back property. On the second floor, a generous master suite has a walk-in closet, a separate shower and a double-bowl vanity.

Width 45'-0"
Depth 36'-11"

Design T232

First Floor: 900 square feet
Second Floor: 870 square feet
Total: 1,770 square feet

Bedrooms: 3
Bathrooms: 2½

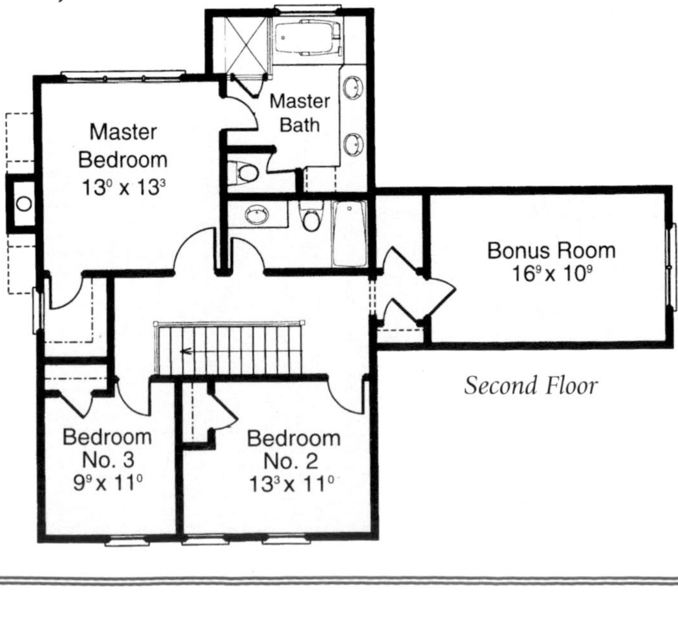

Second Floor

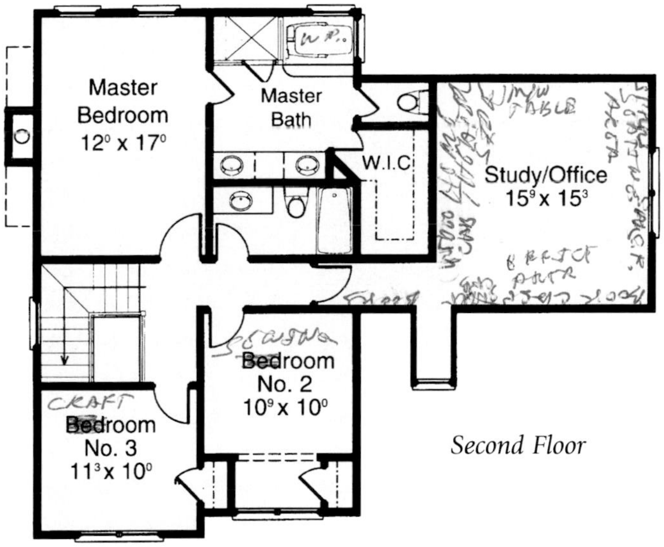

Second Floor

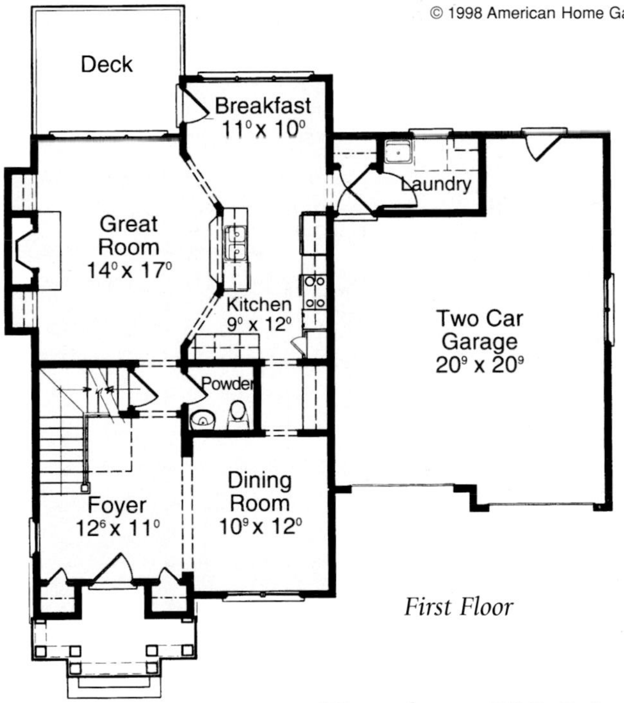

First Floor

FITZGERALD PLACE

The symmetry of the entry's classic pediment is echoed by a sophisticated arrangement of gables plus a charming dormer. These captivating details announce an interior that's no less winsome, starting with a roomy foyer with an L-shaped staircase. A formal dining room is easily served through a convenient butler's pantry by an amenity-rich kitchen. Natural light flows through the breakfast room which allows access to the rear deck. Upstairs, a gallery hall leads to a secluded study or home office.

Width 44'-0"
Depth 41'-4"

Design T231

First Floor: 945 square feet
Second Floor: 825 square feet
Total: 1,770 square feet

Bedrooms: 3
Bathrooms: 2½

Combination brick-and-lap siding with occasional standing-seam copper accents begins this dramatic presentation of Colonial architecture. Highlights include a recessed front entry and a graceful side porch with columns and Colonial-style pickets.

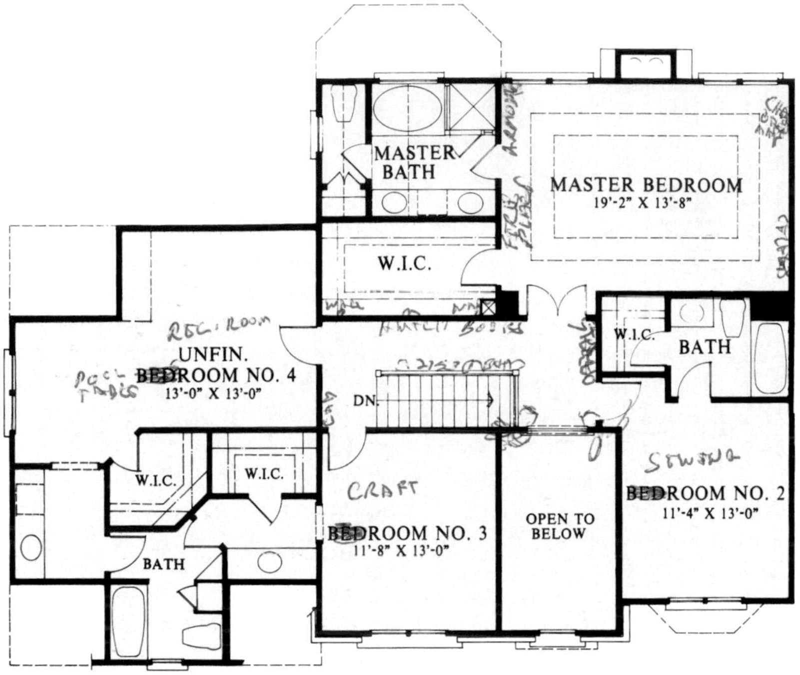

MASTER BATH
MASTER BEDROOM
19'-2" X 13'-8"
W.I.C.
UNFIN.
BEDROOM NO. 4
13'-0" X 13'-0"
DN.
W.I.C.
BATH
W.I.C.
W.I.C.
BATH
BEDROOM NO. 3
11'-8" X 13'-0"
OPEN TO
BELOW
BEDROOM NO. 2
11'-4" X 13'-0"

Second Floor

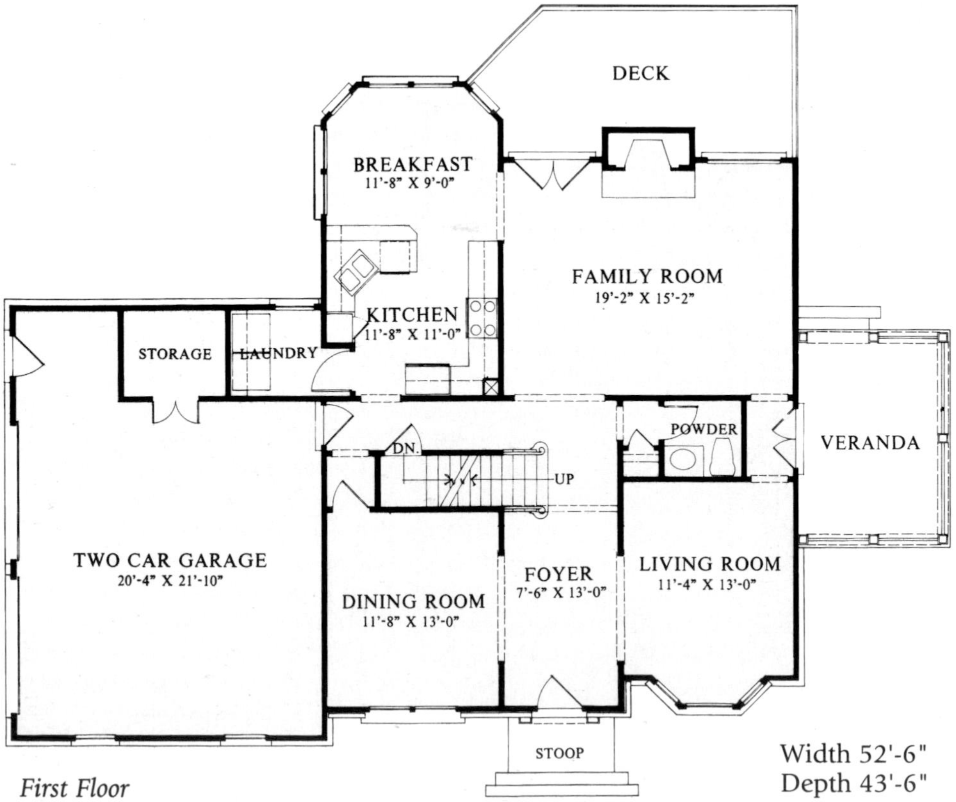

DECK
BREAKFAST
11'-8" X 9'-0"
FAMILY ROOM
19'-2" X 15'-2"
KITCHEN
11'-8" X 11'-0"
STORAGE
LAUNDRY
POWDER
VERANDA
DN.
UP
TWO CAR GARAGE
20'-4" X 21'-10"
DINING ROOM
11'-8" X 13'-0"
FOYER
7'-6" X 13'-0"
LIVING ROOM
11'-4" X 13'-0"
STOOP

First Floor

Width 52'-6"
Depth 43'-6"

MANSFIELD HARBOR

This charming exterior conceals a perfect family plan, with flexible interior spaces designed for the way people live today. The formal dining and living rooms are thoughtfully positioned to either side of the foyer, while the less formal living spaces flow easily into one other from a central stair hall. A kitchen filled with modern amenities features a breakfast area with a bay window that draws in natural light. Upstairs, a tray ceiling highlights the master bedroom, which also boasts a deluxe bath with a garden tub and a knee-space vanity. Each of two additional bedrooms has its own bath, and an unfinished bedroom offers its own compartmented vanity.

Design T088

First Floor: 1,205 square feet
Second Floor: 1,160 square feet
Total: 2,365 square feet

Bedrooms: 4
Bathrooms: 3½

This Revival home has distinctly Southern instincts, with an entry surrounded by glass announced by a classic pediment and rounded columns. Classic formality is modified by an asymmetrical design that makes the house more casual and more appropriate for living today.

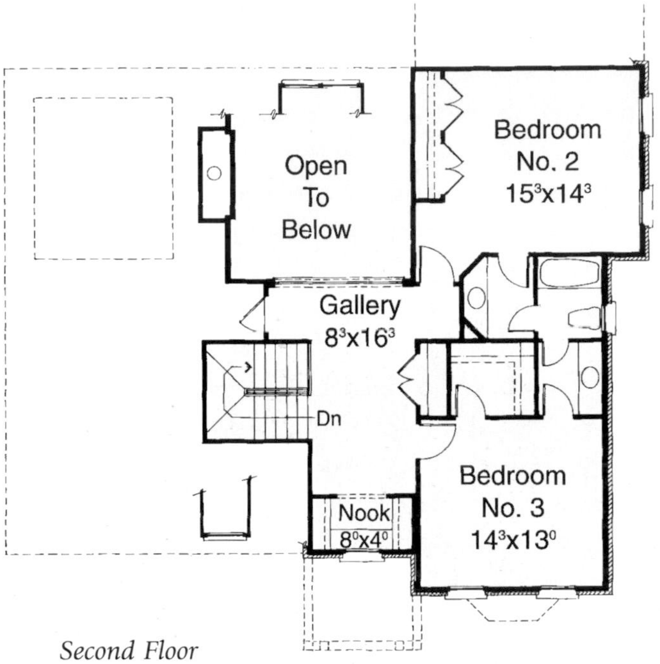

Second Floor

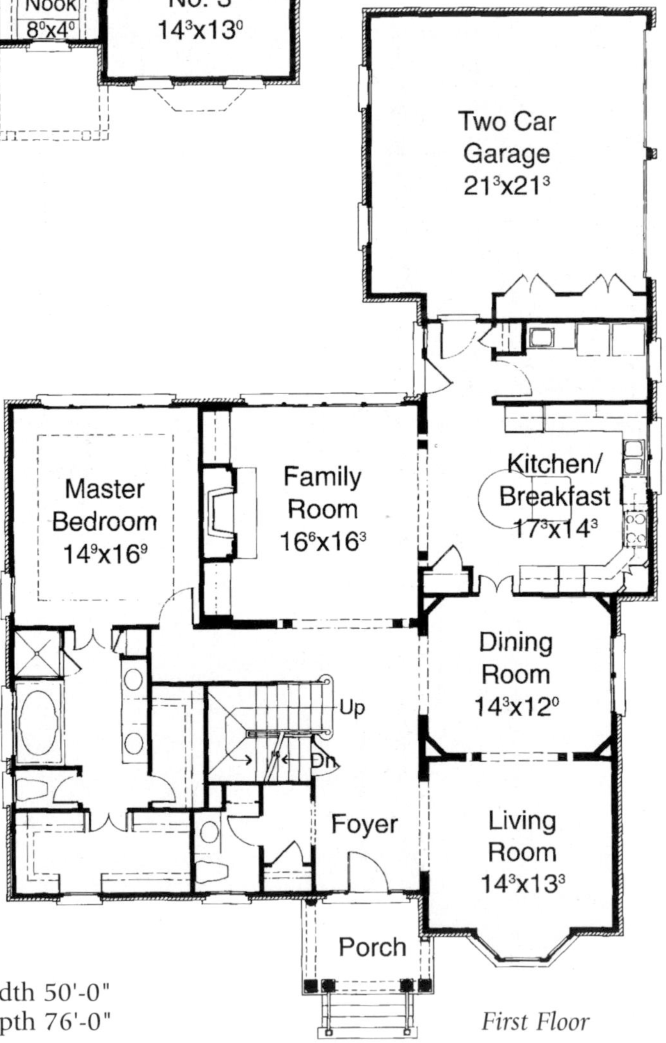

Width 50'-0"
Depth 76'-0"

First Floor

REYNOLDS PLACE

Design T142

First Floor: 2,001 square feet
Second Floor: 864 square feet
Total: 2,865 square feet
Bedrooms: 3
Bathrooms: 2½

The well-known hospitality of the South extends from the welcoming portico to the well-planned interior of this Southern Colonial design. The foyer introduces a formal living room or parlor, which has a lovely bay window. A U-shaped gourmet kitchen offers service to the dining room through French doors. Open planning allows enjoyment of the family room's fireplace in the kitchen, which has a centered food prep island. The private master suite completes the first floor. Two walk-in closets, a double-bowl vanity, a whirlpool tub and a separate shower are featured in the master bath. The second floor includes two bedrooms, a full bath and a gallery hall.

Porter Chase

Design T149

First Floor: 1,465 square feet
Second Floor: 1,332 square feet
Total: 2,797 square feet

Bedrooms: 3
Bathrooms: 2½

Brick, horizontal siding and a columned porch add elements of style to this graceful Georgian Revival design. Formal rooms flank the foyer, which leads to casual living space with a fireplace and French doors to the rear porch. A convenient butler's pantry eases service to the dining room from the well-planned kitchen. Angled counter space allows an overlook to the breakfast room. Upstairs, a rambling master suite has its own hearth and two sets of French doors that lead out to a private porch. The homeowner's bath features a split walk-in closet, an angled shower, a whirlpool tub and a compartmented bath. Each of two family bedrooms enjoys private access to a shared bath.

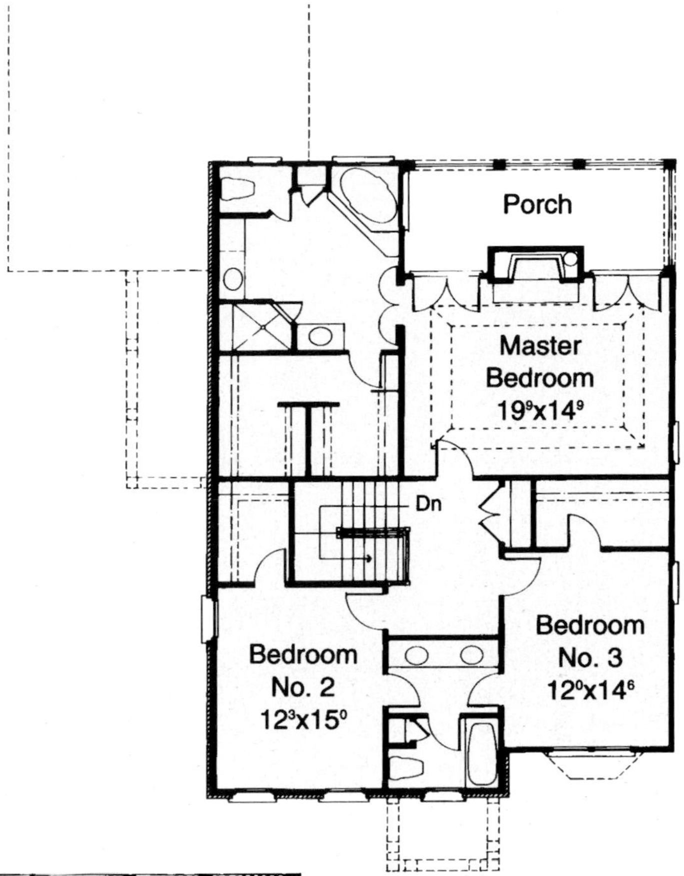

Second Floor

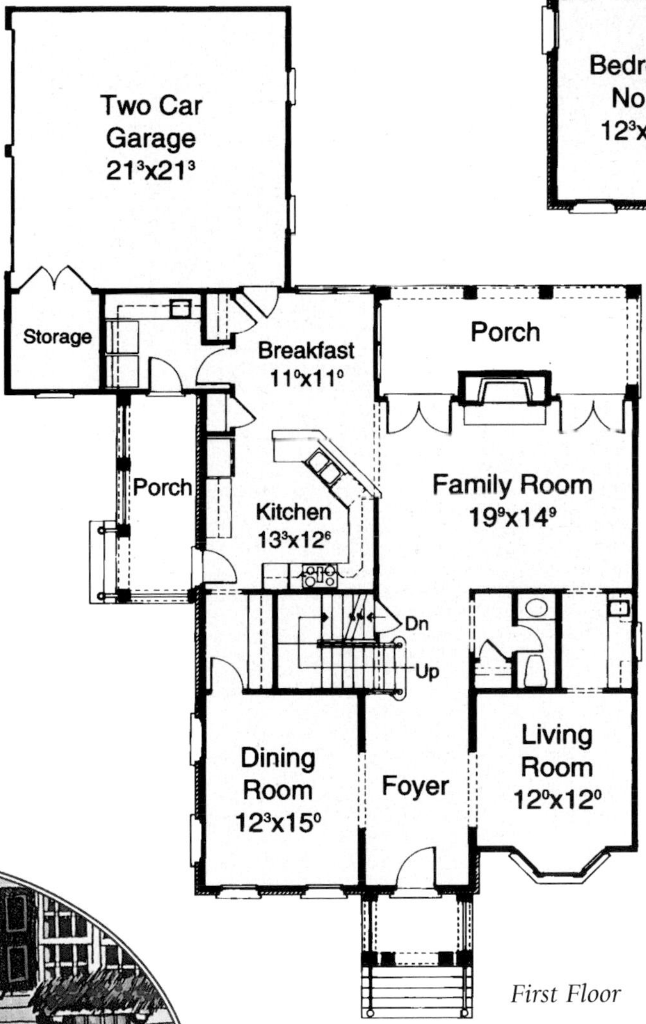

Width 49'-0"
Depth 75'-0"

First Floor

The oval foyer window and detailed surround of this Revival style complement a classic, pedimented entry. A mixture of brick and lap siding inspires a sense of the past and adds to the character and charm of this very modern home.

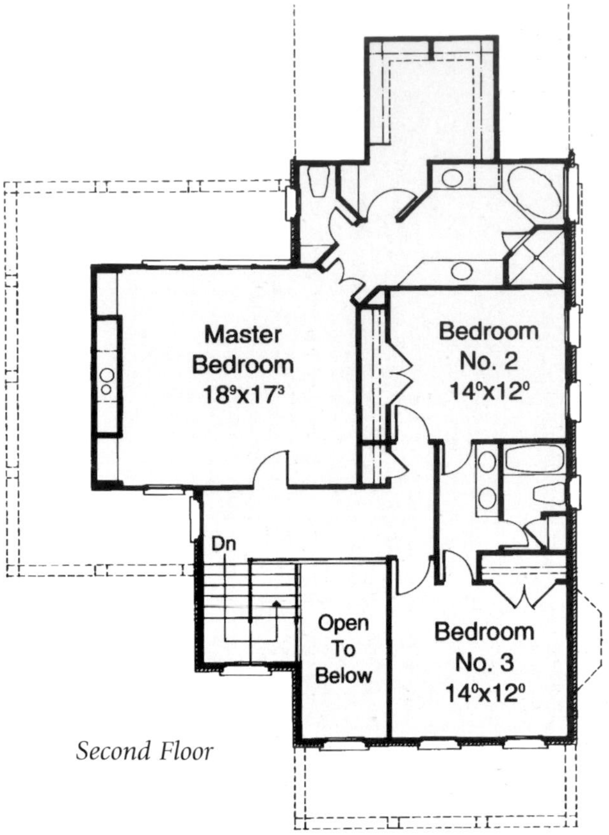

Second Floor

First Floor

Width 47'-6"
Depth 75'-3"

This elevation begins with a three-bay porch on a two-story gable, reminiscent of the classic homes of Charleston. After a large, arched stair window is a side porch with Charleston-style details. The use of lap siding creates the look of a new addition to an older main house.

HAMILTON COURT

Square columns and rounded balusters set off two lovely porches that inspire nostalgia on this Colonial-style home. Just off the foyer, the formal dining room is enhanced by a lovely bay window. Planned events are easily handled with a convenient butler's pantry, which leads to the kitchen. French doors open the great room to the wraparound porch, and a fireplace warms the living space. Second-floor sleeping quarters include the master suite, which has an angled entry to a luxury bath with a corner whirlpool tub, a separate shower and a walk-in closet designed for two. Two additional bedrooms share a full bath and a hall with a balcony overlook to the foyer.

Design T147

First Floor: 1,440 square feet
Second Floor: 1,339 square feet
Total: 2,779 square feet

Bedrooms: 3
Bathrooms: 2½

Stately brick and clapboard siding mix past and present on this Colonial-style country manor. Windows dressed with shutters and brick jack-arches add warmth to its exterior.

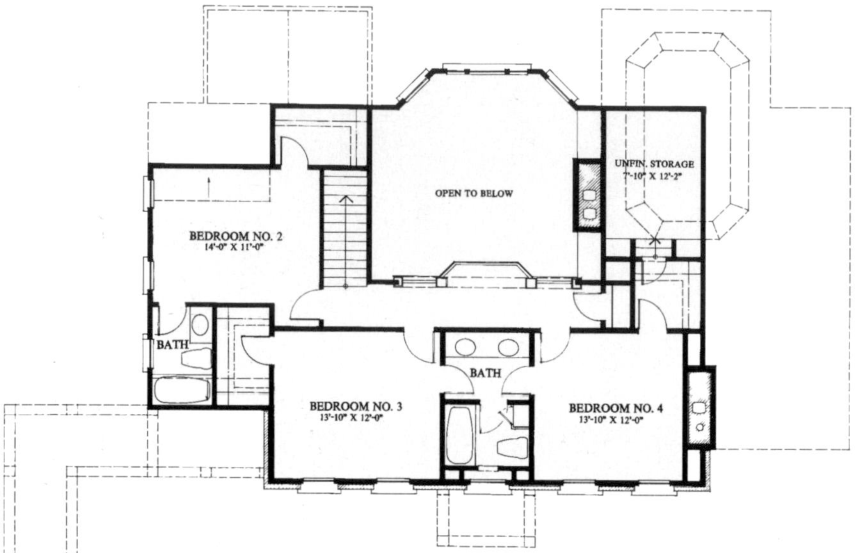

OPEN TO BELOW
UNFIN. STORAGE
7'-10" X 12'-2"
BEDROOM NO. 2
14'-0" X 11'-0"
BATH
BATH
BEDROOM NO. 3
13'-10" X 12'-0"
BEDROOM NO. 4
13'-10" X 12'-0"

Second Floor

BONUS ROOM
10'-0" X 21'-4"
DECK
BREAKFAST
13'-4" X 8'-0"
MASTER BEDROOM
13'-4" X 20'-2"
W.I.C.
TWO STORY
GREAT ROOM
19'-0" X 14'-0"
KITCHEN
14'-0" X 14'-2"
POWDER
MASTER BATH
10'-0" X 15'-0"
LAUNDRY
6'-0" X 9'-10"
DINING ROOM
13'-10" X 12'-0"
FOYER
7'-0" X 12'-0"
LIVING ROOM
13'-10" X 12'-0"
PORCH
BREEZEWAY
STOOP
TWO CAR GARAGE
21'-4" X 21'-4"

First Floor

Width 61'-0"
Depth 70'-6"

CHESTNUT LANE

Design T023

First Floor: 1,960 square feet
Second Floor: 905 square feet
Total: 2,865 square feet

Bedrooms: 4
Bathrooms: 3½

The classical styling of this Colonial home will be appreciated for years. The spacious heart of the home is the two-story great room, which boasts a centered fireplace flanked by built-in bookshelves, as well as a generous bay window. An elegant formal dining room is served by a gourmet kitchen with a center cooktop island and wide wrapping counters. The breakfast room allows wide views through walls of glass and has access to the rear deck. A private vestibule in the master wing offers a convenient powder room and separates the living room and homeowner's retreat. Three second-floor bedrooms share a gallery hall with a balcony overlook to the great room.

Chesterfield

Design T159

Square Footage: 2,914
Bedrooms: 3
Bathrooms: 2½

This Williamsburg Revival home offers entertaining and living quarters on one spacious level. A scallop-shaped porch leads into a foyer that opens first to the gallery, then to the great room. With all three of these public spaces flowing together under 10-foot ceilings, this is a home where hospitality comes naturally. An expansive, covered porch framed with windows runs across the rear elevation of the house. At the same time, the interior space has been carefully ordered for private luxury. The generous master bedroom with a walk-in closet, and a study that has its own fireplace occupy the entire left wing.

© 1998 American Home Gallery, Ltd.

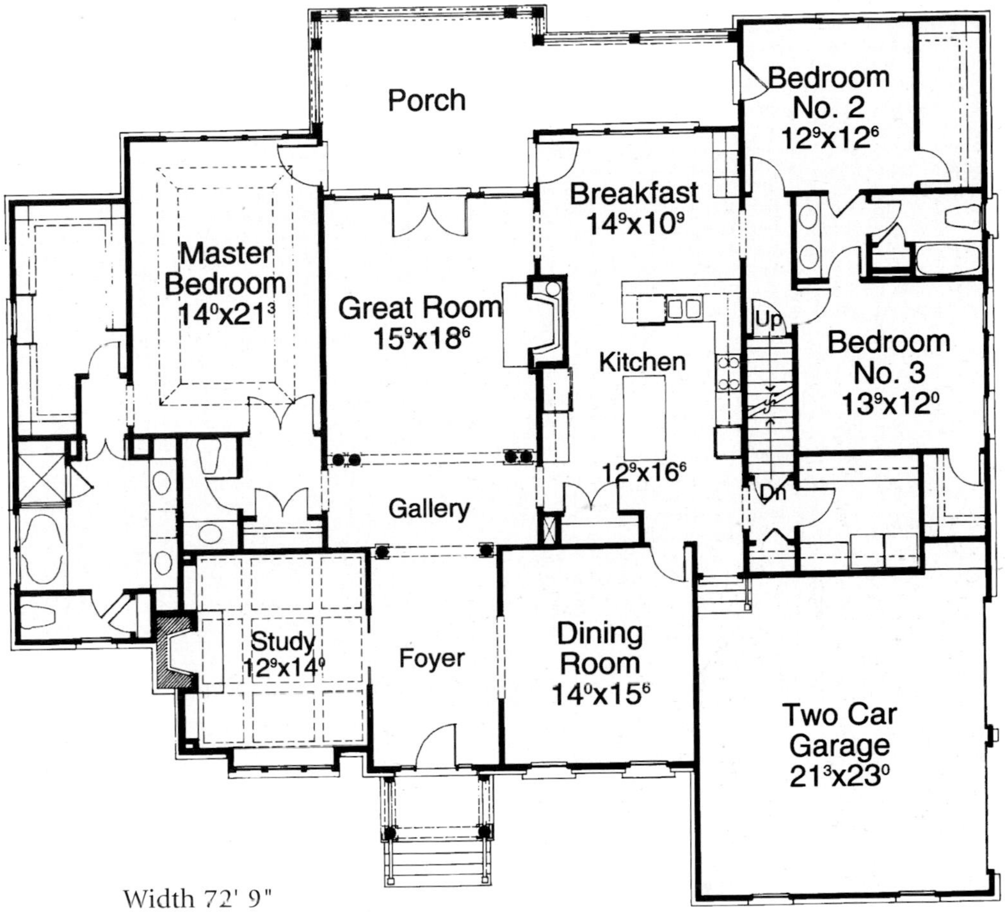
Porch
Bedroom
No. 2
12⁹x12⁶
Master
Bedroom
14⁰x21³
Great Room
15⁹x18⁶
Breakfast
14⁹x10⁹
Kitchen
12⁹x16⁶
Up
Dn
Bedroom
No. 3
13⁹x12⁰
Gallery
Study
12⁹x14⁰
Foyer
Dining
Room
14⁰x15⁶
Two Car
Garage
21³x23⁰

Width 72' 9"
Depth 65'-0"

Rear Elevation

With grace drawn from the 18th Century and comforts that anticipate the 21st, this Revival home comes with a legacy of cordiality that today's family will enjoy continuing. A covered porch framed with windows enhances the rear elevation.

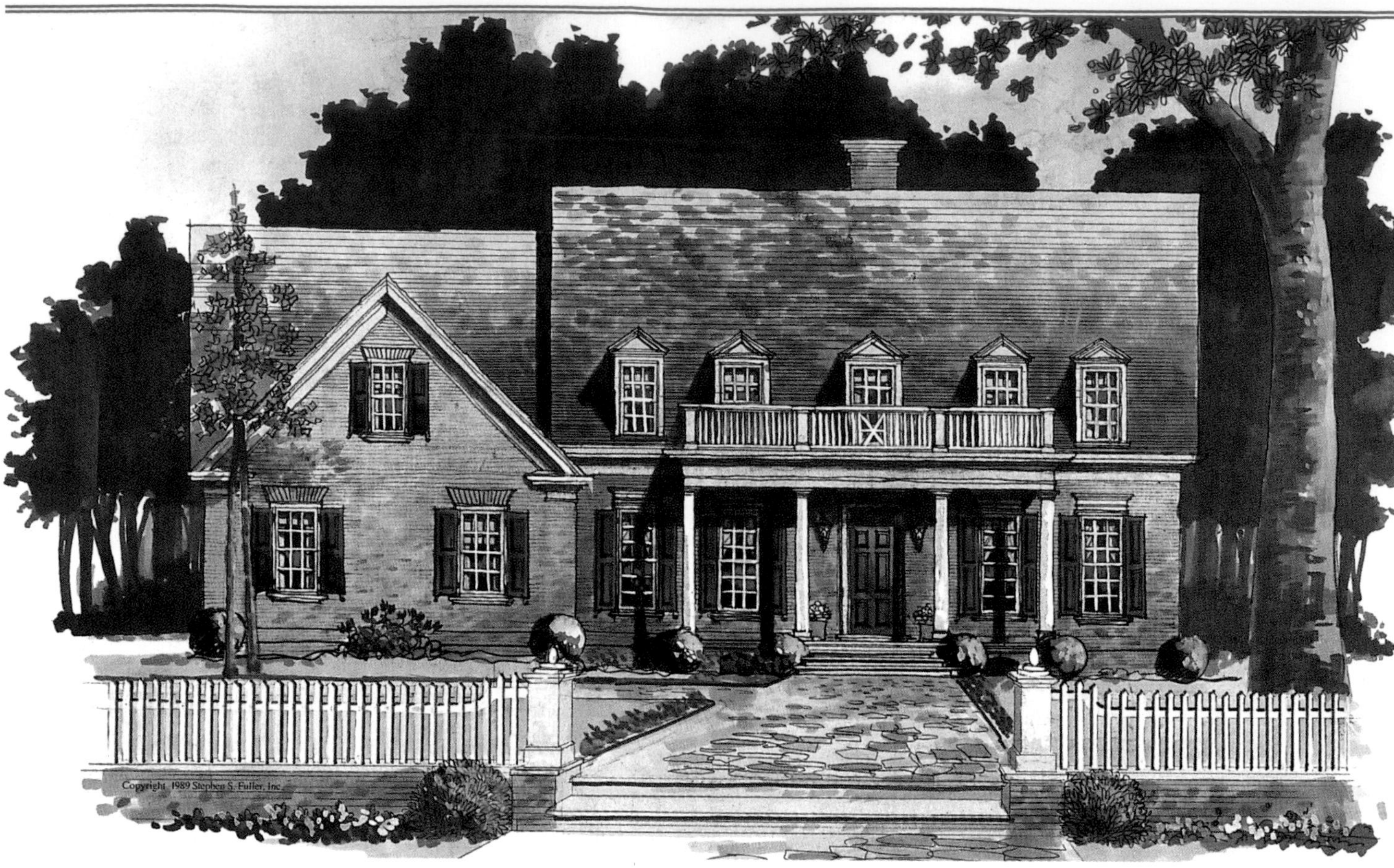

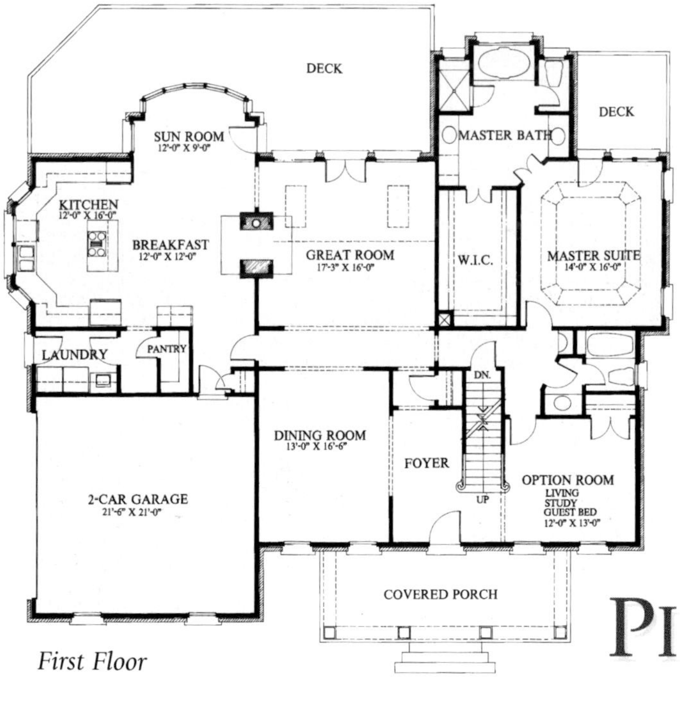
DECK
SUN ROOM
12'-0" X 9'-0"
KITCHEN
12'-0" X 16'-0"
BREAKFAST
12'-0" X 12'-0"
GREAT ROOM
17'-3" X 16'-0"
LAUNDRY
PANTRY
MASTER BATH
DECK
W.I.C.
MASTER SUITE
14'-0" X 16'-0"
DN.
UP
DINING ROOM
13'-0" X 16'-6"
FOYER
OPTION ROOM
LIVING
STUDY
GUEST BED
12'-0" X 13'-0"
2-CAR GARAGE
21'-6" X 21'-0"
COVERED PORCH

First Floor

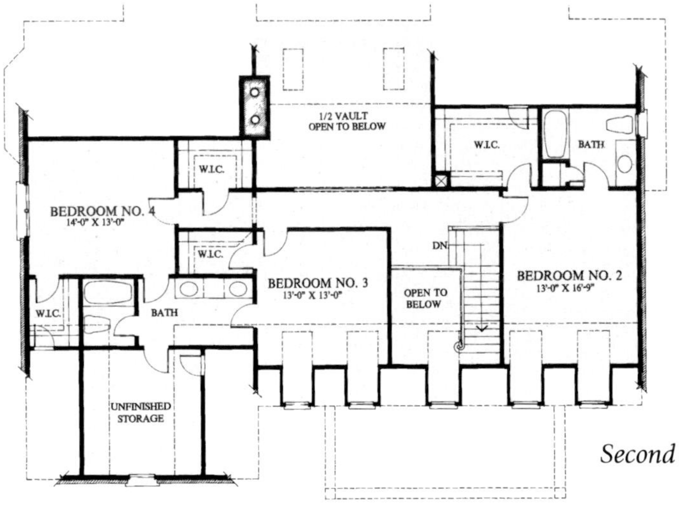
1/2 VAULT
OPEN TO BELOW
W.I.C.
BATH
W.I.C.
BEDROOM NO. 4
14'-0" X 13'-0"
W.I.C.
DN
BEDROOM NO. 3
13'-0" X 13'-0"
OPEN TO
BELOW
BEDROOM NO. 2
13'-0" X 16'-9"
W.I.C.
BATH
UNFINISHED
STORAGE

Second Floor

PIEDMONT FAMILY HOME

Design T005

Width 62'-6"
Depth 54'-3"

First Floor: 2,199 square feet
Second Floor: 1,235 square feet
Total: 3,434 square feet

Bedrooms: 4
Bathrooms: 4

The covered front porch of this Southern Colonial design warmly welcomes family and guests. To the right of the foyer is a versatile option room. On the other side is the formal dining room, located just across from the open great room—which also opens into the breakfast room. The kitchen includes a cooking island/breakfast bar. Adjacent to the breakfast room is a lovely sun room with a curved wall of glass which allows wide views to the back property. On the second floor, three additional bedrooms, two full baths, a balcony hall and unfinished storage space complete the plan.

Design T029

First Floor: 2,380 square feet
Second Floor: 1,295 square feet
Total: 3,675 square feet

Bedrooms: 4
Bathrooms: 3½

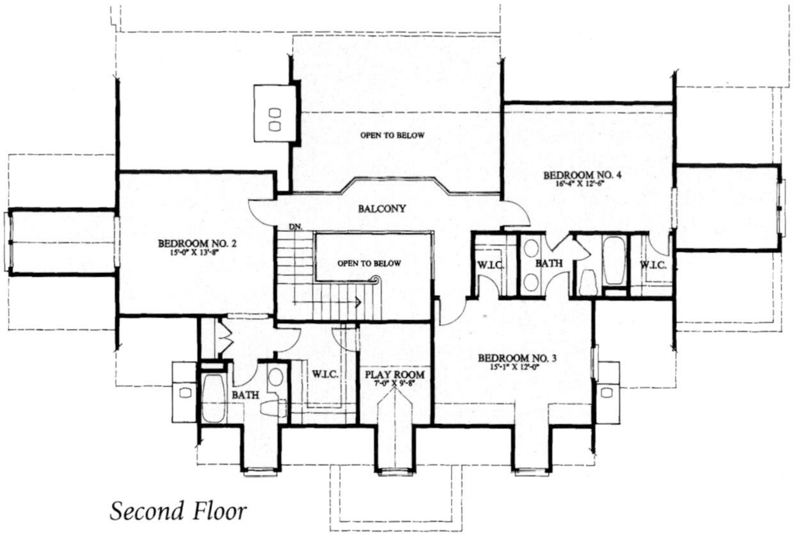

Second Floor

MAPLE GLENN

A beautiful blend of stately brick and finely crafted front and rear porches make this home a standout. An impressive foyer opens through arches and decorative columns to the two formal rooms, each with a fireplace. The central stair hall announces the great room, which leads out to the rear porch through lovely French doors. A gourmet kitchen features a walk-in pantry and overlooks a breakfast room with its own porch, perfect for morning meals. The master suite features a roomy dressing area flanked by walk-in closets, and a through-fireplace it shares with the great room.

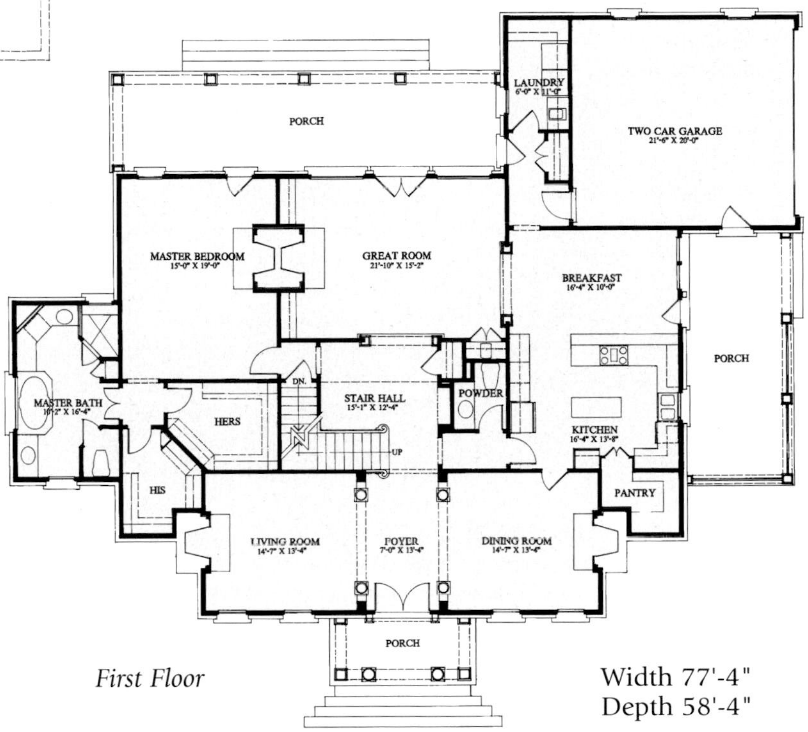

First Floor

Width 77'-4"
Depth 58'-4"

AMESBURY GROVE

Design T179

First Floor: 2,496 square feet
Second Floor: 1,373 square feet
Total: 3,869 square feet

Bedrooms: 4
Bathrooms: 3½

This genteel, 1½-story home, with striking Flemish bond brick pattern and casual wood-sided wings, typifies early Georgian homes along the James River or Chesapeake Bay. A pedimented entry highlights this exterior and conceals an interior that blends past and present. Classical symmetry prevails inside in same-sized living and dining rooms that open off either side of the entrance foyer. The less formal living spaces beyond flow easily into each other from a central stair hall. A gourmet kitchen with a centered food preparation island offers a walk-in pantry and serves a nearby formal dining room. A bumped-out bay highlights the master suite, and a bath offers a garden tub and leads to an ample walk-in closet with its own window.

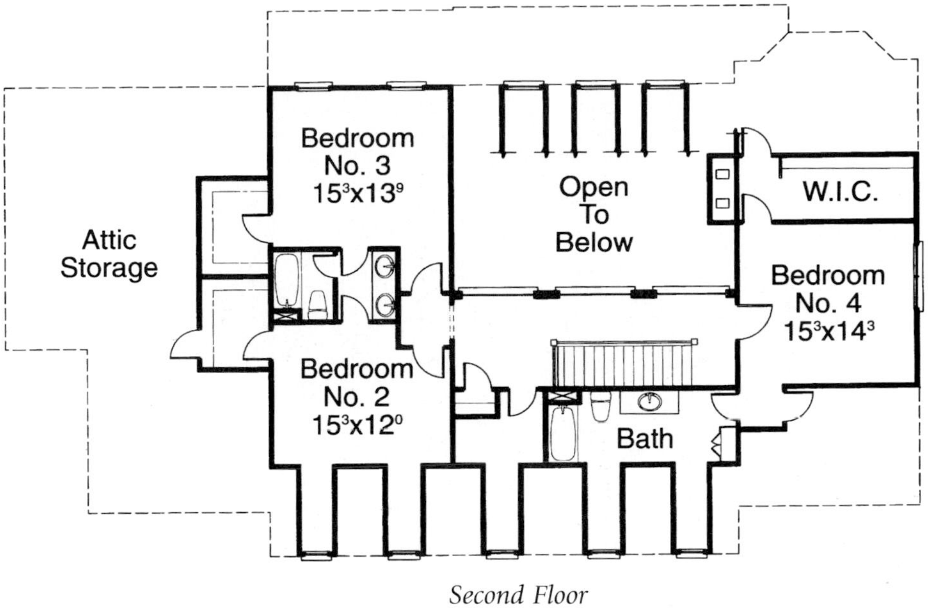

Second Floor

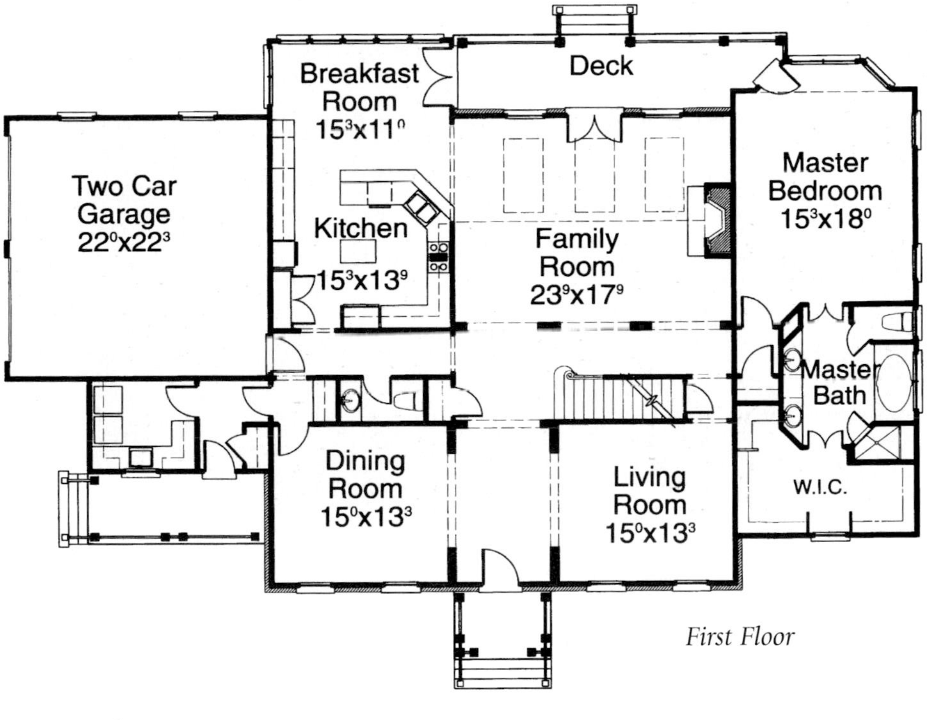

First Floor

Width 78'-0"
Depth 53'-3"

Rear Elevation

Three dormers and a gable on the rear elevation distinguish a second story that includes three bedrooms, two baths and a cozy stair-gallery area. A detailed deck complements a lovely bay window which gives natural light to the master suite.

RUTLEDGE

Design T173

First Floor: 2,191 square feet
Second Floor: 1,228 square feet
Total: 3,419 square feet

Bedrooms: 4
Bathrooms: 3½

Simplicity and symmetry create classic appeal with this Colonial adaptation, enhanced by Doric columns and white balustrades. A harmonious reprise of fanlights decorates the main floor. The lunette window in the center gable is a detail often found in Classic Revival homes. Central to the floor plan, the foyer opens on either side to the living room and dining room, both of which have large, formal entrances set off by beautifully detailed windows. By design, the fireplace in the living room can be seen and enjoyed from the center of the dining room. The kitchen, breakfast room, butler's pantry, small office and laundry are also on this floor. Beyond the dining room, a stair hall leads to the second floor, which has a gallery hall overlooking the great room below.

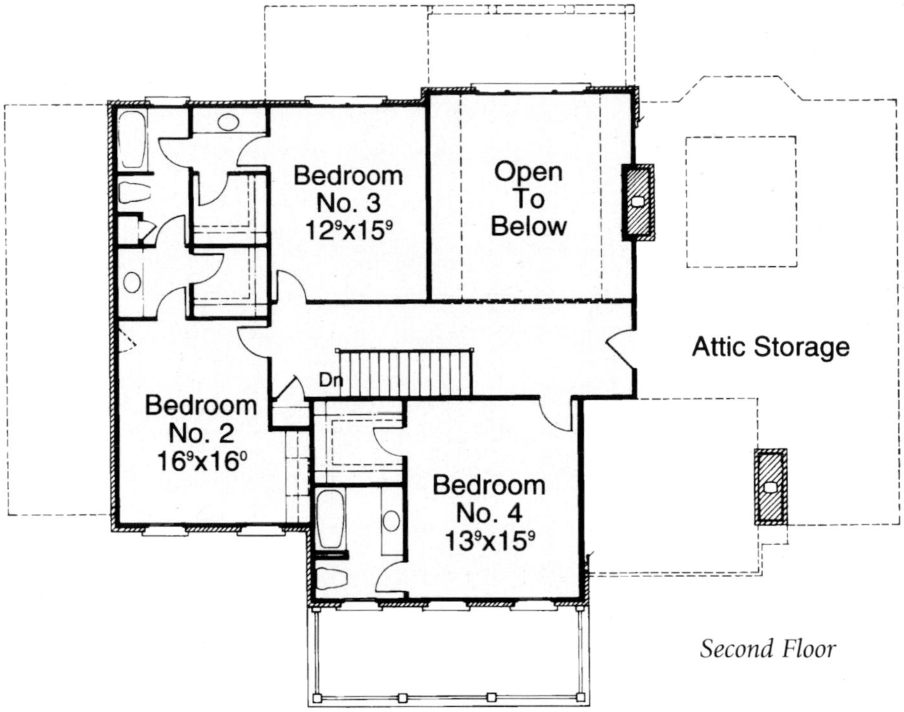

Second Floor

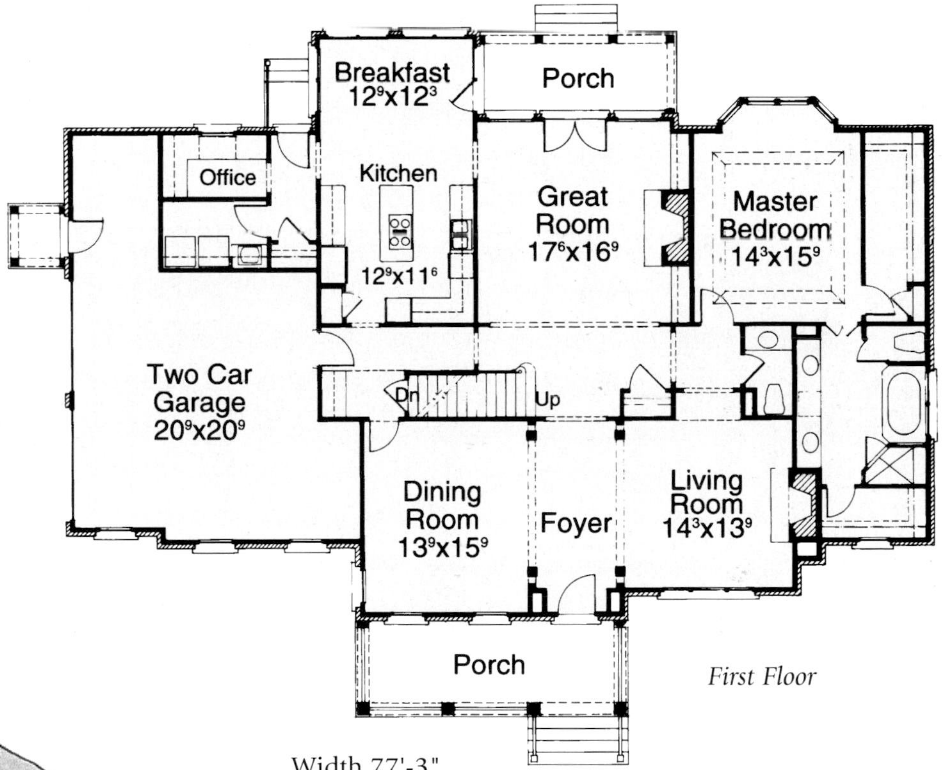

First Floor

Width 77'-3"
Depth 56'-3"

Rear Elevation

Classic elegance, as first defined by Thomas Jefferson, is the keynote of this distinguished home. Yet for all its exterior grandeur, the interior is designed for easy, contemporary family living and entertaining on a memorable scale.

A stunning blend of brick and siding on this stately Revival home embodies the gentrified beauty of its Georgian ancestors. Yet its flowing interior spaces bring a warm, gracious and very today dimension to this most dignified of architectural classics.

Rear Elevation

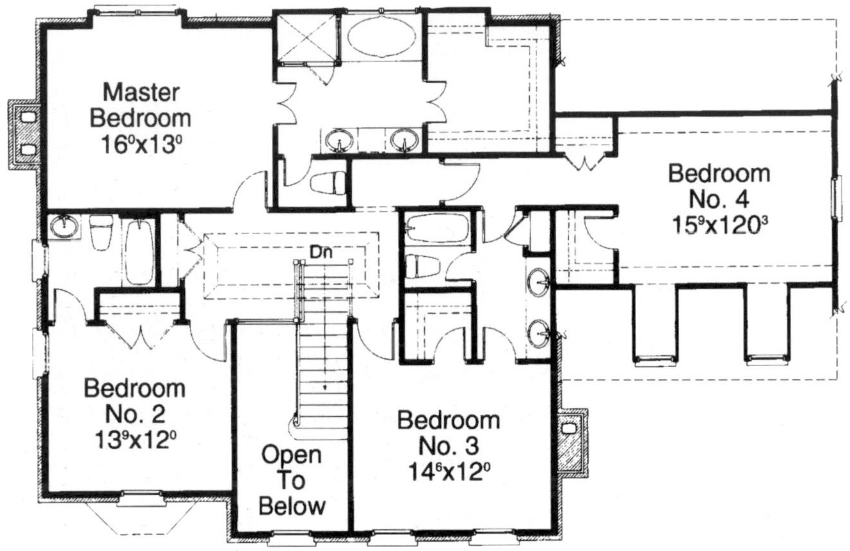

Second Floor

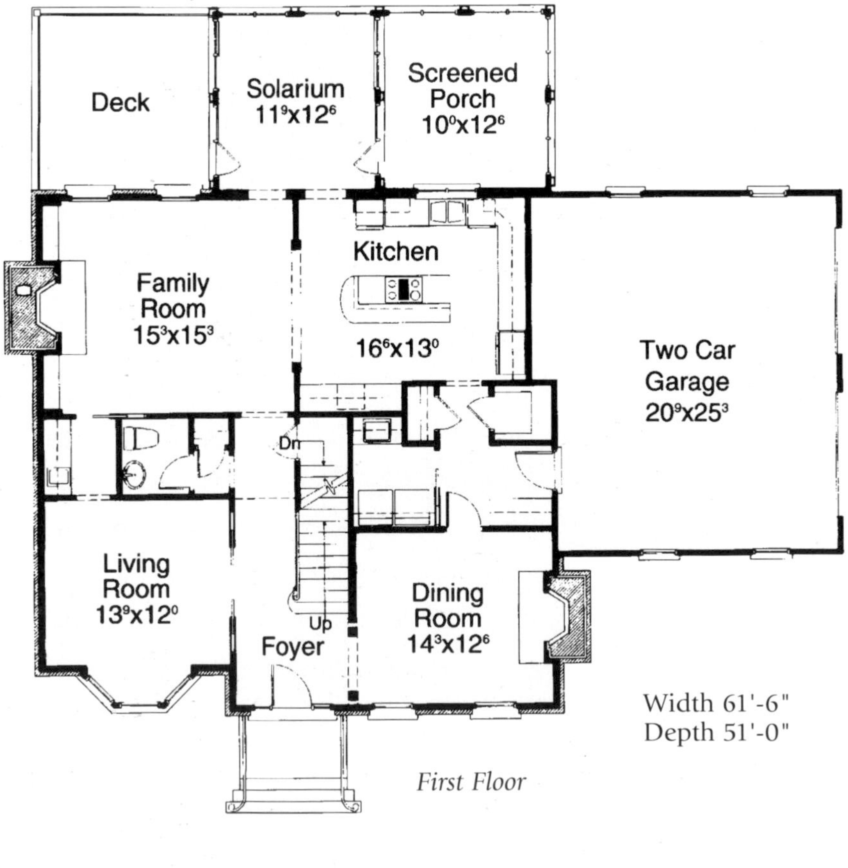

Width 61'-6"
Depth 51'-0"

First Floor

ALBERMARLE

Design T167

First Floor: 1,698 square feet
Second Floor: 1,542 square feet
Total: 3,240 square feet

Bedrooms: 4
Bathrooms: 3½

Classic in proportion and Georgian in attitude, this aristocratic home boasts a rich architectural heritage that traces back to an earlier America. With an enduring, classic style, this design takes tradition a step toward the 21st Century, reordering the usual symmetry of a Georgian plan in favor of the flowing configuration that works so well for modern-day living. The two-story foyer opens to a wing that extends to the left, containing the living room with a bay window and the family room centered around a fireplace. An eat-in kitchen has a cooktop island counter and serves the formal dining room through a convenient butler's pantry. Upstairs is the master suite with a box-bay window and a whirlpool bath, plus three additional bedrooms.

WOODBURY GROVE

Design T196

First Floor: 1,959 square feet
Second Floor: 1,408 square feet
Total: 3,367 square feet

Bedrooms: 4
Bathrooms: 3½

Inspired by Federal-style residences in the Northeast, this design features a monumental front gable and a columned, balustrade-topped covered entrance. Inside, 10-foot ceilings add elegance to an open, flowing floor plan. The foyer opens to formal rooms that offer quiet elegance for planned events and traditional festivities. Casual living space to the rear of the plan features a fireplace and opens to a hospitable rear porch. A U-shaped gourmet kitchen shares natural light from wide windows in the breakfast room. The second-floor bedrooms include a spacious master suite with its own fireplace and a sumptuous bath with a walk-in closet and dressing area. A gallery hall leads to two family bedrooms, each with a walk-in closet, which share a full bath.

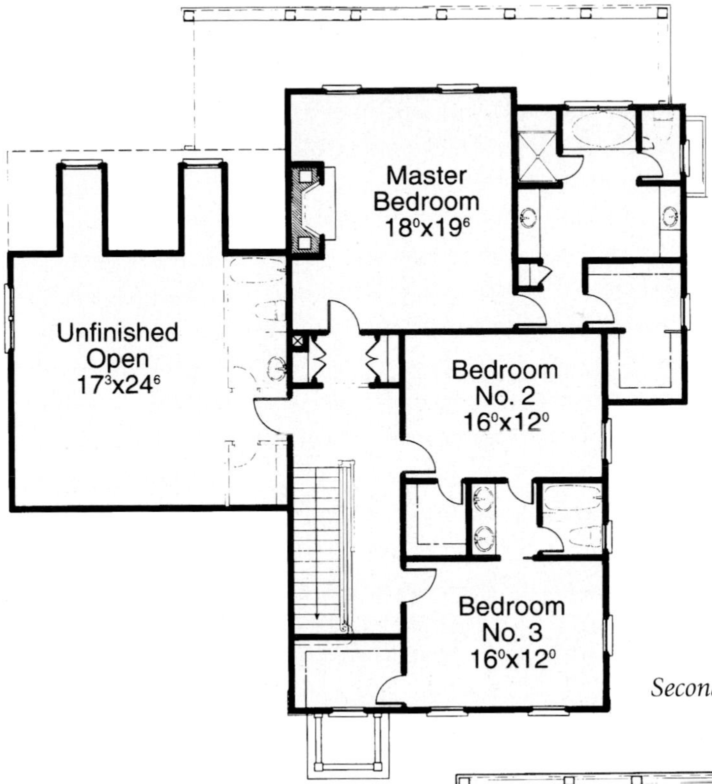

Second Floor

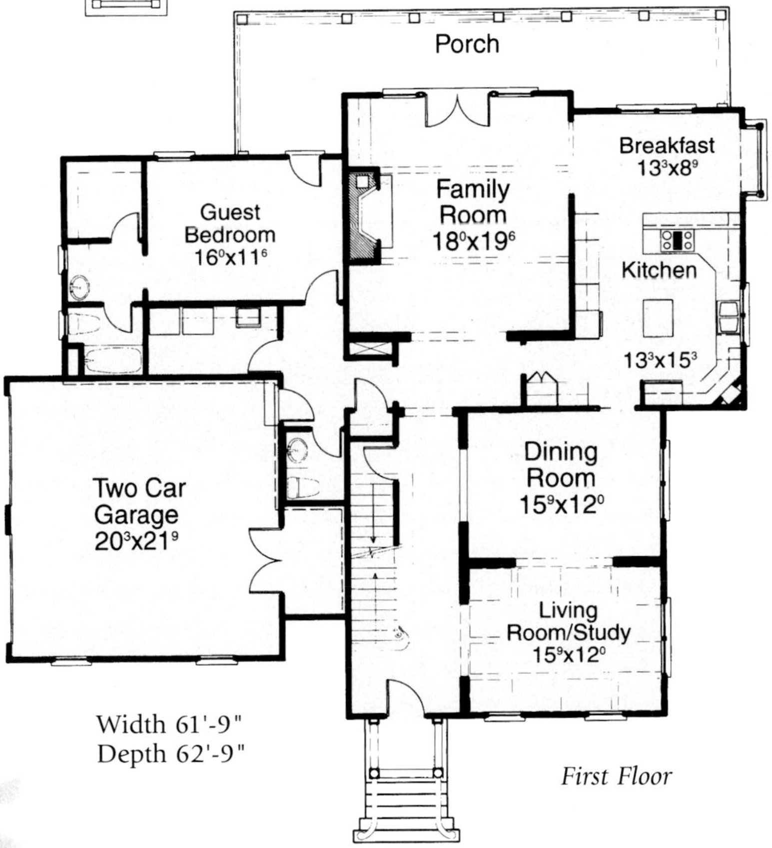

Width 61'-9"
Depth 62'-9"

First Floor

Rear Elevation

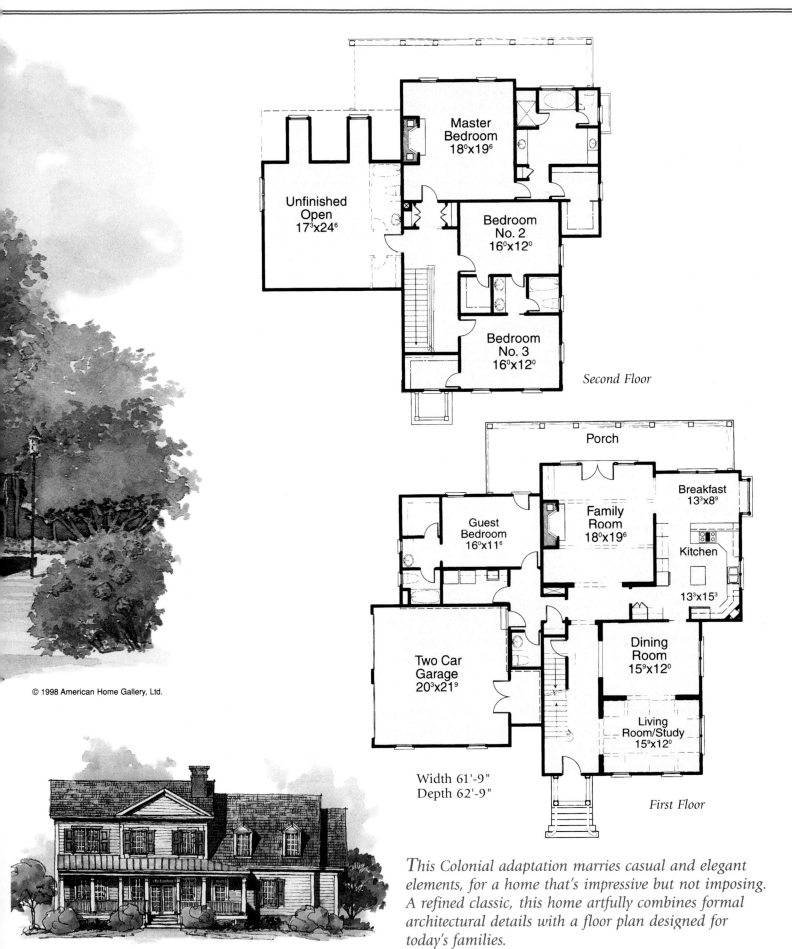

This Colonial adaptation marries casual and elegant elements, for a home that's impressive but not imposing. A refined classic, this home artfully combines formal architectural details with a floor plan designed for today's families.

The harmonious melding of distinctly American influences makes this a comfortable and eminently livable home. An overall simplicity reflects the straightforward building styles that prevailed in colonial New England, with a hint of gracious Georgian hospitality.

Rear Elevation

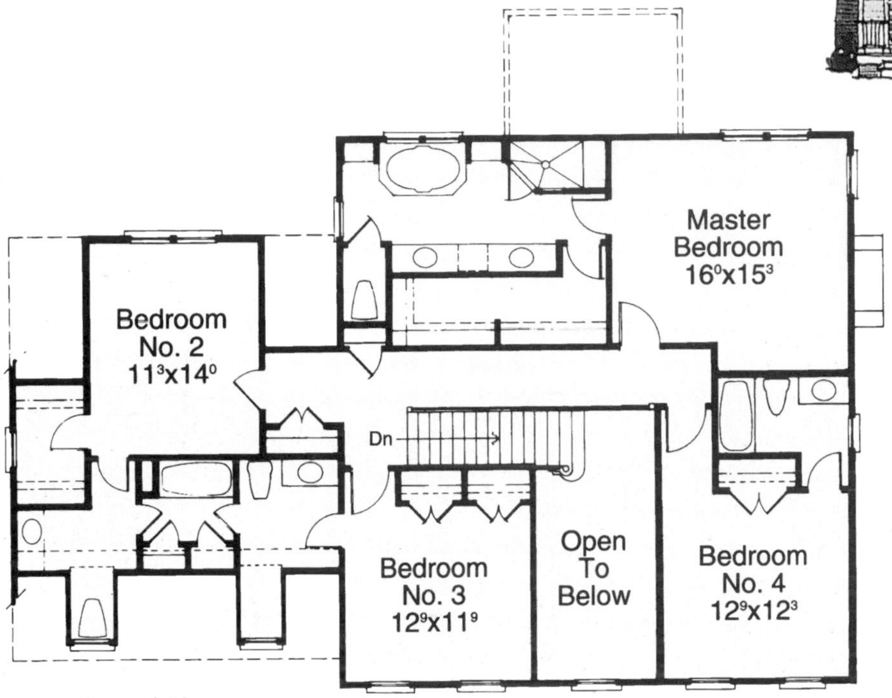

Second Floor

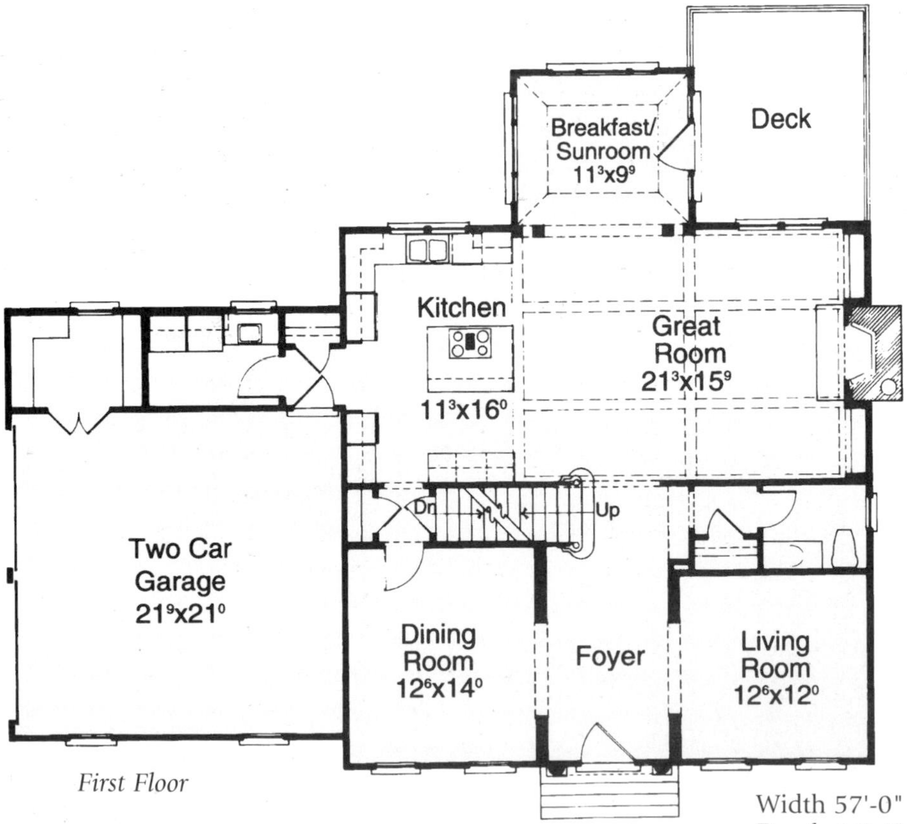

First Floor

Width 57'-0"
Depth 46'-4"

HAWTHORNE

Design T168

First Floor: 1,448 square feet
Second Floor: 1,491 square feet
Total: 2,939 square feet

Bedrooms: 4
Bathrooms: 3½

Two mainstreams of architectural taste in earlier America blend beautifully in this gracious home. The semi-circular fanlight in the low-pitched gable echoes the one over the door, furthering the symmetry that dignifies the exterior of this impressive Traditional home. The wood-sided exterior, centered gable and rounded pilasters point to a Northern heritage, yet there's an aura of Southern hospitality in the open, flowing spaces so conducive to family life and entertaining. Formal living areas are entered from the foyer—to the right is the living room and to the left, the dining room. A butler's pantry links the dining room to the island kitchen.

Design T013

First Floor: 1,580 square feet
Second Floor: 595 square feet
Total: 2,175 square feet

Bedrooms: 3
Bathrooms: 2½

WEATHERBY COTTAGE

Multi-paned windows and ink-black shutters stand out against the rich brick and horizontal clapboard backdrop. Inside, the spacious foyer leads directly to a large vaulted great room with its handsome fireplace. The dining room to the right of the foyer features a dramatic vaulted ceiling. In the privacy and quiet of the rear of the home is the master suite with its luxury bath, double vanities and oversized walk-in closet. The second floor provides two additional bedrooms with a shared bath and balcony that overlook the foyer below.

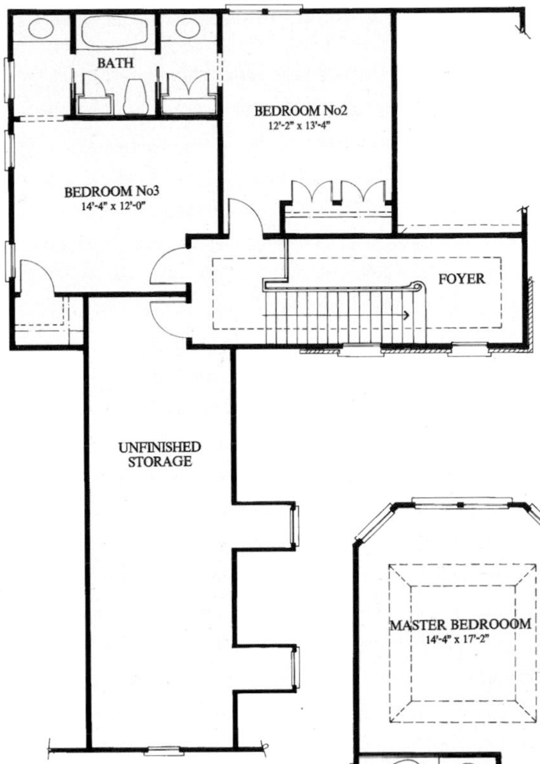
BATH
BEDROOM No2
12'-2" x 13'-4"
BEDROOM No3
14'-4" x 12'-0"
FOYER
UNFINISHED STORAGE

Second Floor

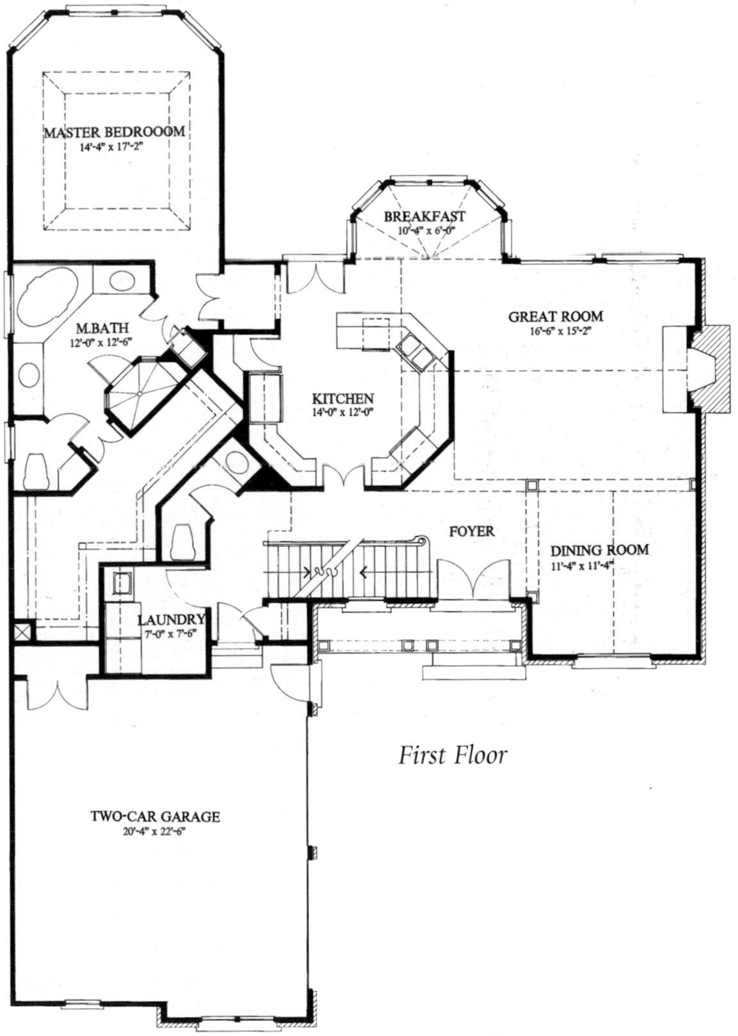
MASTER BEDROOOM
14'-4" x 17'-2"
BREAKFAST
10'-4" x 6'-0"
GREAT ROOM
16'-6" x 15'-2"
M.BATH
12'-0" x 12'-6"
KITCHEN
14'-0" x 12'-0"
FOYER
DINING ROOM
11'-4" x 11'-4"
LAUNDRY
7'-0" x 7'-6"
TWO-CAR GARAGE
20'-4" x 22'-6"

First Floor

Width 48'-6"
Depth 70'-11"

A true American style gently flavored with European elements, this home blends many details to make a big impact on a small lot. The porch comes from cottage styling; the gables and dormers are Colonial, and the garage has a carriage-style roof.

Borrowing from the European vernacular, stucco and brick walls add to the informality of this home along with a random or casual composition. Details that are European are the covered entry, raised arches over windows and paneled shutters.

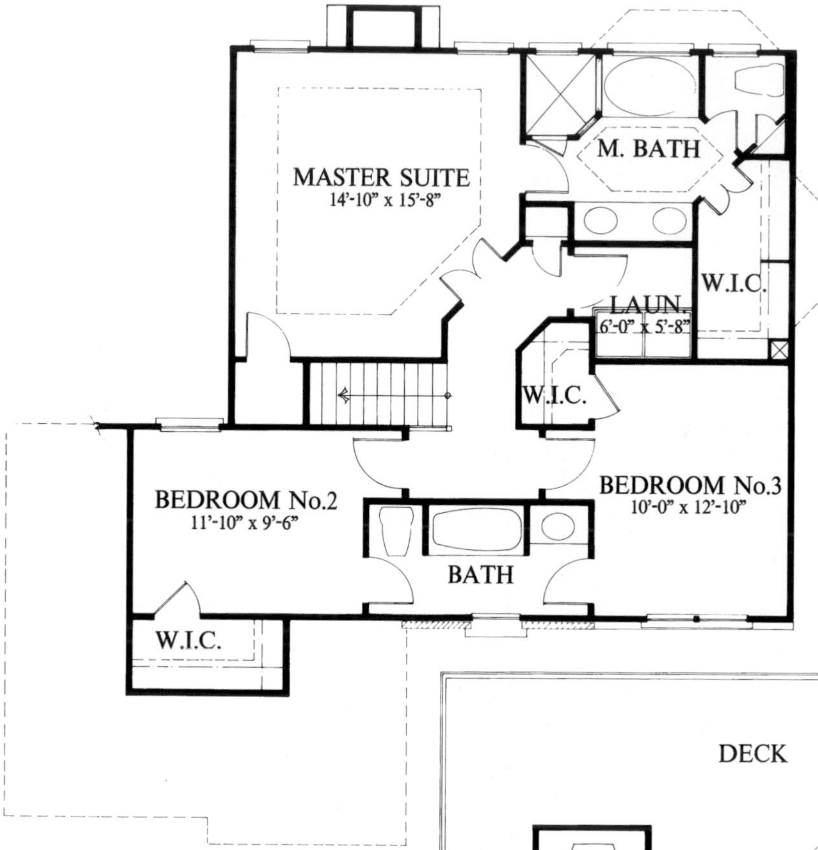
MASTER SUITE
14'-10" x 15'-8"
M. BATH
W.I.C.
LAUN.
6'-0" x 5'-8"
W.I.C.
BEDROOM No.2
11'-10" x 9'-6"
BEDROOM No.3
10'-0" x 12'-10"
BATH
W.I.C.

Second Floor

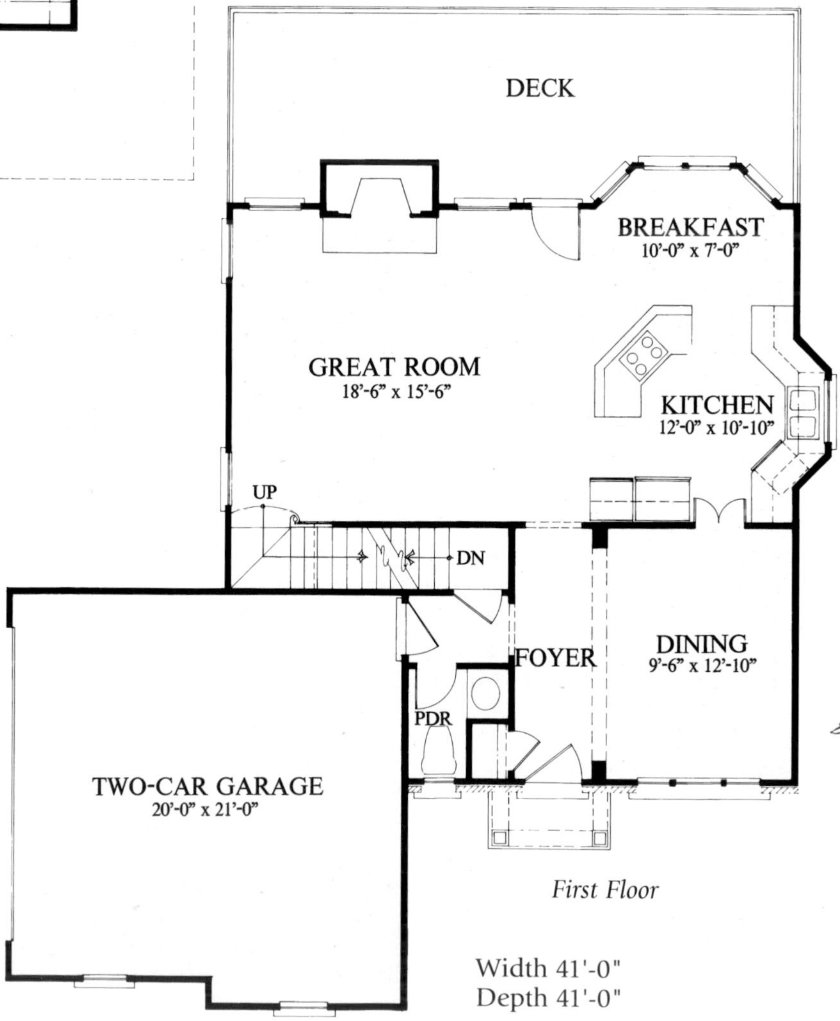
DECK
BREAKFAST
10'-0" x 7'-0"
GREAT ROOM
18'-6" x 15'-6"
KITCHEN
12'-0" x 10'-10"
UP
DN
FOYER
DINING
9'-6" x 12'-10"
PDR
TWO-CAR GARAGE
20'-0" x 21'-0"

First Floor

Width 41'-0"
Depth 41'-0"

WINDERMERE COTTAGE

Design T048

First Floor: 780 square feet
Second Floor: 915 square feet
Total: 1,695 square feet

Bedrooms: 3 630 FOR A STUDY PACKAGE
Bathrooms: 2½ 675 FOR A 4 SET PACKAGE

The clean, traditional lines of this elegant facade describe an architecture that's both formal and casual. Old World window treatments and a copper-seam roof complement a modern mix of brick and stucco. Inside, a convenient powder room is thoughtfully placed to the left of the foyer. French doors open the formal dining room to a well-planned kitchen with an island counter and a bright breakfast room. Wide views abound in the great room, which has a fireplace and a French door to the rear deck. Upstairs, double doors lead to the master suite, which has a tray ceiling and a lovely bath with a walk-in closet designed for two. The second-floor laundry is positioned nearby.

Design T043

Square Footage: 2,090
Bedrooms: 3
Bathrooms: 3

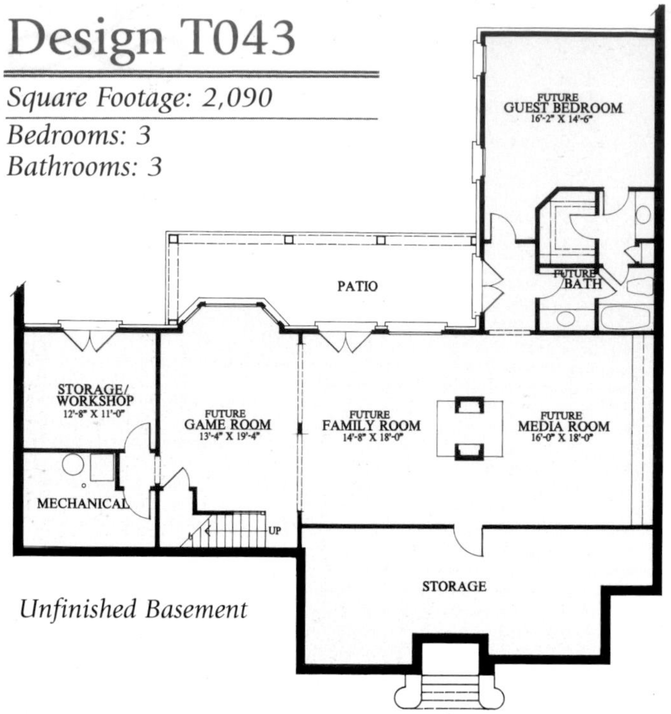

FUTURE GUEST BEDROOM 16'-2" X 14'-6"
FUTURE BATH
PATIO
STORAGE/ WORKSHOP 12'-8" X 11'-0"
FUTURE GAME ROOM 13'-4" X 19'-4"
FUTURE FAMILY ROOM 14'-8" X 18'-0"
FUTURE MEDIA ROOM 16'-0" X 18'-0"
MECHANICAL
UP
STORAGE

Unfinished Basement

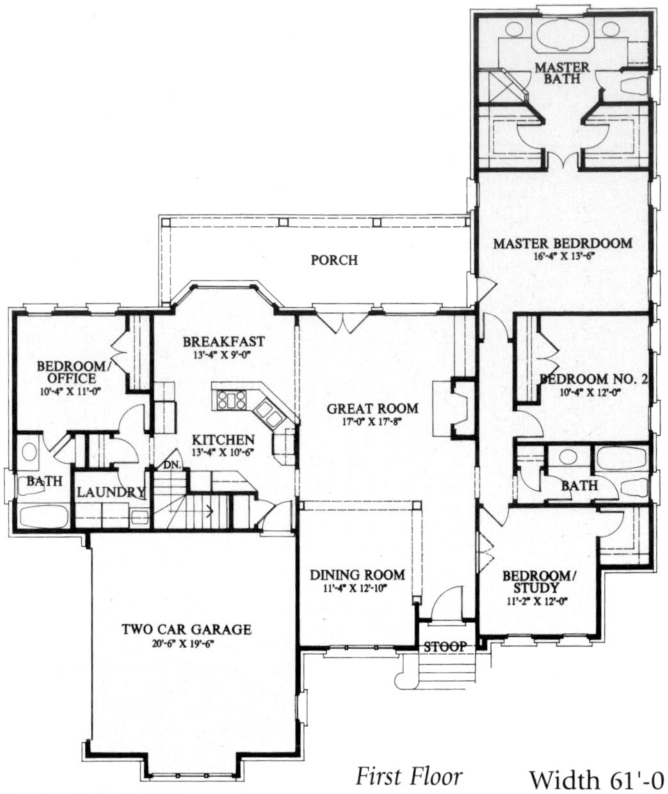

MASTER BATH
PORCH
MASTER BEDRDOOM 16'-4" X 13'-6"
BREAKFAST 13'-4" X 9'-0"
BEDROOM/ OFFICE 10'-4" X 11'-0"
GREAT ROOM 17'-0" X 17'-8"
BEDROOM NO. 2 10'-4" X 12'-0"
KITCHEN 13'-4" X 10'-6"
DN.
BATH
LAUNDRY
BATH
DINING ROOM 11'-4" X 12'-10"
BEDROOM/ STUDY 11'-2" X 12'-0"
TWO CAR GARAGE 20'-6" X 19'-6"
STOOP

First Floor

Width 61'-0"
Depth 72'-6"

JEFFERSON COUNTRY HOME

This graceful English Country facade has a stately presence and a sweet disposition, with an unrestrained, modern personality within. An open plan marries the formal dining room with a spacious great room, dressed with French doors and a focal-point fireplace. In the kitchen, an angled cooktop counter overlooks the breakfast room, which offers wide views through a bay window. Secluded to this side of the plan, a home office or guest suite has a full bath and three lovely windows.

HUNTINGTON WAY

Design T078

Square Footage: 1,770

Bedrooms: 3

Bathrooms: 2½

Asymmetrical gables and keystone arches lend a gentle European flavor to this comfortable traditional home. The foyer opens to interior vistas and outdoor views through the great room, which has a centered fireplace and a vaulted ceiling. Wrapping counters and a corner pantry highlight the well-planned kitchen, while the breakfast room's box-bay window infuses the area with natural light. Double doors open to the master suite from a private hall, which leads to two additional bedrooms and a convenient laundry. The homeowner's bath features separate vanities, a walk-in closet and a garden tub.

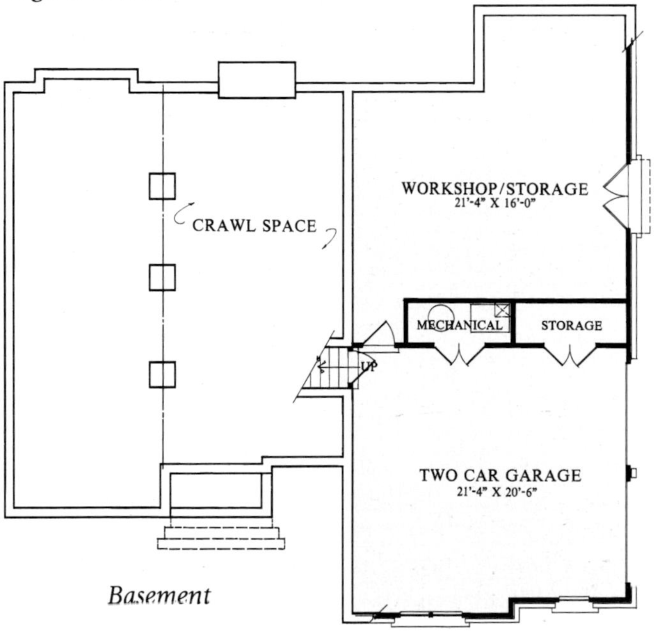

Basement

Width 48'-0"
Depth 47'-0"

First Floor

PETITE ROCHET COTTAGE

Design T046

First Floor: 1,225 square feet
Second Floor: 565 square feet
Total: 1,790 square feet

Bedrooms: 3
Bathrooms: 2½

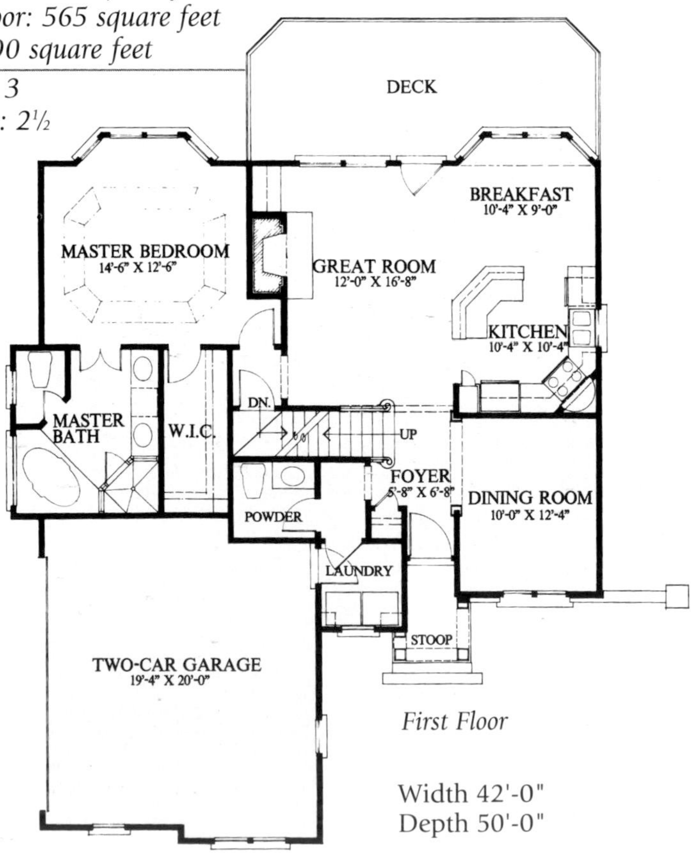

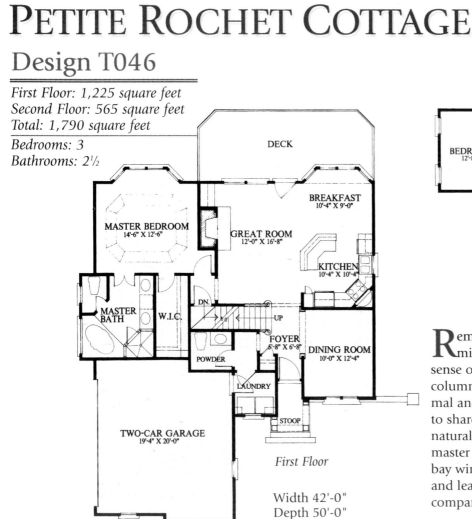

First Floor

Width 42'-0"
Depth 50'-0"

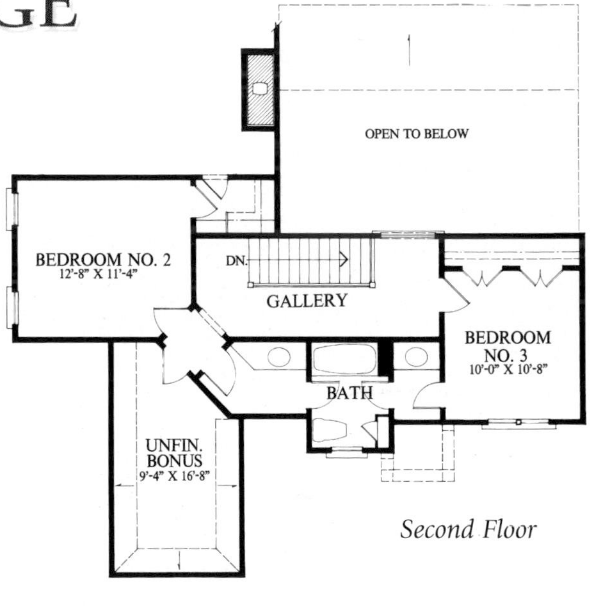

Second Floor

Reminiscent of an English country home, an inviting mix of bold shapes and classic details calls up a sense of the past but steps toward the future. The columned entry leads to a raised foyer that opens to formal and casual areas. Open planning allows the kitchen to share the warmth of the great room's hearth as well as natural light from the breakfast room. The first-floor master suite boasts a tray ceiling, its own fireplace and bay window. The gallery hall overlooks the great room and leads to two additional bedrooms, which share a compartmented bath.

Design T220

First Floor: 1,450 square feet
Second Floor: 1,125 square feet
Total: 2,575 square feet

Bedrooms: 3
Bathrooms: 2½

BRITTANY HEIGHTS

A double-door entry leads to a spacious foyer within this lovely traditional home, which boasts many Old World details. The formal dining room is open on two sides, defined by decorative columns. Nearby, French doors lead out to a patio, where dinner guests may want to linger. Gatherings grand and cozy will be welcomed in the great room, with a centered fireplace framed by French doors. The gourmet kitchen has a food prep island and enjoys great views of the back property. On the second floor, the master suite has a sensational bath with an angled vanity.

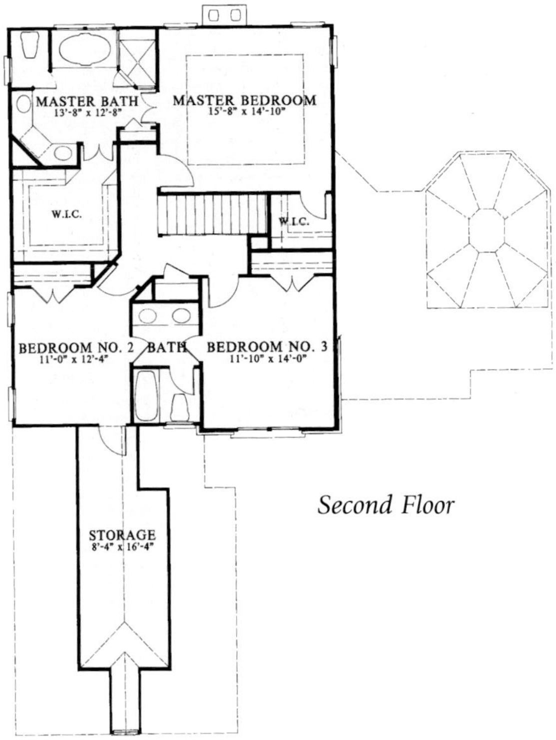

Second Floor

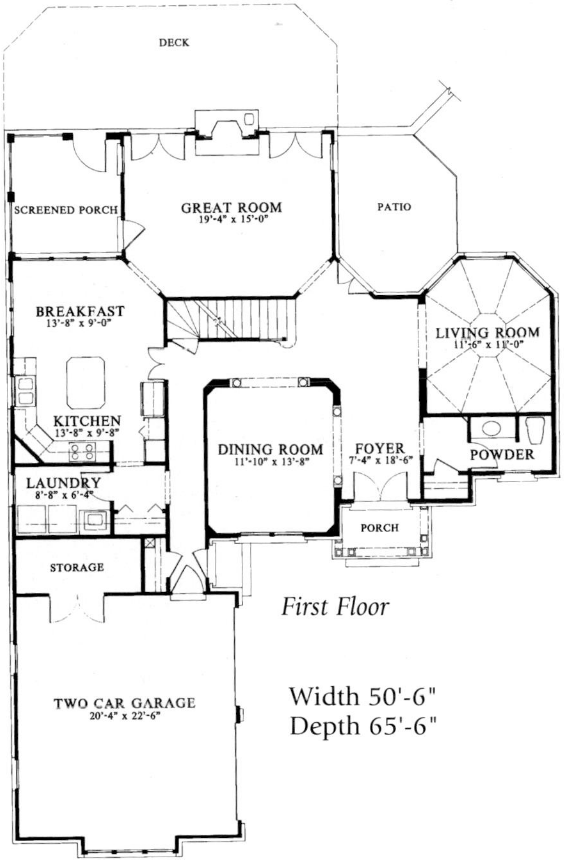

First Floor

Width 50'-6"
Depth 65'-6"

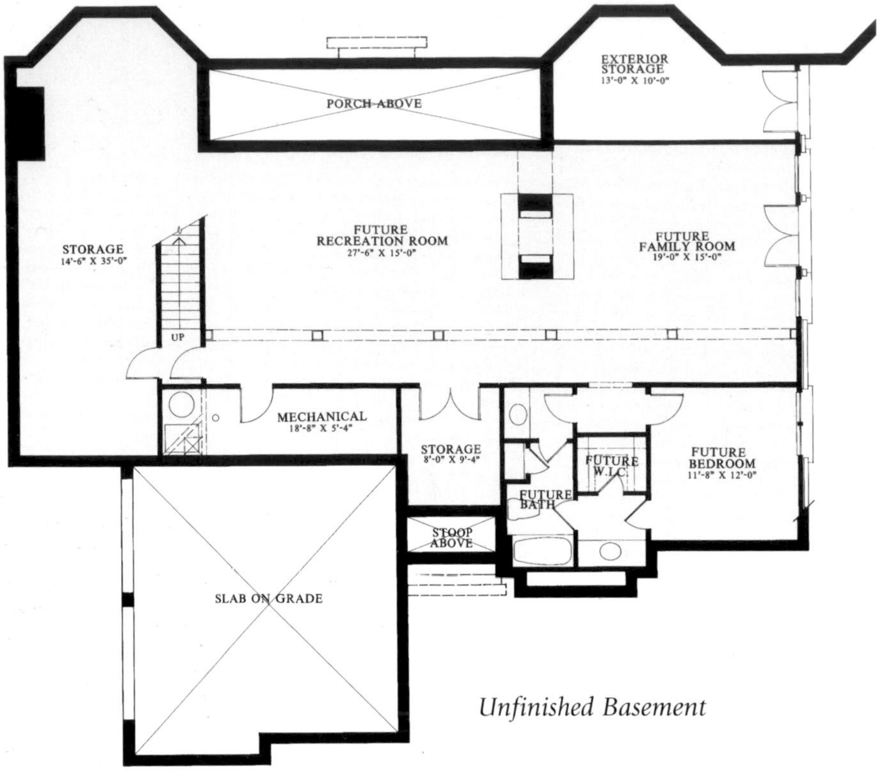
EXTERIOR STORAGE
13'-0" X 10'-0"
PORCH ABOVE
STORAGE
14'-6" X 35'-0"
FUTURE RECREATION ROOM
27'-6" X 15'-0"
FUTURE FAMILY ROOM
19'-0" X 15'-0"
UP
MECHANICAL
18'-8" X 5'-4"
STORAGE
8'-0" X 9'-4"
FUTURE W.I.C.
FUTURE BEDROOM
11'-8" X 12'-0"
FUTURE BATH
STOOP ABOVE
SLAB ON GRADE

Unfinished Basement

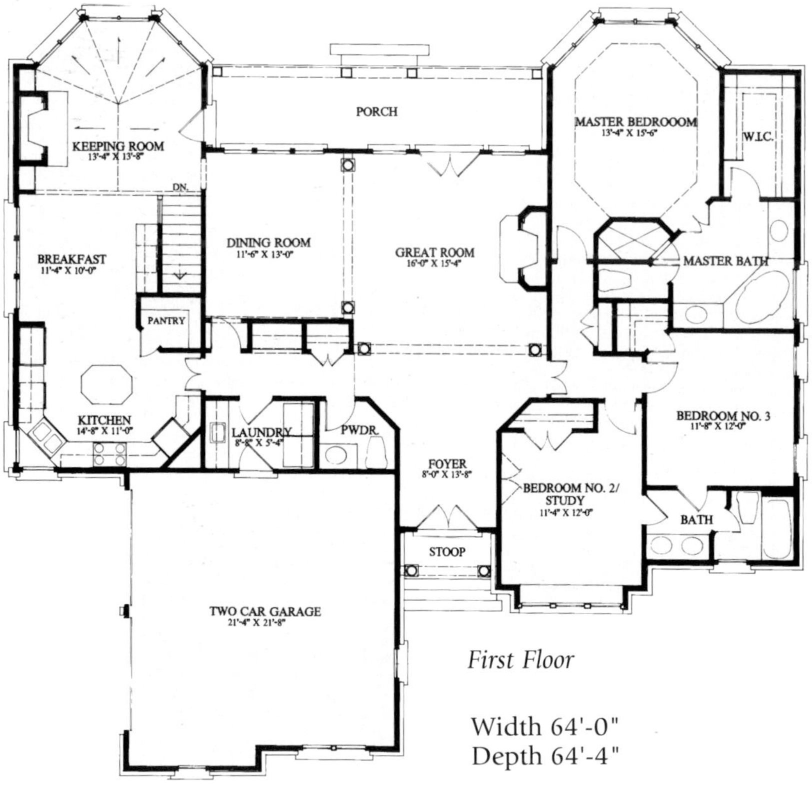
KEEPING ROOM
13'-4" X 13'-8"
PORCH
MASTER BEDROOOM
13'-4" X 15'-6"
W.I.C.
DN.
DINING ROOM
11'-6" X 13'-0"
GREAT ROOM
16'-0" X 15'-4"
BREAKFAST
11'-4" X 10'-0"
MASTER BATH
PANTRY
KITCHEN
14'-8" X 11'-0"
LAUNDRY
8'-8" X 5'-4"
PWDR.
FOYER
8'-0" X 13'-8"
BEDROOM NO. 2/
STUDY
11'-4" X 12'-0"
BEDROOM NO. 3
11'-8" X 12'-0"
BATH
STOOP
TWO CAR GARAGE
21'-4" X 21'-8"

First Floor

Width 64'-0"
Depth 64'-4"

An artful combination of a copper-seam roof and varied yet complementary window treatments create an intriguing and inviting exterior. The unique combination of materials is reminiscent of a French country home, enhanced by a columned entry.

LAUREL HAVEN

Derived from both French and English architectural vocabularies, this distinctive plan would suit a myriad of landscapes, from native woodlands to Arcadian suburbs. Its modish interior steps toward the future with an open floor plan and amenities that add both style and comfort. A massive hearth in the great room extends its warmth to the formal dining room, which is set off by decorative columns. The nearby keeping room has its own fireplace and enjoys wide views through a glorious bay window. A tray ceiling and bumped-out bay highlight the master bedroom, while the deluxe master bath is suited with an angled whirlpool tub.

Design T030

Square Footage: 2,150

Bedrooms: 3

Bathrooms: 2½

The asymmetrical plan that takes the formal edge off this centuries-old English style also opens up an easy flow of contemporary living space. Gracious amenities such as decorative columns and bay windows brighten the thoroughly modern interior.

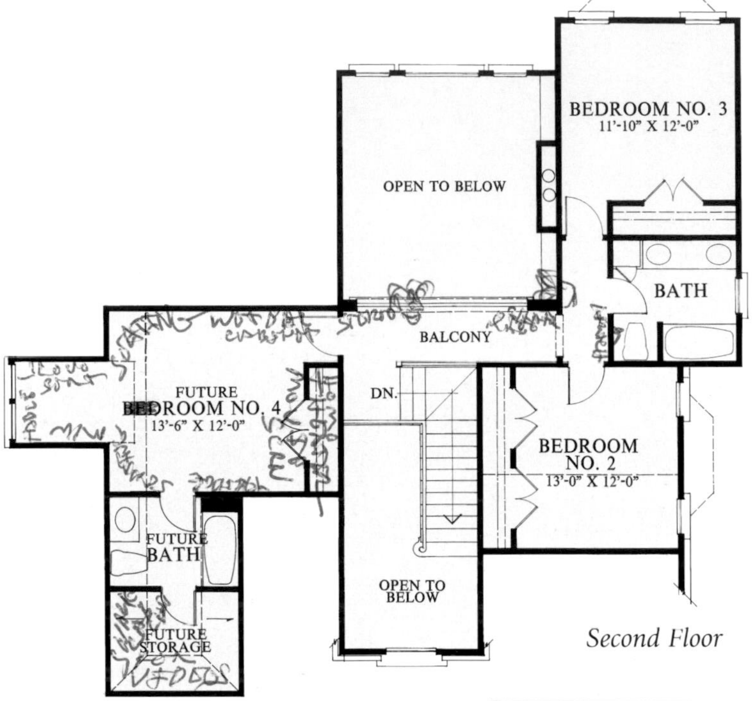

BEDROOM NO. 3
11'-10" X 12'-0"
OPEN TO BELOW
BATH
BALCONY
FUTURE
BEDROOM NO. 4
13'-6" X 12'-0"
DN.
BEDROOM
NO. 2
13'-0" X 12'-0"
FUTURE
BATH
FUTURE
STORAGE
OPEN TO
BELOW

Width 50'-0"
Depth 53'-6"

Second Floor

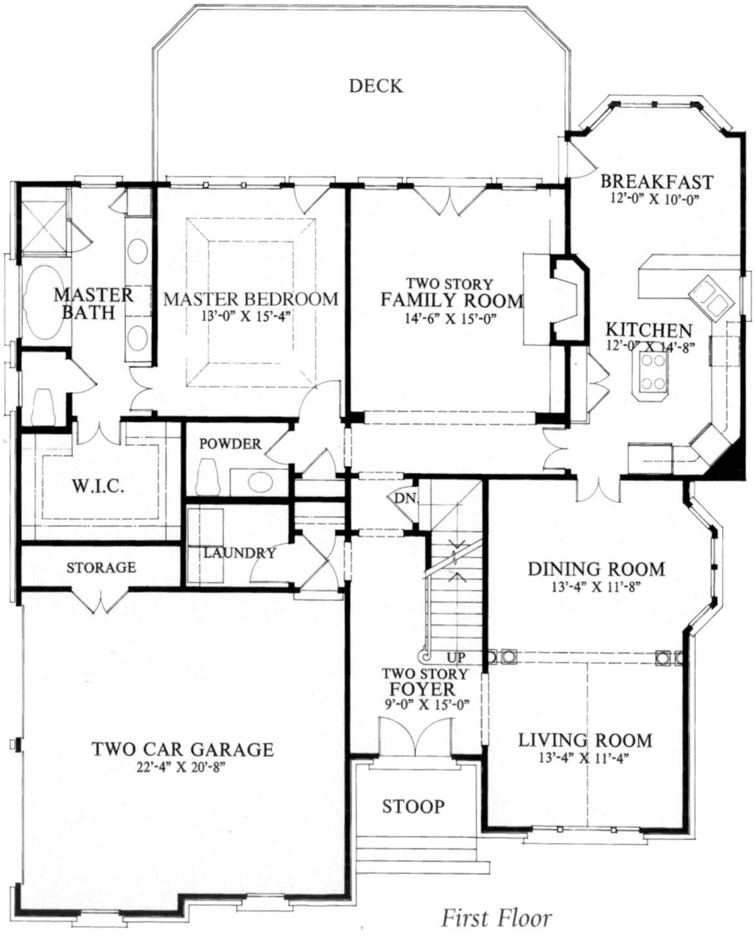

DECK
BREAKFAST
12'-0" X 10'-0"
MASTER
BATH
MASTER BEDROOM
13'-0" X 15'-4"
TWO STORY
FAMILY ROOM
14'-6" X 15'-0"
KITCHEN
12'-0" X 14'-8"
POWDER
W.I.C.
DN.
LAUNDRY
STORAGE
DINING ROOM
13'-4" X 11'-8"
UP
TWO STORY
FOYER
9'-0" X 15'-0"
LIVING ROOM
13'-4" X 11'-4"
TWO CAR GARAGE
22'-4" X 20'-8"
STOOP

First Floor

Quincy Hall

The foyer opens to the living and dining rooms, providing a spectacular entrance to this English country cottage. Just beyond the dining room, a gourmet kitchen with a work island opens onto the breakfast room. Accented by a fireplace and built-in bookcases, the family room with a ribbon of windows is an excellent setting for family gatherings. Remotely located off the central hallway, the master suite includes a rectangular ceiling detail and access to the rear deck. The homeowner's bath features separate vanities, a garden tub and a spacious walk-in closet. The central staircase leads to a hall that connects two additional bedrooms with bonus space that promises a fourth bedroom or guest suite.

Design T075

First Floor: 1,720 square feet
Second Floor: 545 square feet
Total: 2,265 square feet

Bedrooms: 4 630 FOR A STUDY PACKAGE
Bathrooms: $3^1/_2$ 675 4 SET PKG.
730 FOR AN 8 SET PACKAGE

BANFIELD HALL

Design T076

First Floor: 1,660 square feet
Second Floor: 665 square feet
Total: 2,325 square feet

Bedrooms: 4
Bathrooms: 3½

Stately brick and jack-arch detailing create an exterior that may look established—but this floor plan offers 21st-Century living. A dramatic two-story entry is framed by formal living and dining areas. The family room ceiling soars above a cozy fireplace flanked by sensational views to the rear grounds. Nearby, the cheery breakfast nook allows porch access and opens to a kitchen loaded with modern amenities and positioned near the laundry room and garage. A coffered ceiling, sumptuous bath, His and Hers vanities and a walk-in closet highlight the master suite. Upstairs, two additional bedrooms, an optional fourth bedroom and two baths complete the plan.

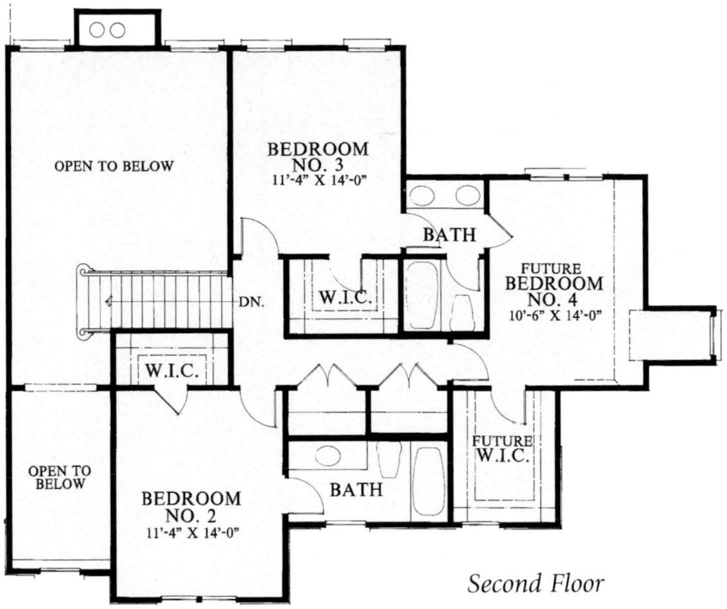
OPEN TO BELOW
BEDROOM NO. 3
11'-4" X 14'-0"
BATH
FUTURE BEDROOM NO. 4
10'-6" X 14'-0"
DN.
W.I.C.
W.I.C.
OPEN TO BELOW
BEDROOM NO. 2
11'-4" X 14'-0"
BATH
FUTURE W.I.C.

Second Floor

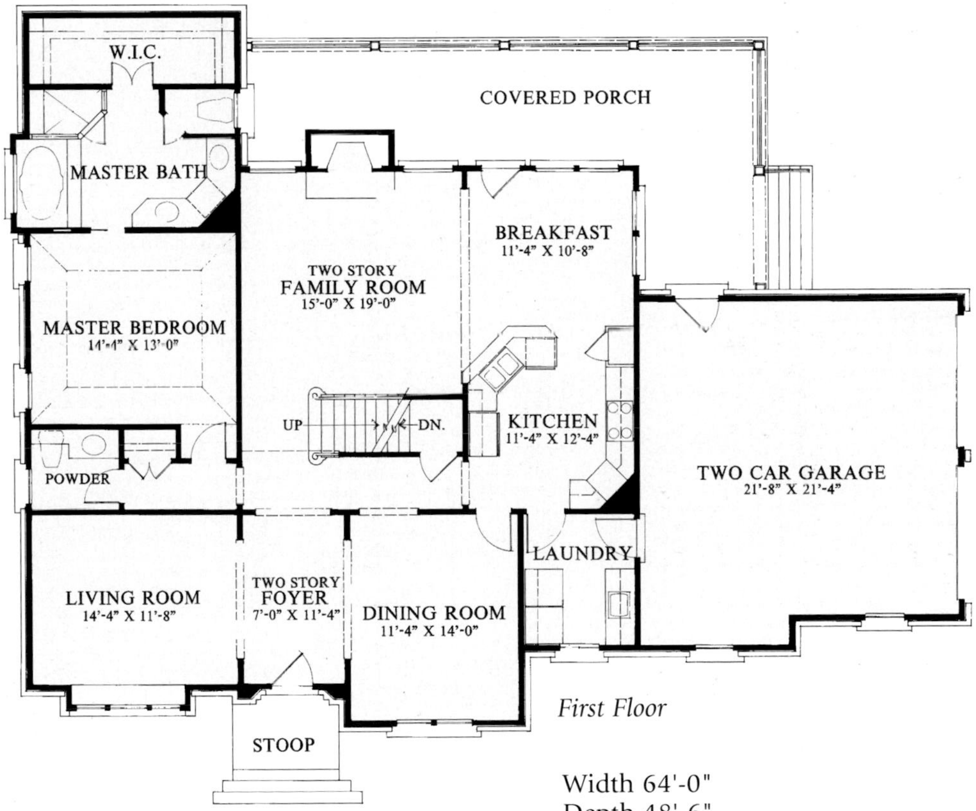
W.I.C.
COVERED PORCH
MASTER BATH
BREAKFAST
11'-4" X 10'-8"
TWO STORY FAMILY ROOM
15'-0" X 19'-0"
MASTER BEDROOM
14'-4" X 13'-0"
UP
DN.
KITCHEN
11'-4" X 12'-4"
TWO CAR GARAGE
21'-8" X 21'-4"
POWDER
LAUNDRY
LIVING ROOM
14'-4" X 11'-8"
TWO STORY FOYER
7'-0" X 11'-4"
DINING ROOM
11'-4" X 14'-0"
STOOP

First Floor

Width 64'-0"
Depth 48'-6"

Characteristic of Colonial homes, a brick facade and central gables begin this Early American presentation. Also typical of the theme, area-raised panel shutters and jack-arch window treatments accent the central gable and complete the design.

Mt. Paran Ranch

Design T009

Square Footage: 2,902
Bedrooms: 3
Bathrooms: 2½

Transoms, arches and sweeping rooflines highlight this French exterior. European styling flavors a thoroughly modern interior, starting with a grand great room, which has a tray ceiling and French doors. Dinner guests will want to kick off their shoes in the spacious keeping room with a cozy hearth. A wet bar serves both the great room and the roomy kitchen. The master suite offers a glass sitting room, a coffered ceiling and a sumptuous bath, while two family bedrooms share a connecting bath.

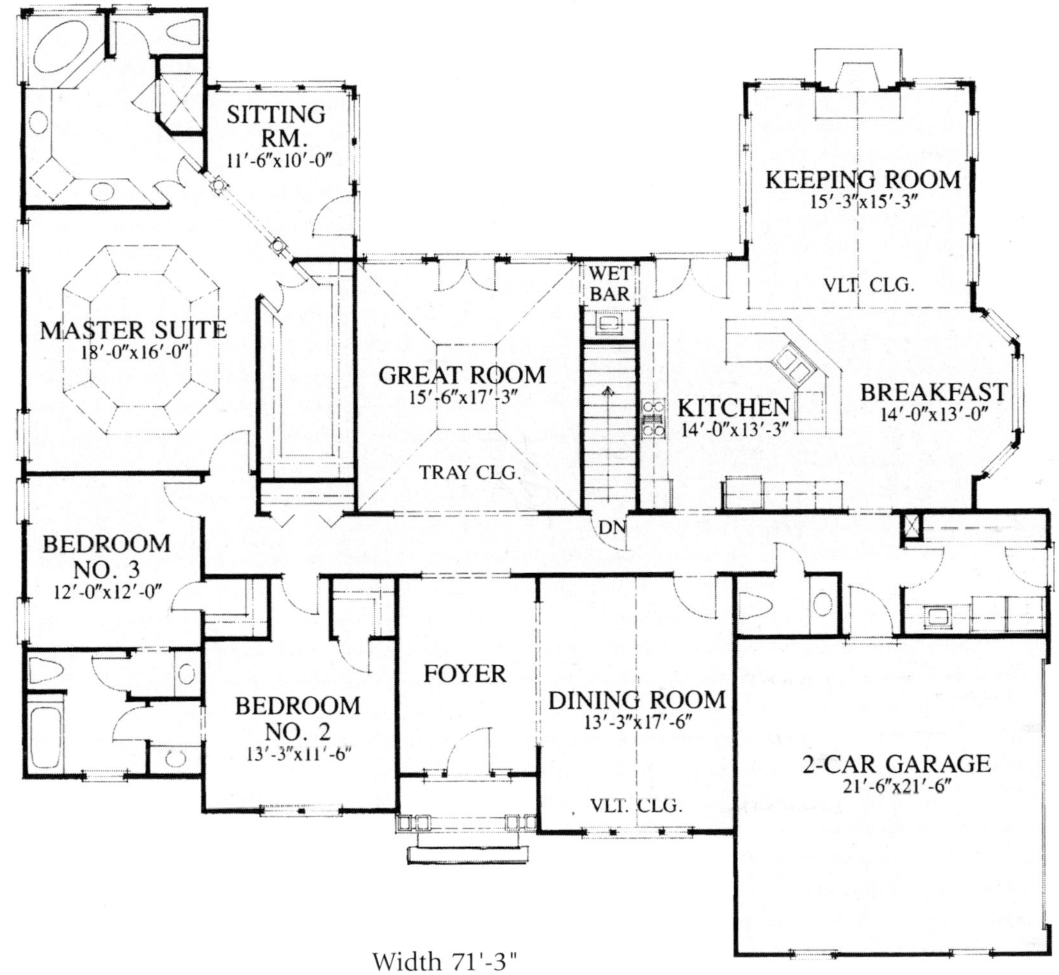
SITTING RM.
11'-6"x10'-0"
MASTER SUITE
18'-0"x16'-0"
GREAT ROOM
15'-6"x17'-3"
TRAY CLG.
WET BAR
DN
KEEPING ROOM
15'-3"x15'-3"
VLT. CLG.
KITCHEN
14'-0"x13'-3"
BREAKFAST
14'-0"x13'-0"
BEDROOM NO. 3
12'-0"x12'-0"
BEDROOM NO. 2
13'-3"x11'-6"
FOYER
DINING ROOM
13'-3"x17'-6"
VLT. CLG.
2-CAR GARAGE
21'-6"x21'-6"

Width 71'-3"
Depth 66'-3"

To highlight the exterior of this brick home, stucco details have been artfully combined with arched transoms and a sweeping roofline. After passage through the handsome entry, one is immediately greeted by the home's architectural warmth.

ANSLEY PARK

Classic in proportion, this picturesque home draws on many traditions, with intricate brick detailing, steeply pitched gables and arched windows. Recessed double doors and a handsome clerestory add interest to the refined exterior presence. Accessed by a two-story foyer, the great room features a centered fireplace framed by a tall window and a lovely French door. In the formal dining room, a triple window allows a generous view of the back property. A secluded master suite with a vaulted ceiling is complemented by three second-floor bedrooms and a loft with an open-rail view to the foyer.

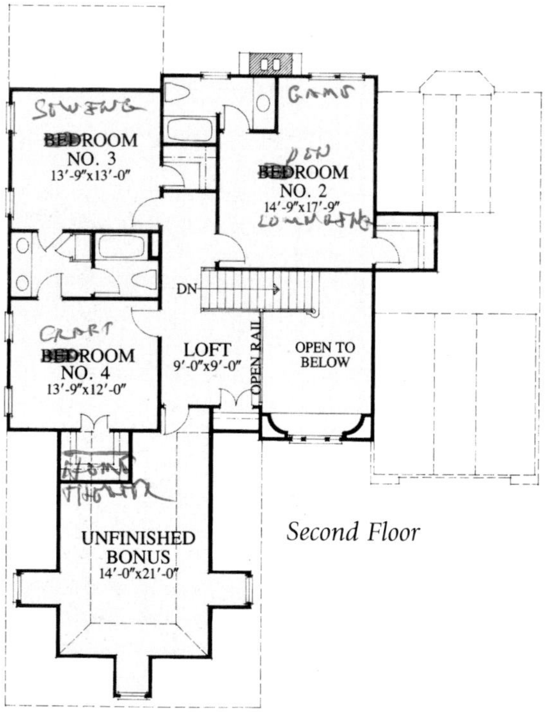

SEWING
BEDROOM
NO. 3
13'-9"x13'-0"
GAME
DEN
BEDROOM
NO. 2
14'-9"x17'-9"
DN
CRAFT
BEDROOM
NO. 4
13'-9"x12'-0"
LOFT
9'-0"x9'-0"
OPEN RAIL
OPEN TO
BELOW
UNFINISHED
BONUS
14'-0"x21'-0"

Second Floor

DINING ROOM
14'-0"x15'-0"
GREAT ROOM
20'-0"x17'-9"
KITCHEN
17'-0"x12'-6"
WET BAR
HIS
HERS
DN
UP
BREAKFAST
11'-0"x12'-0"
FOYER
MASTER SUITE
15'-3"x15'-0"
LAUN.
VLT. CLG.
2-CAR GARAGE
21'-6"x24'-9"

First Floor

Width 50'-9"
Depth 66'-0"

Design T010

First Floor: 1,870 square feet
Second Floor: 1,030 square feet
Total: 2,900 square feet

Bedrooms: 4
Bathrooms: 3½

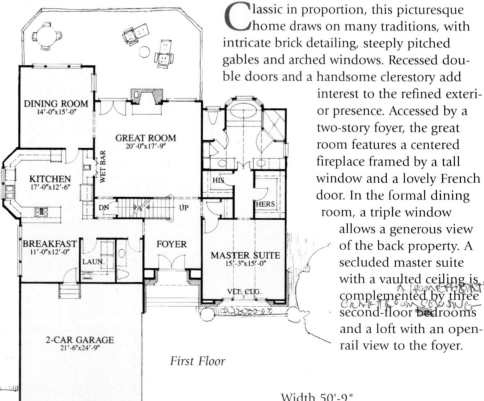

KENNESSAW COUNTRY RETREAT Design T006

A thoughtful blend of brick and stucco, this traditional home presents a specific architectural motif with the repeated arch pattern evident in the window, doorway transom and even dormers. Just off the foyer, the entire right wing of the first-floor plan becomes the sumptuous master suite. The formal dining room and the great room are presented in the center of the plan, with casual living space to the left. A well-planned kitchen has a cooking island, a breakfast area and a keeping room.

Width 61'-6"
Depth 52'-6"

First Floor: 2,355 square feet
Second Floor: 987 square feet
Total: 3,342 square feet

Bedrooms: 4
Bathrooms: 3½

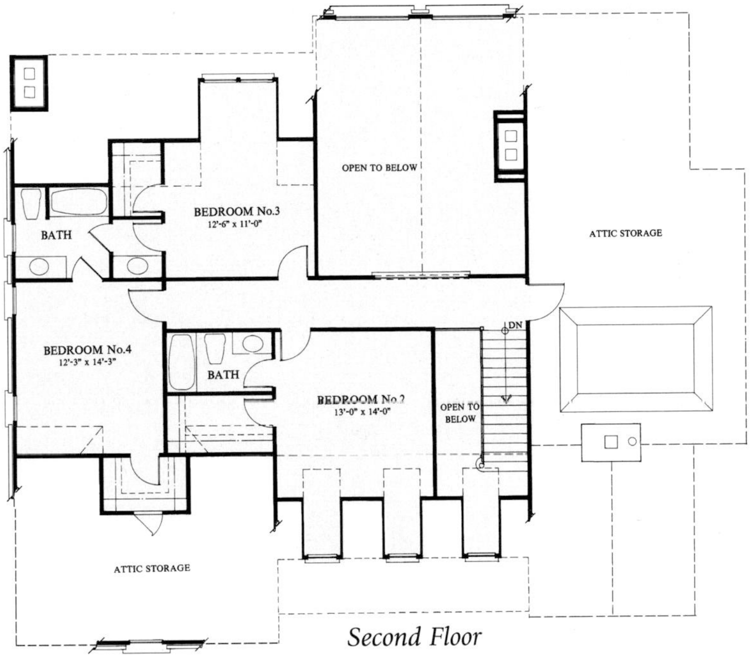

Second Floor

First Floor

Many generously sized, shuttered windows fill this beautiful home with the clear, warming light of the outdoors. Classic styling captures the heart with its varying roofline, double door entry and columned porch.

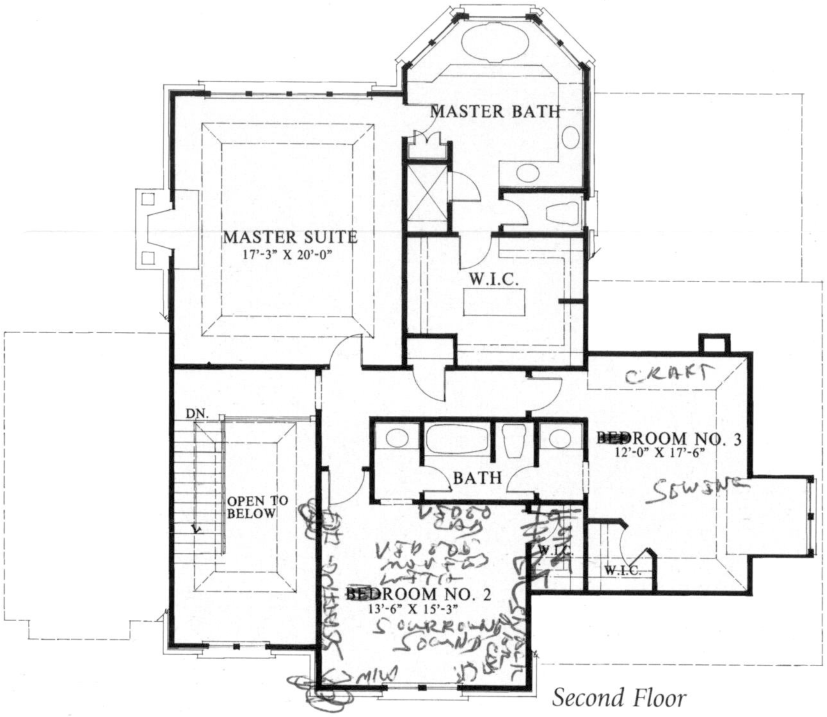
MASTER BATH
MASTER SUITE
17'-3" X 20'-0"
W.I.C.
DN.
OPEN TO BELOW
BATH
BEDROOM NO. 3
12'-0" X 17'-6"
W.I.C.
W.I.C.
BEDROOM NO. 2
13'-6" X 15'-3"

Second Floor

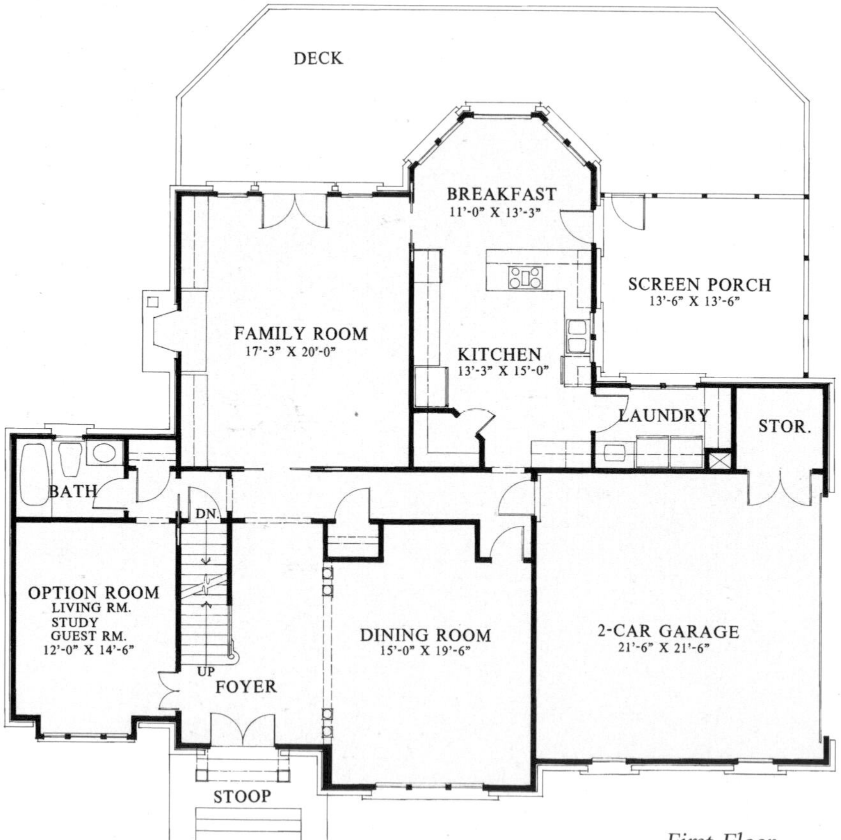
DECK
BREAKFAST
11'-0" X 13'-3"
SCREEN PORCH
13'-6" X 13'-6"
FAMILY ROOM
17'-3" X 20'-0"
KITCHEN
13'-3" X 15'-0"
LAUNDRY
STOR.
BATH
DN.
OPTION ROOM
LIVING RM.
STUDY
GUEST RM.
12'-0" X 14'-6"
DINING ROOM
15'-0" X 19'-6"
2-CAR GARAGE
21'-6" X 21'-6"
UP
FOYER
STOOP

Width 61'-6"
Depth 50'-6"

First Floor

MARIETTA SQUARE TRADITIONAL

Design T065

First Floor: 1,710 square feet
Second Floor: 1,470 square feet
Total: 3,180 square feet

Bedrooms: 3
Bathrooms: 3

A host of shuttered windows dress this traditional exterior with classic style, and allow natural light to fill the interior. The two-story foyer has a tray ceiling and opens to a banquet-sized dining room. The nearby kitchen has an attached breakfast nook with a bright bay window and a door to the screen porch. An optional room to the left of the foyer may be used as a parlor, formal living room, study or guest bedroom. To the rear of the plan, a spacious family room features a fireplace and French doors to the rear deck. Three second-floor bedrooms include a master suite with its own hearth and a lavish bath.

Irving Commons

Design T217

First Floor: 2,225 square feet
Second Floor: 1,225 square feet
Total: 3,450 square feet

Bedrooms: 4
Bathrooms: 3½

The drama of this home through its use of multi-level hipped rooflines is definitely European inspired. The architectural theme begins with the arched recessed entry and is repeated with a graceful transom and an arched front stoop. A ribbon of windows decorates the facade and permits natural light to flow through the interior. The L-shaped foyer brings together the formal elements of the design with an open, casual living space, and leads to a secluded master suite. This private retreat has a tray ceiling and a deluxe bath with a walk-in closet designed for two. On the second floor, two secondary bedrooms with a connecting bath open to a gallery hall that leads to a guest suite or fourth bedroom.

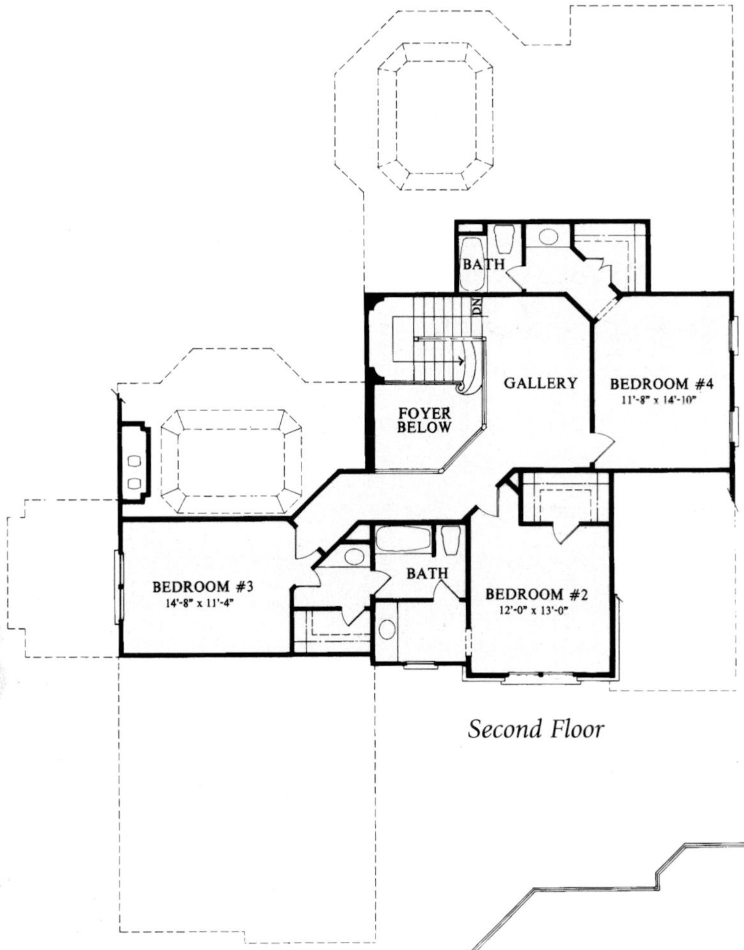
BATH
DN
GALLERY
BEDROOM #4
11'-8" x 14'-10"
FOYER
BELOW
BEDROOM #3
14'-8" x 11'-4"
BATH
BEDROOM #2
12'-0" x 13'-0"

Second Floor

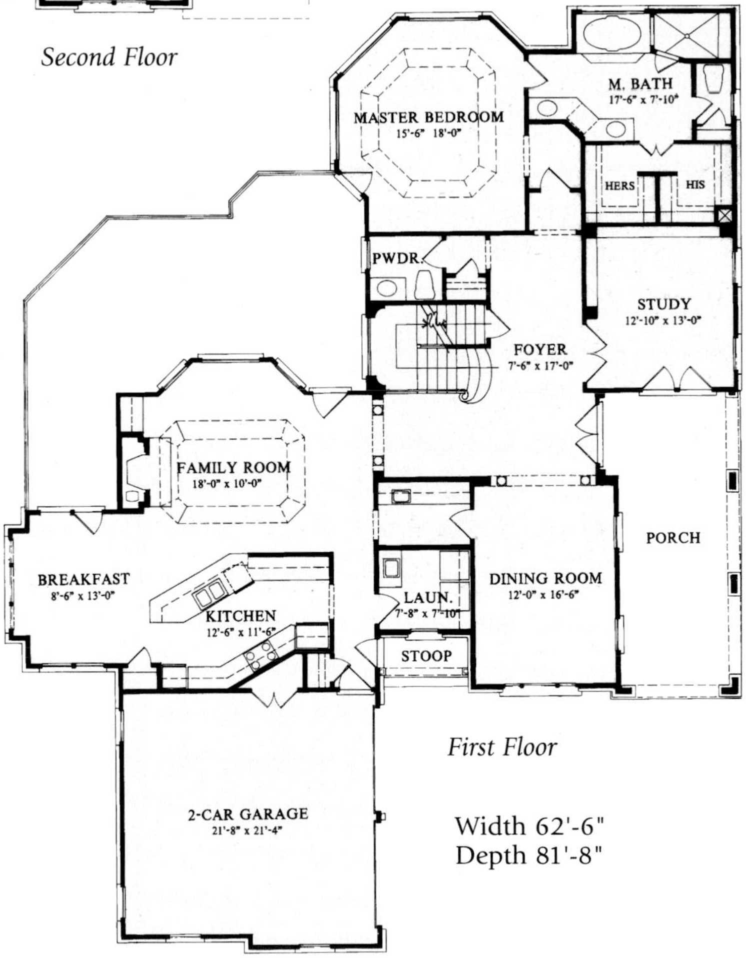
M. BATH
17'-6" x 7'-10"
MASTER BEDROOM
15'-6" 18'-0"
HERS
HIS
PWDR.
STUDY
12'-10" x 13'-0"
FOYER
7'-6" x 17'-0"
FAMILY ROOM
18'-0" x 10'-0"
PORCH
BREAKFAST
8'-6" x 13'-0"
KITCHEN
12'-6" x 11'-6"
LAUN.
7'-8" x 7'-10"
DINING ROOM
12'-0" x 16'-6"
STOOP
2-CAR GARAGE
21'-8" x 21'-4"

First Floor

Width 62'-6"
Depth 81'-8"

Beautiful arches create a look of grandeur and add an inviting quality to the character of this home. An exquisite recessed entry leads to a quiet study through lovely French doors, which add a special touch of European enchantment while allowing plenty of natural light inside.

In a style similar to Federal, simple box shapes are decorated with well-proportioned elements. The style depends on the composition of these elements within the architectural box—such as a paneled entry topped by a round window.

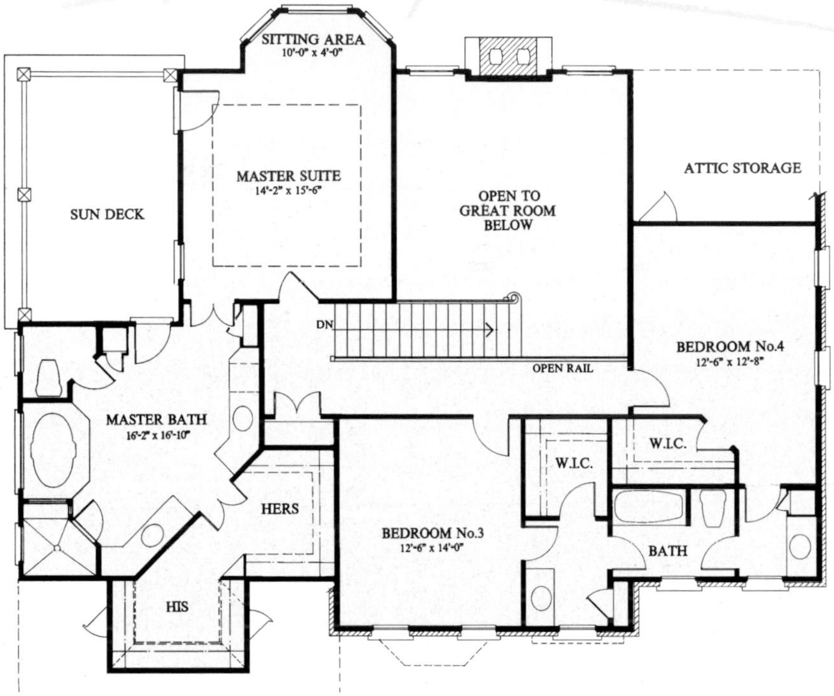
SITTING AREA
10'-0" x 4'-0"
MASTER SUITE
14'-2" x 15'-6"
SUN DECK
OPEN TO
GREAT ROOM
BELOW
ATTIC STORAGE
DN
OPEN RAIL
BEDROOM No.4
12'-6" x 12'-8"
MASTER BATH
16'-2" x 16'-10"
W.I.C.
W.I.C.
HERS
BEDROOM No.3
12'-6" x 14'-0"
BATH
HIS

Second Floor

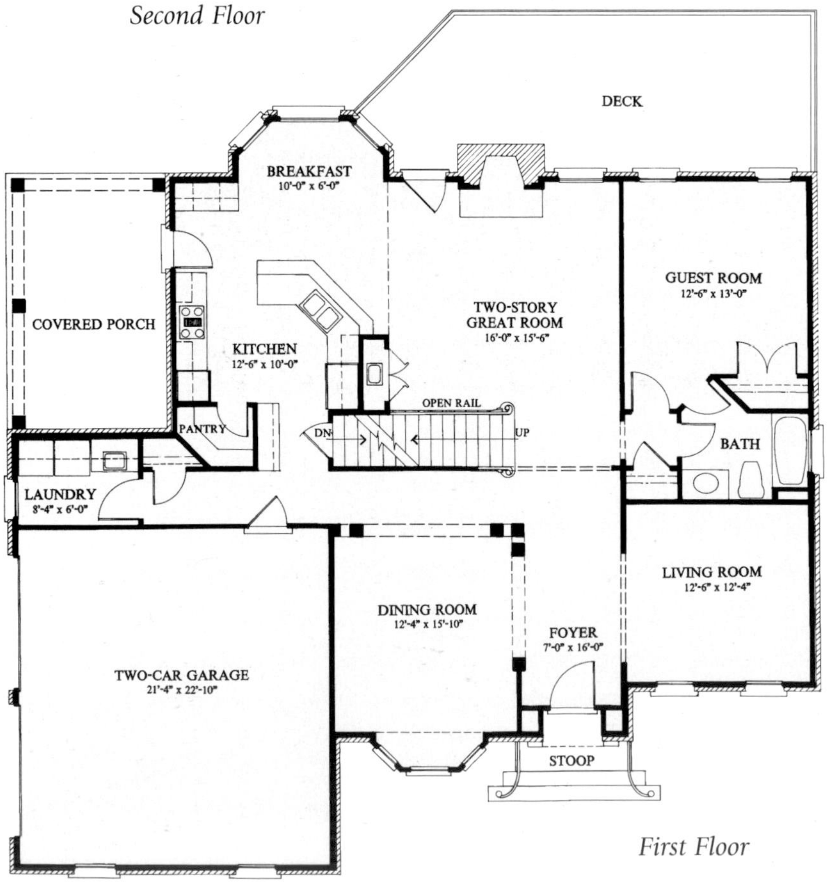
DECK
BREAKFAST
10'-0" x 6'-0"
GUEST ROOM
12'-6" x 13'-0"
TWO-STORY
GREAT ROOM
16'-0" x 15'-6"
COVERED PORCH
KITCHEN
12'-6" x 10'-0"
OPEN RAIL
PANTRY
DN
UP
BATH
LAUNDRY
8'-4" x 6'-0"
LIVING ROOM
12'-6" x 12'-4"
DINING ROOM
12'-4" x 15'-10"
FOYER
7'-0" x 16'-0"
TWO-CAR GARAGE
21'-4" x 22'-10"
STOOP

Width 55'-0"
Depth 52'-0"

First Floor

Somersby Place

Classical details and a stately brick exterior accentuate the grace and timeless elegance of this English Manor home. Inside, the foyer opens to a banquet-sized dining room with an adjacent, equally formal living room. A two-story great room features a wet bar and a warming fireplace. To the left, the sunlit breakfast room and functional kitchen provides a breakfast bar for casual bites and quick meals. Upstairs, the master suite promises gentle comfort with a sitting area bathed in natural light and access to a delightful sundeck. Two bedrooms with a connecting bath that offers private vanities complete the second floor.

Design T028

First Floor: 1,581 square feet
Second Floor: 1,415 square feet
Total: 2,996 square feet

Bedrooms: 4
Bathrooms: 3

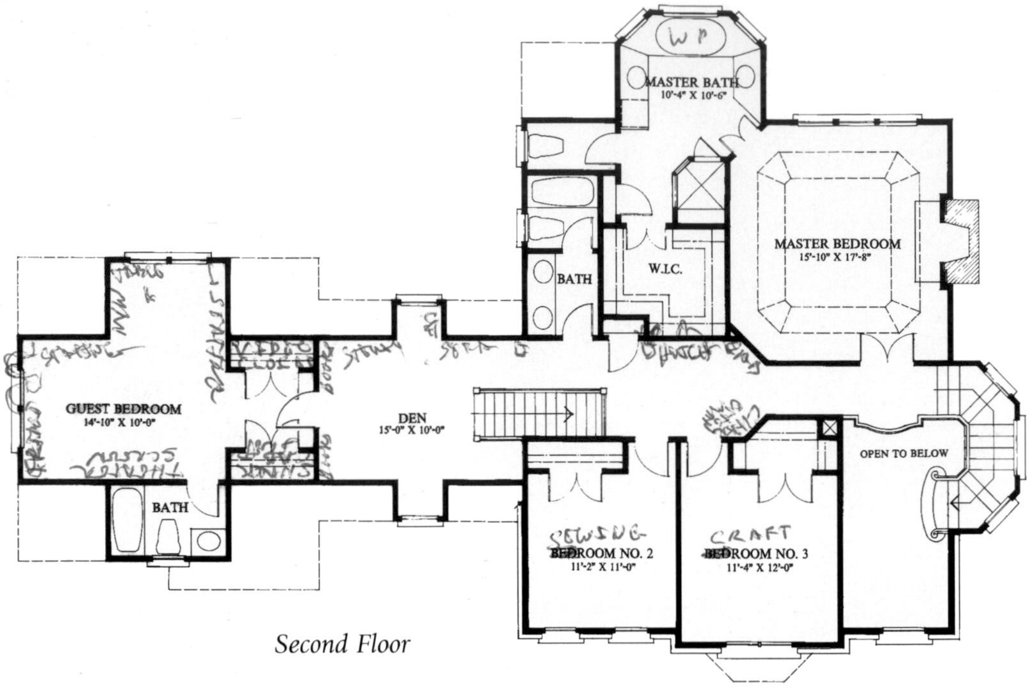
MASTER BATH
10'-4" X 10'-6"
MASTER BEDROOM
15'-10" X 17'-8"
BATH
W.I.C.
GUEST BEDROOM
14'-10" X 10'-0"
DEN
15'-0" X 10'-0"
OPEN TO BELOW
BATH
BEDROOM NO. 2
11'-2" X 11'-0"
BEDROOM NO. 3
11'-4" X 12'-0"

Second Floor

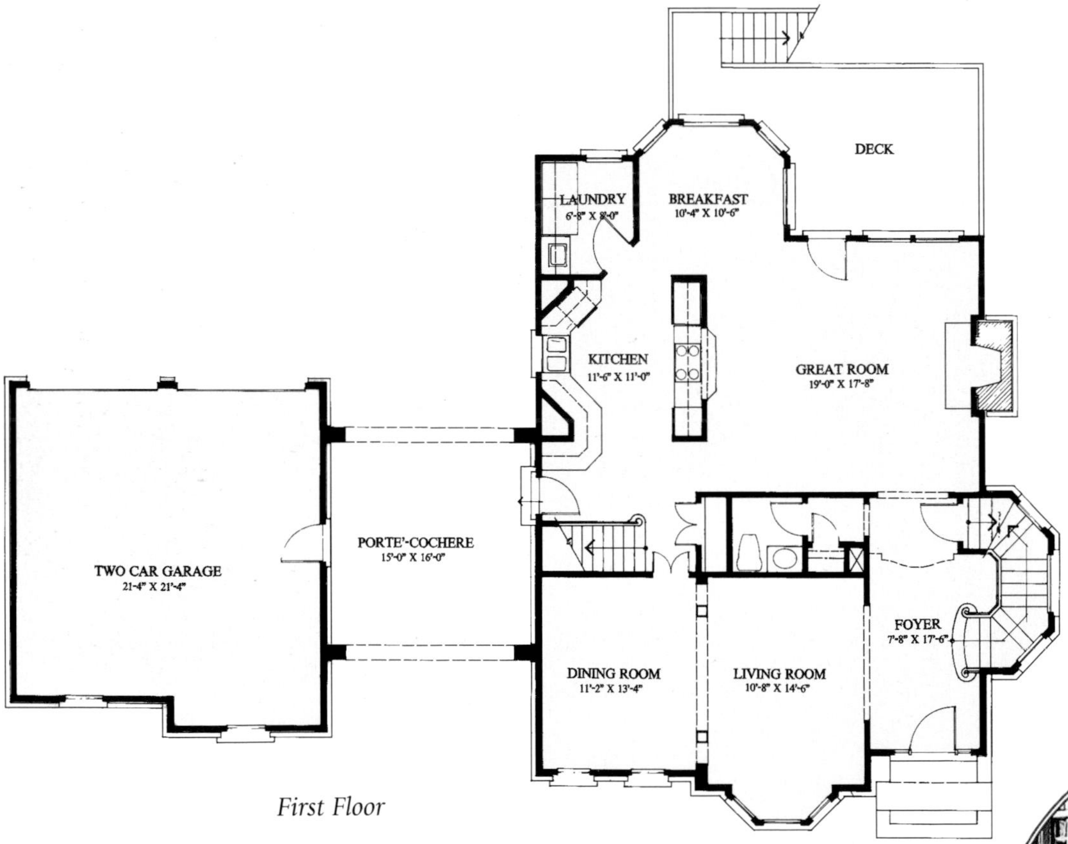
DECK
LAUNDRY
6'-8" X 8'-0"
BREAKFAST
10'-4" X 10'-6"
KITCHEN
11'-6" X 11'-0"
GREAT ROOM
19'-0" X 17'-8"
TWO CAR GARAGE
21'-4" X 21'-4"
PORTE'-COCHERE
15'-0" X 16'-0"
FOYER
7'-8" X 17'-6"
DINING ROOM
11'-2" X 13'-4"
LIVING ROOM
10'-8" X 14'-6"

First Floor

Width 73'-6"
Depth 49'-0"

A graceful arch topped by a keystone makes a classic accent to this dramatic entry. Inspired by neighborhoods of a gentler era, an eclectic blend of architectural elements is drawn together by a simple theme.

Garden Heights

This English Georgian home features a dramatic brick exterior, with jack-arch detailing that complements a charming porte cochere. Inside, a winding staircase and a balcony overlook create an elegant foyer. Defined by a colonnade detail, the formal living and dining rooms make a perfect area for entertaining. The great room features a centered fireplace and opens to the breakfast room and kitchen, which has plenty of cabinets and counter space. The second floor includes a guest suite, a children's den, two family bedrooms and the master suite. A cozy fireplace, coffered ceiling and sumptuous bath highlight this lavish retreat.

Design T015

First Floor: 1,370 square feet
Second Floor: 1,673 square feet
Total: 3,043 square feet
Bedrooms: 4
Bathrooms: 3½

Many traditions drawn from early English architecture come together handsomely in this picturesque home. The steeply pitched, gabled roof might be found in medieval designs but the intricate Tudor detailing, which gives the house its overall character, has been refined.

Rear Elevation

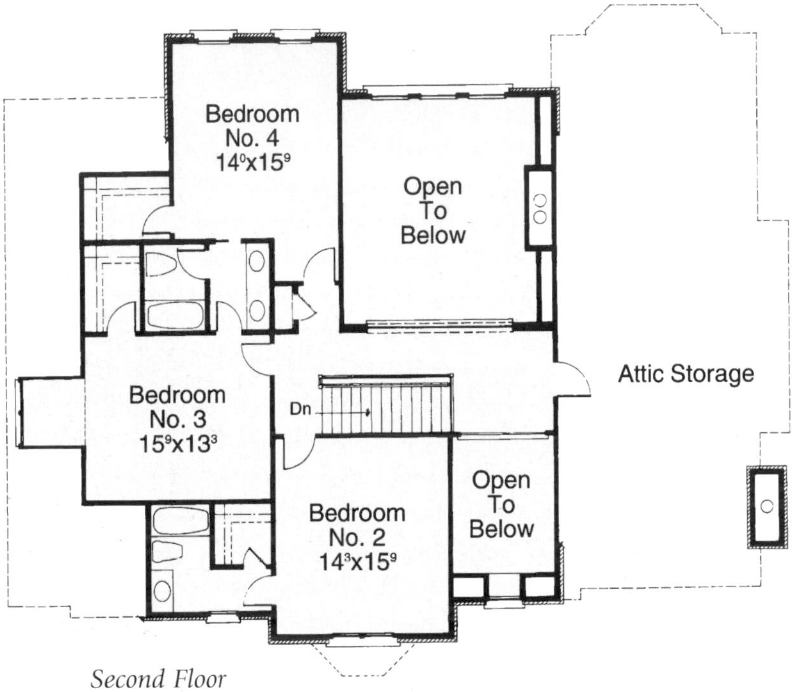

Bedroom
No. 4
14⁰x15⁹
Open
To
Below
Attic Storage
Bedroom
No. 3
15⁹x13³
Dn
Bedroom
No. 2
14³x15⁹
Open
To
Below

Second Floor

Deck
Breakfast
14⁰x12³
Master
Bedroom
16³x15⁰
Great
Room
17³x18³
Office
Kitchen
14⁰x11⁰
Dn
Up
Two Car
Garage
21⁹x22³
Dining
Room
14³x16⁰
Foyer
Living
Room
16⁶x12⁰

First Floor

Width 66'-3"
Depth 57'-9"

BERWICKE

Gently arched cornices and capstones call up a sense of history with this country home. With all the romance of a Tudor folk cottage, the design delivers an elegance and grace that naturally inspire conviviality. Formal rooms flank the two-story foyer, which leads to comfortably elegant living space with an extended-hearth fireplace. A sizable kitchen serves the formal dining room through a butler's pantry and overlooks the breakfast room with wide views of the outdoors. A secluded home office is a quiet place for business conversations. The master suite nestles to the rear of the plan and offers a spider-beam ceiling and a walk-in closet. Upstairs, two family bedrooms share a full bath with two lavatories, while a fourth bedroom, or guest suite, enjoys a private bath.

Design T171

First Floor: 2,302 square feet
Second Floor: 1,177 square feet
Total: 3,479 square feet

Bedrooms: 4
Bathrooms: 3½

RALEIGH COURT

Design T115

First Floor: 2,871 square feet
Second Floor: 1,407 square feet
Total: 4,278 square feet

Bedrooms: 4
Bathrooms: 4½

Brick details and large expanses of glass add to the glamour of this well-proportioned European Country home. The asymmetrical shapes create an interestingly unpredictable arrangement of rooms throughout the interior, while casement windows add an Old World touch on the outside. Sweeping curves of the staircase balustrade highlight the two-story foyer. The available entrances to the study, dining room and vaulted great room make an environment well suited for any lifestyle. The master suite provides retreat with the opportunity to include the vaulted study, bathed in light from the picture window. Three private bedrooms on the second floor have easy access to casual living space via the private staircase.

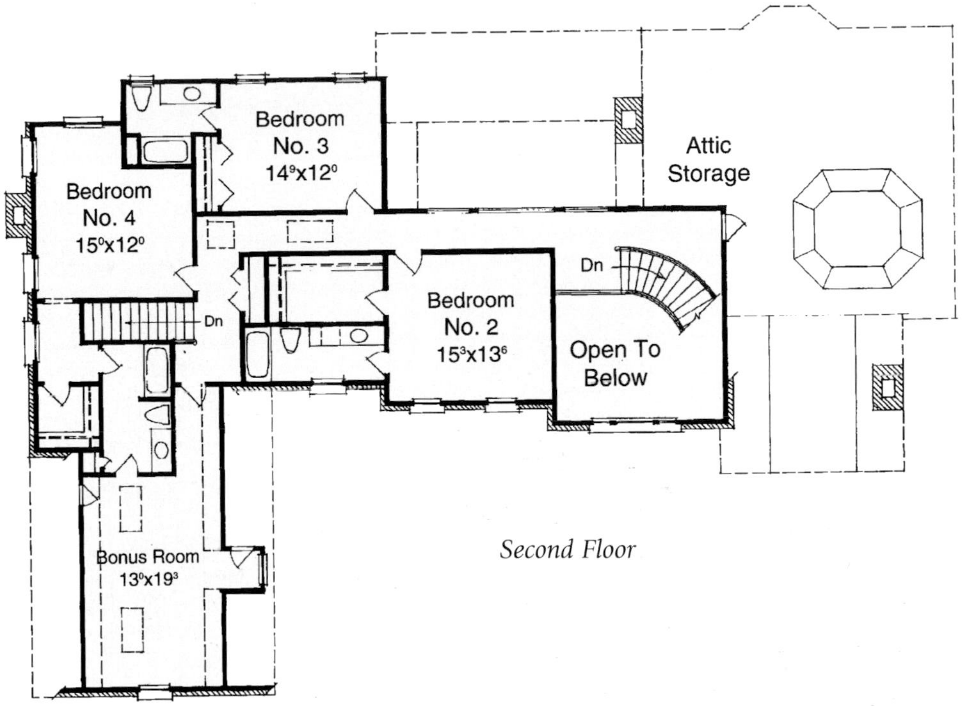

Second Floor

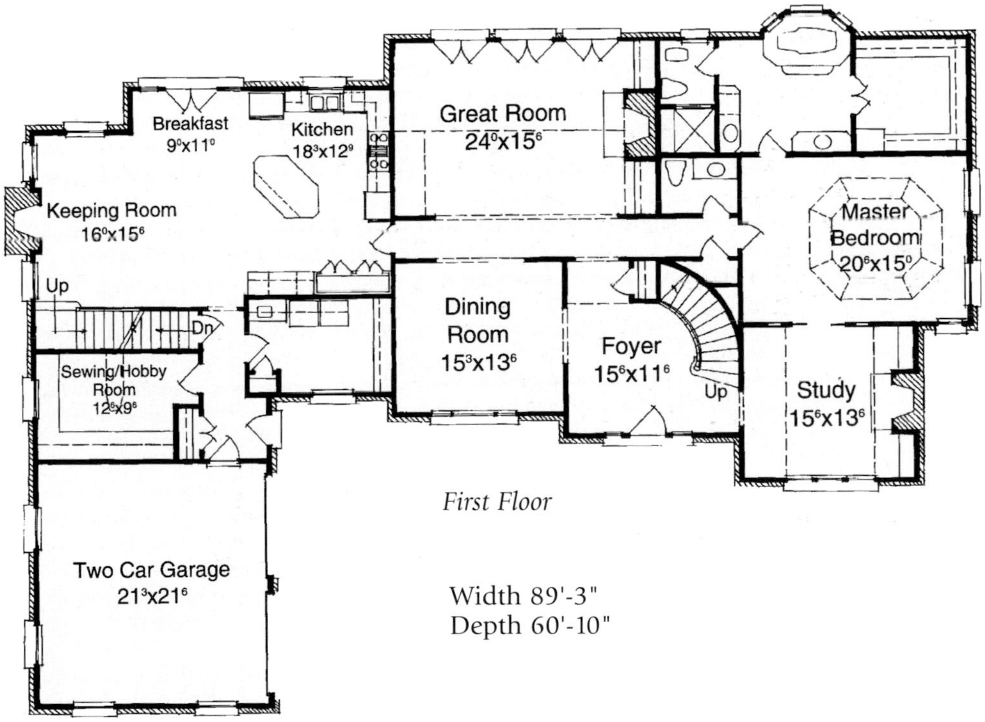

First Floor

Width 89'-3"
Depth 60'-10"

A country estate home designed in a continental or High French Country style. This is not a casual farmhouse, but a landowner's manor home. The time period would be the early 20th Century, when classical details were arranged into a picturesque composition.

Through the use of brick, classical details and symmetrical design, this house displays a stately grace so characteristic of traditional architecture. The symmetry of the facade is repeated in glass on the rear elevation, with French doors that open to the deck.

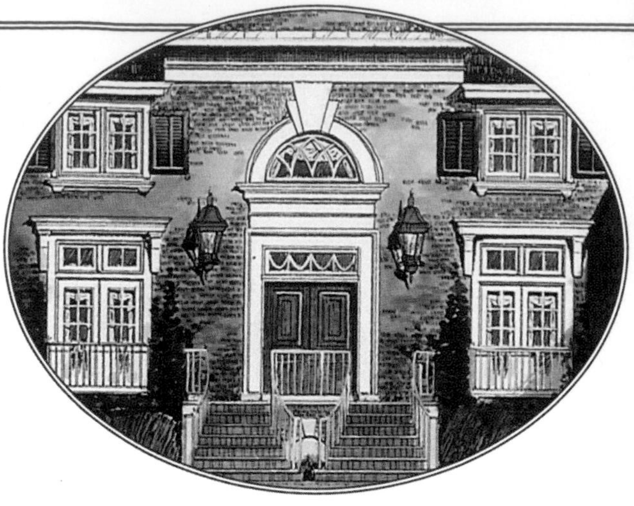

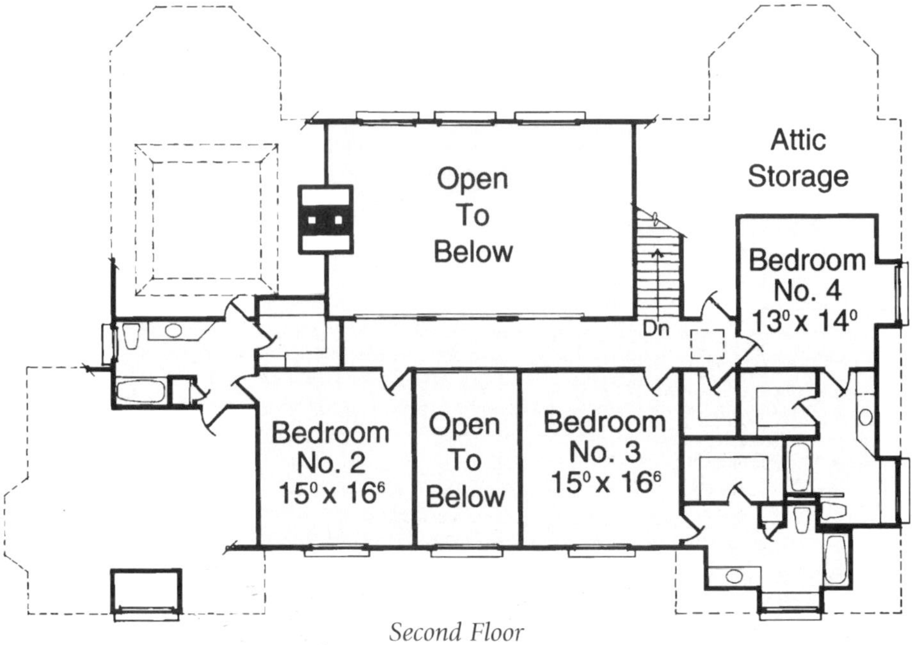

Second Floor

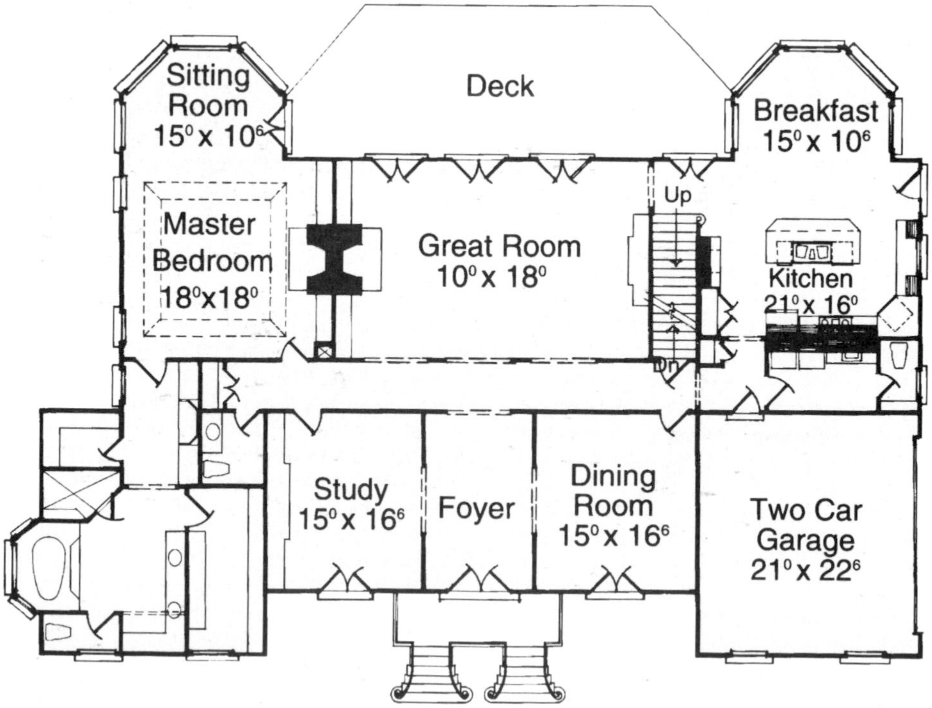

First Floor

Width 86'-9"
Depth 56'-10"

HAMPTON PLACE

Classic detailing and a regal entrance design give this home its traditional and timeless style. Inside the house is a grand exhibition of large, open and flowing rooms. Functional in many respects, the open living areas of this home make entertaining easy and opportunistic. The master suite, secluded in its own wing, offers amenities such as a roomy dressing area with flanking walk-in closets and a sitting room with picturesque views of the back property. Upstairs are three large bedrooms, each with a private bath and a large closet.

Design T128

First Floor: 3,296 square feet
Second Floor: 1,517 square feet
Total: 4,813 square feet

Bedrooms: 4
Bathrooms: 4½

WHEN YOU'RE READY TO ORDER...

Let us show you our home blueprint package.

Our Blueprint Package has nearly everything you'll need to get the job done right, whether you're working on your own or with help from an architect designer, builder or subcontractors.

QUALITY

Hundreds of hours of painstaking effort have gone into the development of your blueprint set. Each home has been quality-checked by professionals to ensure accuracy and buildability.

VALUE

Because we sell in volume, you can buy professional-quality blueprints at a fraction of their development cost. With our plans, your dream home design costs only a few hundred dollars, not the thousands of dollars that custom architects charge.

SERVICE

Once you've chosen your favorite home plan, you'll receive fast, efficient service whether you choose to mail or fax your order to us or call us toll free at 1-800-521-6797.

SATISFACTION

Over 50 years of service to satisfied home plan buyers provide us unparalleled experience and knowledge in producing quality blueprints. What this means to you is satisfaction with our product and performance.

ORDER TOLL FREE 1-800-521-6797

After you've looked over our Blueprint Package and Important Extras on the following pages, simply mail the order form on page 159 or call toll free on our Blueprint Hotline: 1-800-521-6797.

For customer service, call toll free 1-888-690-1116.

THE BLUEPRINT PACKAGE

Each set of home plan blueprints is a related gathering of plans, diagrams, measurements, details and specifications that precisely show how your new residence will come together. Each home design receives careful attention and planning from our expert staff to ensure quality and buildability.

Designer's Rendering of Front Elevation

The artist's sketch of the full exterior of the house provides a projected view of how the home will look when built and landscaped. Large ink-line floor plans show all levels of the house and offer an overview of your new home's livability.

SAMPLE PACKAGE

Foundation Plan
This sheet shows the foundation layout including support walls, excavated and unexcavated areas, if any, and foundation notes. All of the homes in this collection are designed with a basement foundation.

Dimensioned Floor Plans
These sheets show the layout of each floor of the house. Rooms and interior spaces are carefully dimensioned and keys are given for cross-section details provided later in the plans. The positions of electrical outlets and switches are shown.

House Cross-Sections
Large-scale views show sections or cut-aways of the foundation, interior walls, exterior walls, floors, stairways and roof details. Additional cross-sections may show important changes in floor, ceiling or roof heights of the relationship of one level to another. Extremely valuable for construction, these sections show exactly how the various parts of the house fit together.

Interior Elevations
Many of our drawings show the design and placement of kitchen and bathroom cabinets, laundry areas, fireplaces, bookcases and other built-ins. Little "extras," such as mantelpiece and wainscoting drawings, plus moulding sections, provide details that give your home a custom touch.

Exterior Elevations
These drawings show the front, rear and sides of your house and give necessary notes on exterior materials and finishes. Particular attention is given to cornice detail, brick and stone accents or other finish items that make your home unique.

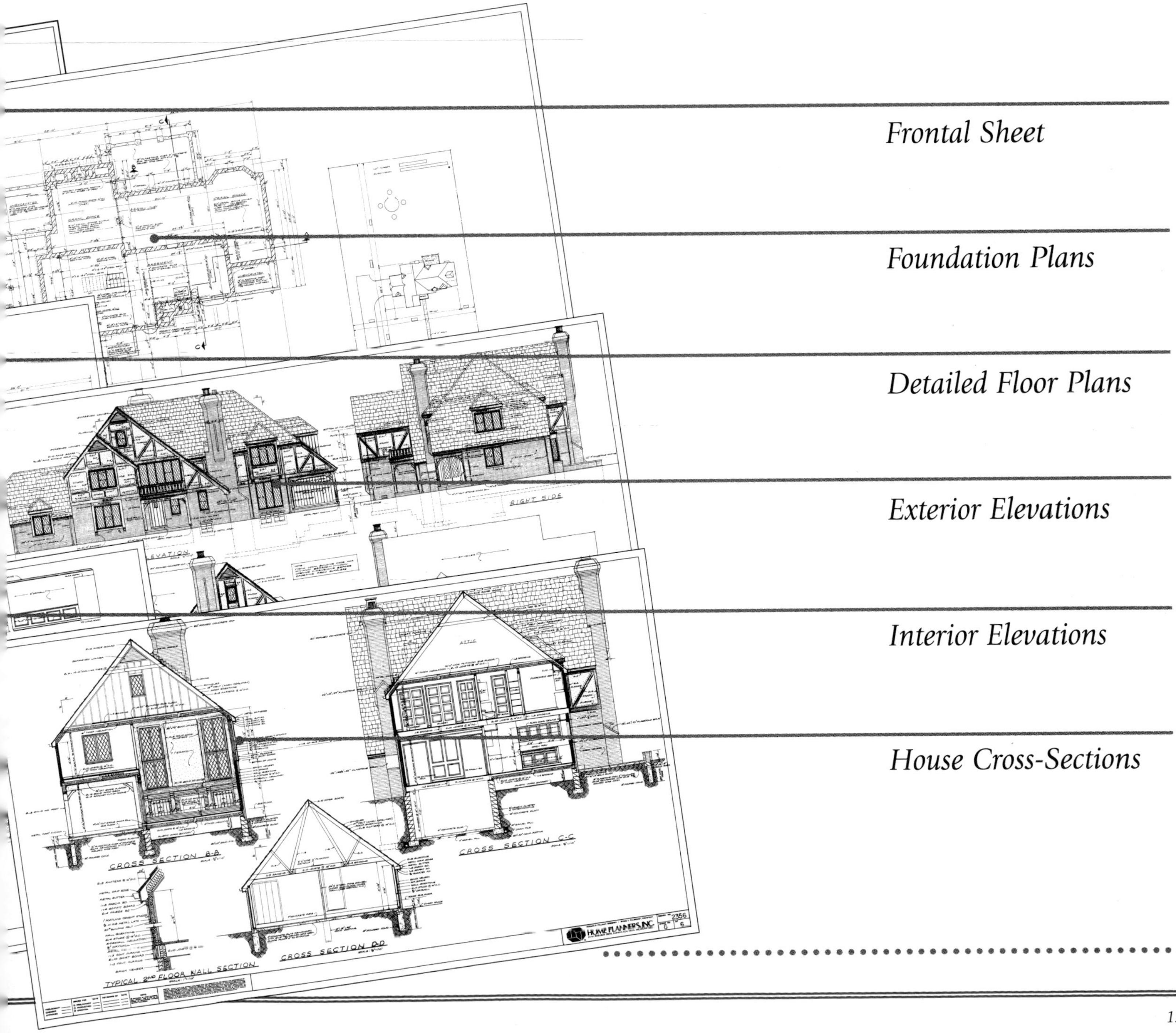

IMPORTANT EXTRAS TO DO THE JOB RIGHT!

Introducing eight important planning and construction aids developed by our professionals to help you succeed in your home-building project.

MATERIALS LIST

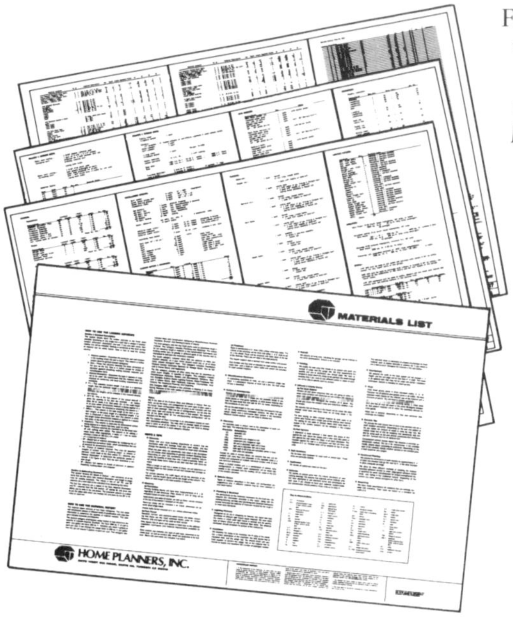

For many of the designs in our portfolio, we offer a customized materials take-off that is invaluable in planning and estimating the cost of your new home. This Materials List outlines the quantity, type and size of materials needed to build your house (with the exception of mechanical system items). Included are framing lumber, windows and doors, kitchen and bath cabinetry, rough and finish hardware, and much more. This handy list helps you or your builder cost out materials and serves as a reference sheet when you're compiling bids. A Materials List cannot be ordered before blueprints are ordered.

(Note: Because of the diversity of local building codes, our Materials List does not include mechanical materials.)

QUOTE ONE®

SUMMARY COST REPORT/MATERIALS COST REPORT

A new service for estimating the cost of building select designs, the Quote One® system is available in two separate stages: The Summary Cost Report and the Materials Cost Report.

The Summary Cost Report shows the total cost per square foot for your chosen home in your zip-code area and then breaks that cost down into ten categories showing the costs for building materials, labor and installation. The total cost for the report (which includes three grades: Budget, Standard and Custom) is just $19.95 for one home, and additionals are only $14.95. These reports allow you to evaluate your building budget and compare the costs of building a variety of homes in your area.

Make even more informed decisions about your home-building project with the second phase of our package, our Materials Cost Report. This tool is invaluable in planning and estimating the cost of your new home. The material and installation (labor and equipment) cost is shown for each of over 1,000 line items provided in the Materials List (Standard grade) which is included when you purchase this estimating tool. It allows you to determine building costs for your specific zip-code area and for your chosen home design. Space is allowed for additional estimates from contractors and subcontractors, such as for mechanical materials, which are not included in our packages. This invaluable tool is available for a price of $110, which includes a Materials List. A Materials Cost Report cannot be ordered before blueprints are ordered.

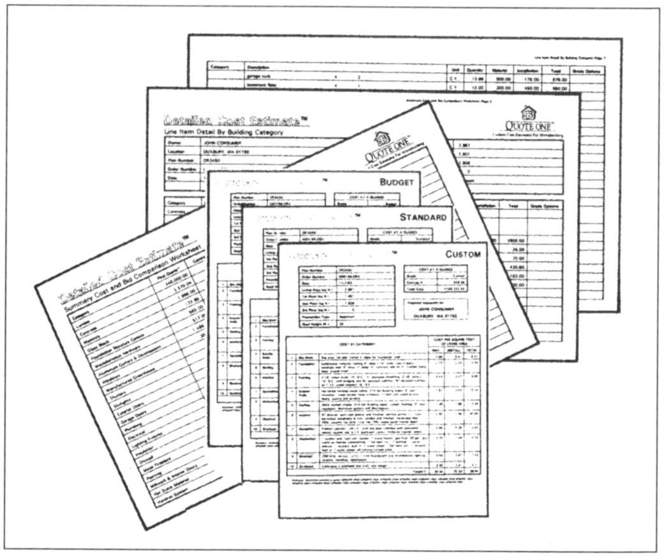

The Quote One® program is continually updated with new plans. If you are interested in a plan that is not indicated as Quote One®, please call to verify the status. To order these invaluable reports, use the order form on page 159 or call **1-800-521-6797**.

DETAIL SETS

Each set is an excellent tool that will add to your understanding of these technical subjects and help you to deal more confidently with subcontractors.

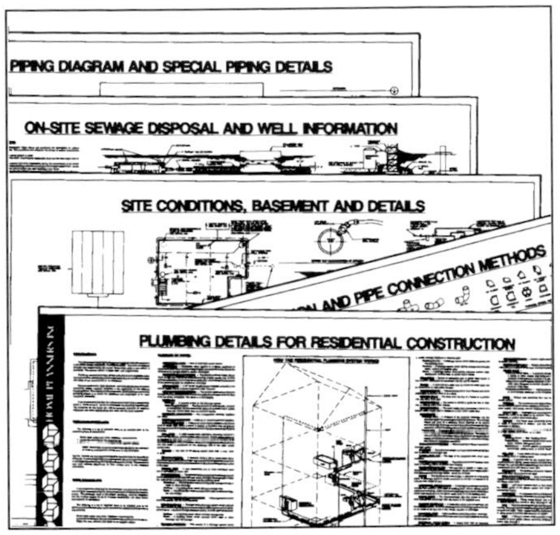

PLUMBING

If you want to know more about the complete plumbing system, these 24x36-inch detail sheets will prove very useful. Prepared to meet requirements of the National Plumbing Code, these six fact-filled sheets give general information on pipe schedules, fittings, sump-pump details, water-softener hookups, septic system details and much more. Color-coded sheets include a glossary of terms.

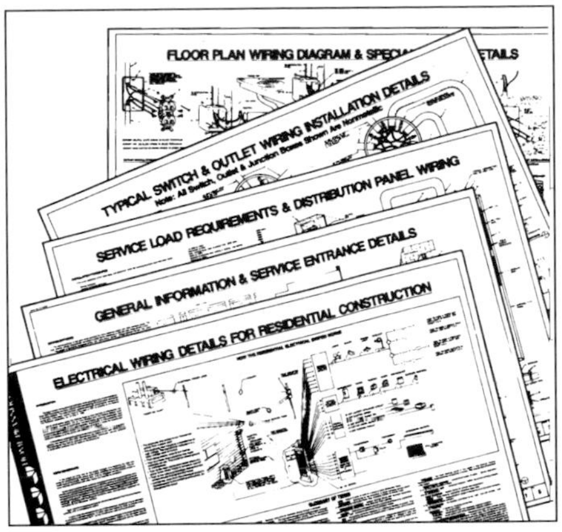

ELECTRICAL

Prepared to meet requirements of the National Electrical Code, these comprehensive 24x36-inch drawings come packed with helpful information, including wire sizing, switch-installation schematics, cable-routing details, appliance wattage, doorbell hookups, typical service panel circuitry and much more. Six sheets are bound together and color-coded for easy reference. A glossary of terms is also included.

Design T201

16"x20" COLOR RENDERING

Full-color renderings suitable for framing are available for all of the plans contained in this book. For prices and additional information, please see page 156 or call the toll-free number listed below.

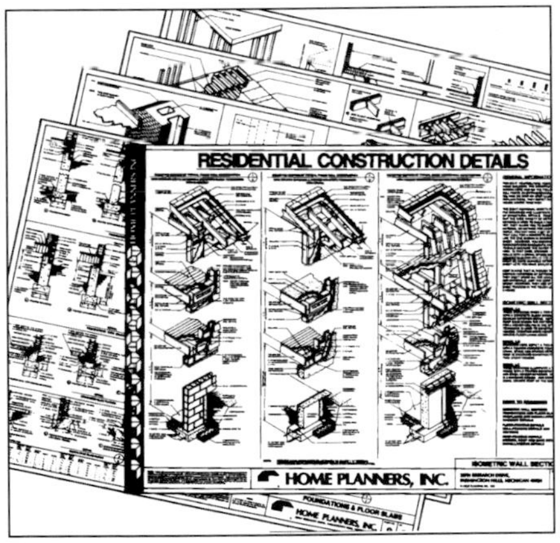

CONSTRUCTION

To help you understand how your house will be built—and offer additional techniques—this set of drawings depicts the materials and methods used to build foundations, fireplaces, walls, floors and roofs. Where appropriate, the drawings show acceptable alternatives. These six sheets will answer questions for the advanced do-it-yourselfer or home planner.

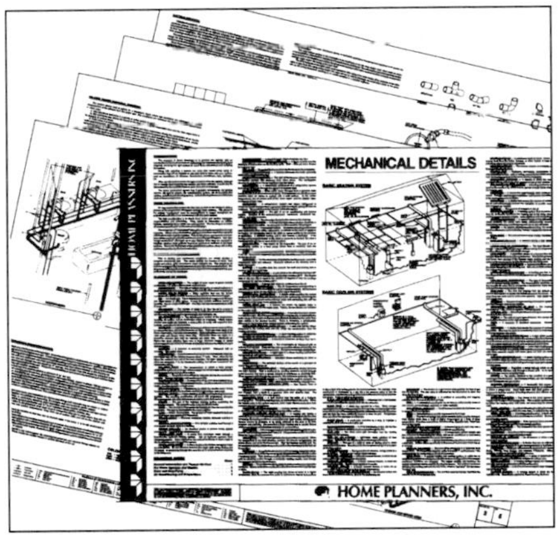

MECHANICAL

This package will help you make informed decisions and communicate with subcontractors about heating and cooling systems. The 24x36-inch drawings contain instructions and samples that allow you to make simple load calculations and preliminary sizing and costing analysis. Covered are today's most commonly used systems from heat pumps to solar fuel systems. The package is full of illustrations and diagrams to help you visualize components and how they relate to one another.

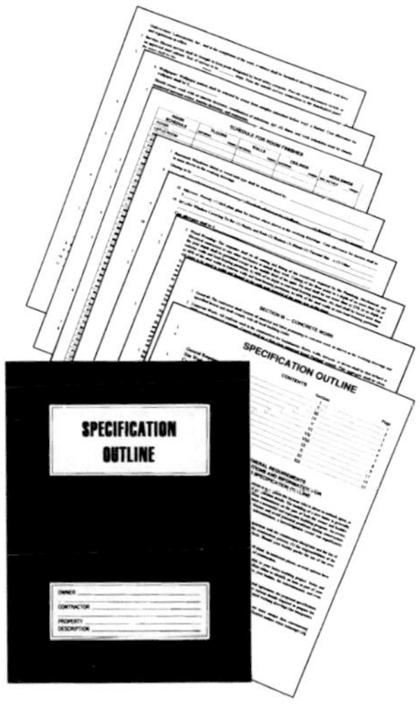

SPECIFICATION OUTLINE

This 16-page document is critical to building your house correctly. Designed to be filled in by you or your builder, this book lists 166 stages or items crucial to the building process. It provides a comprehensive review of the construction process and helps in making choices of materials. When combined with the blueprints, a signed contract, and a schedule, it becomes a legal document and record for the building of your home.

To Order, Call Toll Free 1-800-521-6797

To add these important extras to your Blueprint Package, simply indicate your choices on the order form on page 159 or call us toll free 1-800-521-6797.

House Blueprint Price Schedule

(Prices guaranteed through December 31, 1999)

	1-set Study Package	4-set Building Package	8-set Building Package
Package Schedule E	$630	$675	$735

All of the plans featured in this publication are Schedule E.

Prices for 4- or 8-set Building Packages honored only at time of original order.

Additional Identical Blueprints in same order ....$50 per set
Reverse Blueprints (mirror image) ....$50 per set
Specification Outlines ....$10 each

Materials Lists ....$60 each
(available only for those plans marked with a ◆)

Exchanges..........$ 50 exchange fee for first set; $10 for each additional set
$ 70 exchange fee for 4 sets
$100 exchange fee for 8 sets

16"x20" Color Rendering, Front Perspective $125

All prices are subject to change without notice and subject to availability.

Reversed plans are mirror-image sets with lettering and dimensioning shown backwards. To receive plans in reverse, specifically request this when placing your order. Since lettering and dimensions appear backward on reverse blueprints, we suggest you order one set reversed for siting and the rest as shown for construction purposes.

Purchase Policy
Accurate construction-cost estimates should come from your builder after review of the blueprints. Your purchase includes a license to use the plans to construct one single-family residence. These plans may NOT be reproduced, modified or used to create derivative works. Additional sets of the same plan may be ordered within a 60-day period at $50 each, plus shipping and tax, if applicable. After 60 days, re-orders are treated as new orders.

Plans are designed to meet the requirements of the Building Officials and Code Administrators (BOCA) Intl, Inc.; the International Conference of Building Officials; or the Council of American Building Officials (CABO). Because codes are subject to various changes and interpretations, the purchaser is responsible for compliance with all local building codes, ordinances, site conditions, subdivision restrictions and structural elements by having their builder review the plans to ensure compliance. We also recommend that you have an engineer in your area review your plans before actual construction begins.

Index

To use the Index below, refer to the design number listed in numerical order (a helpful page reference is also given). Refer to the price description on page 156 for the cost of one, four or eight sets of blueprints. Additional prices are shown for identical and reverse blueprint sets.

To Order: Fill in and send the order form on page 159 ,or if you prefer , fax to 1-800-224-6699 or 520-544-3086 —or call toll free 1-800-521-6797 or 520-297-8200.

Before You Order . . .

Before filling out the coupon at right or calling us on our Toll-Free Blueprint Hotline, you may want to learn more about our services and products. Here's some information you will find helpful.

Quick Turnaround
We process and ship every blueprint order from our office within 2 business days. Because of this quick turnaround, we won't send a formal notice acknowledging receipt of your order.

Our Exchange Policy
Since blueprints are printed in response to your order, we cannot honor requests for refunds. However, we will exchange your entire first order for an equal number of blueprints at a price of $50 for the first set and $10 for each additional set; $70 total exchange fee for 4 sets; $100 total exchange fee for 8 sets . . . plus the difference in cost if exchanging for a design in a higher price bracket or less the difference in cost if exchanging for a design in lower price bracket. One exchange is allowed within a year of purchase date. (Sepias are not exchangeable.) All sets from the first order must be returned before the exchange can take place. Please add $18 for postage and handling via ground service; $30 via Second Day Air; $40 via Next Day Air.

About Reverse Blueprints
If you want to build in reverse of the plan as shown, we will include an extra set of reverse blueprints (mirror image) for an additional fee of $50. Although lettering and dimensions will appear backward, reverses will be a useful aid if you decide to flop the plan.

Revising, Modifying and Customizing Plans
The wide variety of designs available in this publication allows you to select ideas and concepts for a home to fit your building site and match your family's needs, wants and budget. Like many homeowners who buy these plans, you and your builder, architect or engineer may want to make changes to them. Some minor changes may be made by your builder, but we recommend that most changes be made by a licensed architect or engineer. As set forth below, we cannot assume any responsibility for blueprints which have been changed, whether by you, your builder or by professionals selected by you or referred to you by us, because such individuals are outside our supervision and control.

Architectural and Engineering Seals
Some cities and states are now requiring that a licensed architect or engineer review and "seal" a blueprint, or officially approve it, prior to construction due to concerns over energy costs, safety and other factors. Prior to application for a building permit or the start of actual construction, we strongly advise that you consult your local building official who can tell you if such a review is required.

Local Building Codes and Zoning Requirements
Each plan was designed to meet the requirements of a nationally recognized model building code in effect at the time and place the plan was drawn. Because national building codes change from time to time, plans may not comply with any such code at the time they are sold to a customer. In addition, building officials may not accept these plans as final construction documents of record as the plans may need to be modified and additional drawings and details added to suit local conditions and requirements. We strongly advise that purchasers consult a licensed architect or engineer, and their local building official, before starting any construction related to these plans. At the time of creation, our plans are drawn to specifications published by the Building Officials and Code Administrators (BOCA) International, Inc.; the Southern Building Code Congress (SBCCI) International, Inc.; the International Conference of Building Officials; or the Council of American Building Officials (CABO). Our plans are designed to meet or exceed national building standards. Because of the great differences in geography and climate throughout the United States and Canada, each state, county and municipality has its own building codes, zone requirements, ordinances and building regulations. Your plan may need to be modified to comply with local requirements regarding snow loads, energy codes, soil and seismic conditions and a wide range of other matters. In addition, you may need to obtain permits or inspections from local governments before and in the course of construction. Prior to using blueprints ordered from us, we strongly advise that you consult a licensed architect or engineer—and speak with your local building official—before applying for any permit or beginning construction. We authorize the use of our blueprints on the express condition that you strictly comply with all local building codes, zoning requirements and other applicable laws, regulations, ordinances and requirements. Notice: Plans for homes to be built in Nevada must be re-drawn by a Nevada-registered professional. Consult your building official for more information on this subject.

Foundation and Exterior Wall Changes
All plans are drawn with a basement foundation. Depending on your specific climate or regional building practices, you may wish to change this basement to a slab or crawlspace. Most professional contractors and builders can easily adapt your plans to alternate foundation types. Likewise, most can easily change 2x4 wall construction to 2x6, or vice versa.

Disclaimer
We have put substantial care and effort into the creation of our blueprints. However, because we cannot provide on-site consultation, supervision and control over actual construction, and because of the great variance in local building requirements, building practices and soil, seismic, weather and other conditions, WE CANNOT MAKE ANY WARRANTY, EXPRESS OR IMPLIED, WITH RESPECT TO THE CONTENT OR USE OF OUR BLUEPRINTS, INCLUDING BUT NOT LIMITED TO ANY WARRANTY OF MERCHANTABILITY OR OF FITNESS FOR A PARTICULAR PURPOSE.

Terms and Conditions
These designs are protected under the terms of United States Copyright Law and may not be copied or reproduced in any way, by any means. We authorize the use of your chosen design as an aid in the construction of one single family home only. You may not use this design to build a second or multiple dwellings without purchasing another blueprint or blueprints or paying additional design fees.

How Many Blueprints Do You Need?
A single set of blueprints is sufficient to study a home in greater detail. However, if you are planning to obtain cost estimates from a contractor or subcontractors—or if you are planning to build immediately—you will need more sets. Because additional sets are cheaper when ordered in quantity with the original order, make sure you order enough blueprints to satisfy all requirements. The following checklist will help you determine how many you need:

____Owner

____Builder (generally requires at least three sets; one as a legal document, one to use during inspections, and at least one to give to subcontractors)

____Local Building Department (often requires two sets)

____Mortgage Lender (usually one set for a conventional loan; three sets for FHA or VA loans)

____TOTAL NUMBER OF SETS

Toll Free 1-800-521-6797

Regular Office Hours:
8:00 a.m. to 8:00 p.m. Eastern Time, Monday through Friday
Our staff will gladly answer any questions during regular office hours. Our answering service can place orders after hours or on weekends.

If we receive your order by 4:00 p.m. Eastern Time, Monday through Friday, we'll process it and ship within 48 hours. When ordering by phone, please have your charge card ready. We'll also ask you for the Order Form Key Number at the bottom of the coupon.

By FAX: Copy the Order Form on the next page and send it on our FAX line: 1-800-224-6699 or 1-520-544-3086.

Canadian Customers
Order Toll-Free 1-800-561-4169

For faster service and plans that are modified for building in Canada, customers may now call in orders directly to our Canadian supplier of plans and charge the purchase to a charge card. Or, you may complete the order form at right, adding 40% to all prices and mail in Canadian funds to:

The Plan Centre 60 Baffin Place
Unit 5
Waterloo, Ontario N2V 1Z7

OR: Copy the Order Form and send it via our Canadian FAX line: 1-800-719-3291.

Title. You have purchased a license to use the plans. The title to and intellectual property rights in the plans shall remain with American Home Gallery, Ltd. Use of the plans in a manner inconsistent with this agreement is a violation of U.S Copyright laws. These designs are protected under the terms of the United States Copyright Law and may not be copied or reproduced in any way. We authorize the use of your chosen design as an aid in the construction of one single family home only. You may not use this design to build a second or multiple dwellings without purchasing another blueprint or blueprints or paying additional design fees.

Modifications and warranties. Any modifications made to the vellums by parties other than American Home Gallery, Ltd. voids any warranties express or implied including the warranties of fitness for a particular purpose and merchantability. American Home Gallery, Ltd. is an architectural design firm. Our house plans are not intended to eliminate the use of local architects or engineers. We recommend that an architect or engineer in your area review your plans before actual construction begins.

ORDER TOLL FREE!
1-800-521-6797 or
520-297-8200

For Customer Service,
call toll free 1-888-690-1116.

By fax: Copy the Order Form and send it to 1-800-224-6699 or 1-520-544-3086.

BLUEPRINTS ARE NOT RETURNABLE

ORDER FORM

HOME PLANNERS, LLC
Wholly owned by Hanley-Wood, Inc.
3275 WEST INA ROAD, SUITE 110
TUCSON, ARIZONA 85741

THE BASIC BLUEPRINT PACKAGE
Rush me the following (Please refer to the Plans Index and Price Schedule on pages 156, 157):
___ Set(s) of Blueprints for Plan Number(s)_______. $_______
___ Additional Identical Blueprints in same order @$50 per set $_______
___ Reverse Blueprints @$50 per set_______. $_______

ADDITIONAL PRODUCTS
Rush me the following:
___ 16"x20" Color Rendering(s) for Plan Number(s)_______@ $125.00 ea. $_______
___ Specification Outlines @ $10 each. $_______
___ Materials List @$60 each. $_______
___ Detail Sets @$14.95 each; any two for $22.95; any three for $29.95; all four for $39.95 (Save $19.85). $_______
___Plumbing___Electrical___Construction___Mechanical
(These helpful details provide general construction advice and are not specific to any single plan.)
___ Quote One® Summary Cost Report @$19.95 for 1, $14.95; for each additional, for plans_______ $_______
Building location City___________________ Zip Code___________
___ Quote One® Materials Cost Report @$110, for plans_______ $_______
(Must be purchased with Bluepints set.)
Building location City___________________ Zip Code___________

POSTAGE AND HANDLING	1-3 sets	4 or more sets
Signature and street address required for all deliveries.		
• Regular Service (Allow 7-10 days delivery)	$15.00	$18.00
• Priority (Allow 4-5 days delivery)	$20.00	$30.00
• Express (Allow 3 days delivery)	$30.00	$40.00
CERTIFIED MAIL (Requires signature) (Allow 7-10 days delivery)	$20.00	$30.00
OVERSEAS DELIVERY: Fax, phone or mail for quote.		
NOTE: All delivery times are from date Blueprint Package is shipped.		

POSTAGE (From box above) $_______
SUB-TOTAL $_______
SALES TAX (AZ, CA, DC, IL, MI, MN, NY & WA residents please add appropriate state & local sales tax.) $_______
TOTAL (Sub-total and Tax) $_______

YOUR ADDRESS (Please print) (Street address required)
Name ____________________
Street ____________________
City__________State__________Zip__________
Daytime telephone number (_____) ____________________

FOR CREDIT CARD ORDERS ONLY Please fill in the information below:
Credit card number ____________________
Exp. Date: Month/Year ____________________
Check one ❒ Visa ❒ MasterCard ❒ Discover Card ❒ American Express

Signature ____________________
Please check appropriate box: ❒ Licensed Builder-Contractor ❒ Homeowner

Order Form Key
TB58

Stephen Fuller